She City

She City

Designing Out Women's Inequity in Cities

NICOLE KALMS

BLOOMSBURY VISUAL ARTS
LONDON · NEW YORK · OXFORD · NEW DELHI · SYDNEY

BLOOMSBURY VISUAL ARTS
Bloomsbury Publishing Plc
50 Bedford Square, London, WC1B 3DP, UK
1385 Broadway, New York, NY 10018, USA
29 Earlsfort Terrace, Dublin 2, Ireland

BLOOMSBURY, BLOOMSBURY VISUAL ARTS and the Diana logo are trademarks of Bloomsbury Publishing Plc

First published in Great Britain 2023
Reprinted 2024

Copyright © Nicole Kalms, 2023

Nicole Kalms has asserted her right under the Copyright, Designs and Patents Act, 1988, to be identified as Author of this work.

For legal purposes the Acknowledgements on p. xiv constitute an extension of this copyright page.

Cover design: Eleanor Rose
Cover image: © Gene Bawden

All rights reserved. No part of this publication may be reproduced or transmitted in any form or by any means, electronic or mechanical, including photocopying, recording, or any information storage or retrieval system, without prior permission in writing from the publishers.

Bloomsbury Publishing Plc does not have any control over, or responsibility for, any third-party websites referred to or in this book. All internet addresses given in this book were correct at the time of going to press. The author and publisher regret any inconvenience caused if addresses have changed or sites have ceased to exist, but can accept no responsibility for any such changes.

A catalogue record for this book is available from the British Library.

Library of Congress Cataloging-in-Publication Data
Names: Kalms, Nicole, author.
Title: She city : designing out women's inequity in cities / Nicole Kalms.
Description: New York : Bloomsbury Publishing, [2024] | Includes bibliographical references and index. |
Identifiers: LCCN 2023011569 (print) | LCCN 2023011570 (ebook) | ISBN 9781350153080 (hardback) | ISBN 9781350153073 (paperback) | ISBN 9781350153097 (pdf) | ISBN 9781350153103 (epub) | ISBN 9781350153110
Subjects: LCSH: Urban women—Social conditions—Case studies. | Women—Violence against—Case studies. | City and town life—Case studies. | Sex role—Case studies.
Classification: LCC HQ1155 .K355 2024 (print) | LCC HQ1155 (ebook) | DDC 305.42—dc23/eng/20230623
LC record available at https://lccn.loc.gov/2023011569
LC ebook record available at https://lccn.loc.gov/2023011570

ISBN: HB: 978-1-3501-5308-0
PB: 978-1-3501-5307-3
ePDF: 978-1-3501-5309-7
eBook: 978-1-3501-5310-3

Typeset by RefineCatch Limited, Bungay, Suffolk
Printed and bound in Great Britain

To find out more about our authors and books visit www.bloomsbury.com and sign up for our newsletters.

CONTENTS

List of Illustrations vii
Preface x
Acknowledgments xiv

1 Women in Cities: An Introduction 1

PART ONE Resisting Sexist Cities 31

2 Don't Stand So Close to Me: Sexist Street Harassment and Women's Safety Work 33
3 Fake Happy: Hypersexual Cities and Women's Inequity 63
4 Missing Women: Smart Women in the Data Gap 83

PART TWO Designing Feminist Cities 101

5 Girls to the Front: Mainstreaming Women's Needs 103
6 Not Neutral: Designing Cities for Women 118
7 Expanding Expertise: Women's Safety Audits 135

PART THREE Prioritizing Safer Cities 155

8 Train Wreck: Public Transport and Women's Safety 157
9 Eyes on the Street: Women and Urban Crime Prevention 187
10 On the Edge of the Night: Women and the Night-Time Economy 208
11 Run the World: Co-design in a Feminist Framework 229

Notes 244
References 248
Index 284

ILLUSTRATIONS

1.1 The book focuses on four of the sustainable development goals. Adapted from the United Nations (2015).   5
1.2 Continuum of violence diagram. Adapted from Liz Kelly, (1996), "Continuum of sexual violence," in Marianne Hester, Liz Kelly and Jill Radford (eds.), Women, Violence, and Male Power, Buckingham, UK: Open University Press. Diagram further adapted by Dr. Gill Matthewson (2021) and Isabella Webb (2022), Monash University XYX Lab.   10
1.3 Perception of safety. Adapted and expanded by Gill Matthewson, Monash University XYX Lab from Yavuz and Welch 2010.   20
1.4 Chapter matrix and discipline reference.   24
2.1 Sexual Harassment is defined by a range of behaviors across verbal, non-verbal, physical and digital, and may escalate to violent crime and sexual assault.   37
2.2 An inventory of things that some women and girls to do to stay safe when out in public. Image Isabella Webb, Monash University XYX Lab, 2022.   40
2.3 The daily mobility of women with a comparison to men. Adapted from Rahul Goel, Oyinlola Oyebode, Louise Foley, Lambed Tatah, Christopher Millett, and James Woodcock (2022).   46
2.4 Typical responses to sexual harassment reporting. Adapted from Gwen Kash (2019) and Anna Gekoski, Jacqueline M. Gray, Miranda A.H. Horvath, Sarah Edwards, Aliye Emirali & Joanna R. Adler, (2017). Collated by Dr. Gill Matthewson and Isabella Webb, Monash University XYX Lab.   50

2.5 Alternative forums for collective action against sexist street harassment have been developed internationally with various modes for gathering women's experiences of sexist harassment. Note: crowd mapping and geo-locative data collection with women and girls is discussed in Chapter 4. Image Isabella Webb, Monash University XYX Lab. 54
2.6 Illustration of sexual harassment campaign, "Respect women 'Call it Out' 2018, Australia." Illustration Isabella Webb, Monash University XYX Lab 2022. 58
3.1 Example of type of pornographication in public space infrastructure. Illustration Isabella Webb, Monash University XYX Lab 2022. 68
3.2 Types of representations of women and girls. Adapted from Nicole Kalms (2017); Lauren Rosewarne (2007a); Leena–Maija Rossi (2007). 70
3.3 Sites of urban media infrastructure in cities. 73
3.4 Example of type of pornographication and iteration in public space. Illustration Isabella Webb, Monash University XYX Lab 2022. 79
4.1 Data sources that may provide sex- and gender disaggregated indicators. 88
5.1 Phases of gender mainstreaming in urban planning. 107
5.2 Domination and oppression adapted from the "matrix of domination" developed by Patricia Hill Collins. Illustration Isabella Webb, Monash University XYX Lab 2022. 115
6.1 "Probable/Plausible/Possible/Preferable/Possibility" cone adapted from Anthony Dunne and Fiona Raby (2013). 127
7.1 Safety Audit developed by Casey City Council, Australia. This safety audit tool is used to evaluate the public environment through the four categories of "safety and security," "connection and belonging," "access and movement," and the "look and feel" of urban spaces and inform future strategies for the local community. 142
7.2 The impact of the use of women's safety audits. Table based on findings from Women's Safety Audits: What Works and Where? UN-Habitat: Safer Cities

Programme, Melanie Lambrick, & Kathryn Travers, 2008. Research suggests that positive outcomes that result from the use of women's safety audits. 153

8.1 Gender differences in use of public transport in major cities across the world, adapted from Rahul Goel, Oyinlola Oyebode, Louise Foley, Lambed Tatah, Christopher Millett, and James Woodcock 2022. 164

8.2 Women's mobility patterns versus "traditional" commuter mobility. Diagram Isabella Webb, Monash University XYX Lab 2022. 166

8.3 Factors affecting perceptions of safety on public transport. Adapted and expanded by Gill Matthewson, Monash University XYX Lab from Yavuz and Welch 2010. 173

9.1 The principles of crime prevention through environmental design are often viewed as "best-practice" by local government and city stakeholders who implement a series of measures, aimed at assisting designers to meet metrics for safety. This mode fails to seek insights from the diverse communities these practices should ostensibly benefit. The absence of community contribution leads to "neutral" guidelines often uninformed by the influencing factors of race, indigeneity, class, ability, age, sexuality and gender. Diagram Isabella Webb, Monash University XYX Lab 2022. 197

10.1 Proportion of women who say they feel safe walking home at night compared to men. Adapted from OECD Better Life Index (2020). 213

11.1 Modes for feminist participatory co-design. 233

11.2 Feminist participatory co-design process. Diagram Isabella Webb, Monash University XYX Lab 2022. 240

11.3 Feminist participatory co-design workshop in action. Monash University XYX Lab. 242

PREFACE

She City compiles a range of principles, practices and strategies that aim to re-design cities with the rights of women and girls at the center. It consolidates an intense period of applied research in the design team I lead, based in Melbourne, Australia. As the founding director of the Monash University XYX Lab, I am committed to examining the relationship between gender and urban space. This has often involved facilitating collaborative engagements between diverse groups of women and girls with policymakers, planners, and designers. Together, we work through design methods and processes to find solutions to the issues women face in cities.

One of the most challenging aspects of the research we undertake at the XYX Lab is that our expertise in the field of feminist urban design is in huge demand. And for all the wrong reasons. Intense periods of research and requests for our skills are often contextualized by devastating and violent events in public spaces. When women are victims of unthinkable crimes, our workload peaks and we are called upon to speak, design and problem-solve.

By examining women's marginalization in cities, the XYX Lab extends traditional modes of creative practice, using feminist methodologies and activist techniques. The inception of these modes and the title of this book, *She City*, were catalysed by a series of workshops which questioned the status quo and framed urban problems from women's lived experience.[1] Our research has involved partnerships with communties across six continents and has evolved into a range of XYX Lab techniques, tool kits, and professional training credentials that will mean more women can participate fully in cities.

In this current book format, *She City* speaks to the (de)politicization of women's inequality and calls for a deliberate shift from a gender-neutral position to an active series of gender-sensitive responses which insist that it is women's right to actively occupy, connect and belong in their cities and communities. Its conceptualization draws upon a concerning and deeply unnerving international backdrop in which women are frequently raped and murdered in public space.

It seems we have come to accept that no woman is immune to random acts of male violence. These high-profile cases are distributed in media, in image and in text and mulled over; time and time again they claim a troubled space in our urban imagination that is perplexing, unresolved and persistent. Women's last moments are replayed in CCTV footage on the evening news and then repeated in whispers between friends, family, colleagues, and acquaintances.

In my hometown of Melbourne, many victims' names continue to ring in our ears: journalist Jill Meagher (2012), sex worker Tracey Connelly (2013), pastry chef Renae Lau (2014), high-school student Maša Vukotić (2015), comedian Eurydice Dixon (2018) and student Aiia Massawre (2019). We hear echoes and similarities from elsewhere, we know that more names will follow and are simultaneously aware that some women's stories never surface.

Many women are likely to be "uncounted" because of their age, disability, ethnicity, gender, geographic location, income, indigeneity, migratory status, race, religion, and sexuality. This vague and muted context characterizes the issue that there is ongoing resistance to getting a full picture of men's public violence against women. The government, justice system and media intervene to decide who and what is made visible. These missing women remind us that the work toward change is yet to be done.

Of course, women and girls take these issues into their own hands to insist their voices be heard—in social media, press media, vigils, events, policy demands, campaigns, symposia, and strikes. Their actions confirm—rather than deny—that feminism is alive and kicking and is needed more than ever. Women are here. Wanting liberation. Demanding their right to live in cities safely.

My role at Monash University has provided me with the opportunity to listen to the stories of women internationally and it leaves me in no doubt that women's negative experiences in cities are shared and pervasive. Women's collective protests give this book immediate political relevance everywhere and acknowledge that achieving women's equity is one of the most important things we can do for achieving urban sustainability.

And so, these previous ties are reflected in the title of the book and hope to speak to women's ongoing demand to be heard. The use of "she" as a prefix for "city" indicates an active, central position for women and girls in the definition and design of cities. *She City* is therefore both a description of the book's provocation as well as signaling women's interconnectedness across the globe.

Although *She City* is written with academic, professional, and disciplinary-specific readers in mind, recent events make it particularly relevant for readers from many vocations. *She City* unifies both design theory and practice (or praxis) by providing a practical and accessible context within which to describe, discuss and strategize the many barriers to women's equity in cities, including men's violence against women, sexist stereotypes, personal safety, and gender bias in the built environment.

One of the benefits of working in a collaborative design environment is that research evolves in the context of an ongoing conversation. I am at my best when inspired by the provocative discussion with the XYX Lab team. Despite the politically contentious context of sex and gender, the XYX Lab does not aim for consensus. It is an extraordinary achievement that we undertake award-winning, global research, that we produce exhibitions, reports, communication campaigns, that we teach students and practitioners and raise awareness of gender-sensitive cities, *despite* holding divergent perspectives on issues of sex and gender. For this reason, it is important to acknowledge that, while this book's foundations are set firmly in the strengths of the XYX Lab, it does not reflect the position of others in the team. In this book, I am drawing on my own individual research position.

This position is shaped by my personal experience as a white, able bodied, educated female and scholar. I have benefited from a position of privilege—notably, in the country where I was born—and where I now work and live on Indigenous land that was never ceded. My networks and the support I have received influence my research. As I have gained visibility and a voice from the work that I do, I am committed to undertaking research with and for women that are less visible or yet to be heard.

While I aim to undertake research and amplify insights that impact a diverse range of women and thinkers, my attempts will likely fall short and will not reflect every woman's perspective nor every woman's needs, wants and desires. Nonetheless, my hope is that this book can provide a synopsis and guide to challenge women's shared oppression in cities and that there can be positive change.

And so, as governments continue to deliberate about whether the rights of women and girls are a priority, what is required is not more rhetoric, wavering and silencing, but radical action through a strong and enduring, women-centered framework.

Nicole Kalms
Wadawurrung Country

ACKNOWLEDGMENTS

I wish to acknowledge and pay my respects to the people of the Kulin Nations who are the Traditional Owners and Custodians of the land in which the writing of this book has taken place. I especially pay my humble respect to the Wadawurrung people and wish to recognize their continuing connection to land, water, and culture. I pay my respects to Elders past, present and emerging. Given the ongoing and devastating impacts of colonization, any initiatives and commitments to women's equality need to be underpinned by a commitment to reconciliation.

This book has been in the making for many years and during this time many people have provided direction, encouragement and support. Firstly, I would like to thank the Dean of the Faculty of Art Design and Architecture at Monash University—Professor Shane Murray—for his continued and candid mentorship and support since my undergraduate years. Under his leadership, the faculty has provided me with numerous opportunities to develop my research and I am lucky to be a part of the Monash's extraordinary community.

Professor Melissa Miles and Professor Diego Ramirez-Lovering have both been significant mentors since commencing at Monash over a decade ago. I have yet to meet two scholars with more generosity and commitment and they have been invaluable to my career progression. I have relied on their experience and direction. They have provided assurance (and the occasional nudge) at critical junctures.

Much of the thinking that underpins *She City* has been undertaken in the context of the Monash University XYX Lab where our aim is to understand how sex and gender limit participation in cities. Since founding the Lab in 2016 I have worked with an extraordinary team to deliver an array of research projects, exhibitions, public engagements and scholarly outputs. I am grateful to this dedicated team, energized by our work together and privileged to have the opportunity to discuss feminist design praxis with such esteemed colleagues. Thank you to XYX Lab co-director and Head of Design, Associate Professor Gene Bawden, for bearing the pressures of leading a busy research lab among many competing commitments. Shared research with Gene informs Chapter 11. Research with Dr. Gill Matthewson has been infinitely rewarding and significantly shapes my thinking and impacts chapters 4, 7, 8 and 9. Thank you, Associate Professor Jess Berry; our shared research into women's experiences of the night-time economy has informed Chapter 10. Thank you, Dr. Timothy Moore for your candid perspectives on architectural practice and generosity as a colleague. Isabella Webb requires additional thanks for her assistance with the drawing production, diagrams and graphics. A very special thanks to Dr. Teagan Larin who is an inspiring early career researcher and who assisted with the case studies and definitions and has provided insightful feedback on the feminist position of the book during the writing process. The XYX Lab are, quite simply, an outstanding team of researchers and colleagues. The good humor we generate lightens the weight of some heavy research issues. We know how to have a good time and this makes the tough bits, the hard work and the late nights worth it.

As well as the core XYX Lab team there is an extended network of Monash University PhD students and project assistants who have contributed their time to individual XYX Lab initiatives, and I thank them. Their contributions are detailed under individual projects and are available to view on the XYX Lab website.

A special thank you to long-term collaborators, Anthony Aisenberg from CrowdSpot, Susanne Legena and Hayley Cull from Plan International and Kristy Nicholson from Casey City Council—our shared research has shaped the following pages and surfaced experiences from women who have shared their stories of urban spaces. Special thanks to these women for their contribution to the book, as their perspectives bring out the issues more effectively than my writing ever could.

Thank you to Ella Mitchell, Anna Lensky and Hayden Dowd for making many ambitious projects possible. Professor Angela Taft—chair and collaborator on the TramLab project—thank you for the invitation to join such an important project which progressed the transport research for the XYX Lab. Thank you, Professor Lisa

Grocott, for indoctrinating Gene and me into the co-design cult that summer in NYC.

Tim Hunt and Hoa Yang from ARUP Melbourne led research with XYX Lab and Plan International on lighting that informs the insights in Chapter 10. Christina Houen has, once again, provided skilled and professional copyediting for *She City*. Denise Taylor provided professional feedback in the book's early stages. Aspects of Chapter 3 draw on previous research into sexualization from my 2018 monograph—*Hypersexual City: The Provocation of Soft-Core Urbanism*.

Finally, I am indebted to my parents, Lynette Kalms and Peter Kalms, who have supported me financially and emotionally throughout many years of study and who continue to provide support to me and my son Luca.

CHAPTER ONE

Women in Cities
An Introduction

Cities are always on the cusp of transformation and change. As the scale and density of cities increase, so too does the inequity of the women and girls who live and work within them. Understanding the challenges faced by women in cities requires understanding how sex and gender shape both the practicalities of designing cities and the gendered experiences of those living within them. Some practitioners struggle to recognize how cities impact women's experiences of sexism, of discrimination or their fear of men's violence. There may be resistance to deepening their understanding or they may believe that feminism is passé and does not warrant their serious consideration (Gamble 2006: 38). For those that are curious, questions commonly asked indicate uncertainty and ambiguity, and often include:

How and why do women experiences cities differently?
What does the built environment have to do with women's oppression?
Why do women feel more at risk in cities than men do?
Can design address the complex concerns of women moving through cities?

These questions have been the focus of research by feminist planners, urban geographers and architects for many decades. Despite their interrogation of these questions—and their agitation for alternative approaches to policy, practice and design—evidence reiterates time and again that women's use and occupation of public space continues to be inhibited. The barriers women face when trying to freely access public spaces include hetero/sexism encountered in cities, discrimination and bias, which result in a lack of attention to their practical daily urban needs, as well as in the social tolerance toward and normalization of men's violence.

> ### Feminism
>
> Feminism is a contested term, with various interpretations and definitions. Feminist theorist Catharine MacKinnon has described the different strands of feminism as subsidiary considerations of larger projects, such as liberalism or socialism, whereas radical feminism stands on its own, it is "feminism unmodified" (MacKinnon 1989: 117). Radical feminism is a social and political theory and movement for the liberation of women from male domination. Whereas the goal of liberal feminism is gender equality, that is, for women to be equal to men, radical feminism seeks to dismantle the gender hierarchy altogether.[1] From a disciplinary-specific perspective, the architectural text, *Gender, Space, Architecture*, maintains that feminism is contextualized by "an understanding that in all countries where the sexes are divided into separate cultural, political and economic spheres and where women are less valued than men, their sexuality is held as the cause of their oppression" (Rendell et al. 2000: 16).

Feminist architect and activist Leslie Kanes Weisman (1981: 6) addressed these issues over four decades ago, and her position is still characteristic of women's predicament today. She described how "women's lives are profoundly affected by the design and use of public spaces and buildings, transportation systems, neighbourhoods and housing," where "the man-made environments" which surround women "reinforce conventional patriarchal definitions of women's role in society"; these spaces imprint "sexist messages" and condition communities into an "environmental myopia which limits our concepts." Similarly, geographer Gill

Valentine's critique began over thirty years ago when she wrote that "women's inhibited use and occupation of public space is ... a spatial expression of patriarchy" (1989: 389). Scholars and practitioners, Sandercock and Forsyth, problematized the lack of women's engagement in the process of creating neighborhoods, where women's presence seems always limited, if not invisible (1992: 55). Others have promoted alternative urban policy scenarios to address the "imprint of gender forces" within the built environment (Greed 2006: 268).

Many feminists have initiated responses to this issue with a range of strategies and interventions developed and tested successfully across government policy, urban design planning and community activism. These initiatives share the uptake of a gendered lens to accelerate understanding of how the built environment perpetuates inequity in the everyday experiences of women and girls.

Yet the uptake of women-centered strategies in the built environment is at best inconsistent and at worst imperceptible—and the consequences are evident. By 2050, more than two-thirds of the world's population will live in urban areas (Ritchie et al. 2018) and around half of them will be women (that is, over 3.2 billion women). Disappointingly it is estimated that at the current rate of progress, when measuring economic participation, opportunity, educational attainment, health, survival and political empowerment and the removal of discriminatory laws worldwide gender parity is at least 135 years away (Devlin 2021; UN 2022: 11).

At present, the minimal resources afforded to women in public spaces authorize entrenched inequality. If the issues women face in cities have been minimized to date, these numbers should provide ample incentive for transformation.

Public space

> Public space is for shared public use and should be accessible and enjoyable by all. A primary function of public spaces is to provide connection for social wellbeing, and to contribute to meaningful expressions of a community's diversity. In this way, public spaces shape identity, belonging and the relationships between members of communities.

Activating a feminist-focused, women-centered approach to designing cities for women's rights and needs is more critical than ever. Women have the right to be part of their cities and their communities, and of all the culture that cities might offer, including access to education, training and employment, to health care and social services, as well as to leisure and recreation. This requires that women and girls move freely and safely in public spaces and transport networks, as these rights are critical for ensuring a cycle of social and economic inclusion for women and girls into the future. Addressing women's needs means recognizing that cities are not simply defined by materiality and infrastructure, but that the urban environment is equally defined by its capacity to shape the interactions which take place within it. And yet, without these foundational concepts most practitioners will fall short when asked to address inequity in cities.

Understanding how gender impacts urban experience and, in turn, policy, planning and practice, is not a core part of the education of engineers, architects, planners and designers, yet there is increasing pressure from communities and governments alike to align with local and national targets for gender equality in cities. While many will agree that identifying and fiercely challenging the tendency to create androcentric, heterosexist and heteronormative urban places is vital, they may also concede that they lack confidence to enact change, and they view the task as anything but straightforward.

This book offers a way to navigate the territory of urban intervention, plotting a path through a range of feminist frameworks. These include pragmatic and applied approaches to designing cities and operate across traditional material interventions, but also include digital, experiential and political approaches in their scope. Some readers may be familiar with these strategies; others may find the content innovative or at the margins of their disciplinary expertise. The operation between disciplinary fields is purposeful—linking practitioners, academic scholars and feminist-informed action with women themselves. The overall intention is to support practitioners and research students to engage in the creation of more equitable cities and communities.

Why Women?

Feminists are regularly reminded of the many social, environmental and economic problems that are more important or more pressing than women's oppression. The inference is that women and girls must go to the back of the queue and wait their turn. Focusing on improving women's rights and safety in cities does not preclude other explorations and the urgent action for other critical causes. In fact, it is predicted that by redressing the disproportionate allocation of resources in cities to support women's safe access, there will be significant positive impacts on a myriad of other social issues (Lomazzi et al. 2019: 152).

The positions in this book are shaped by the priorities of the United Nations (2015), which aims to promote social progress with better living standards and human rights at its core. Under the

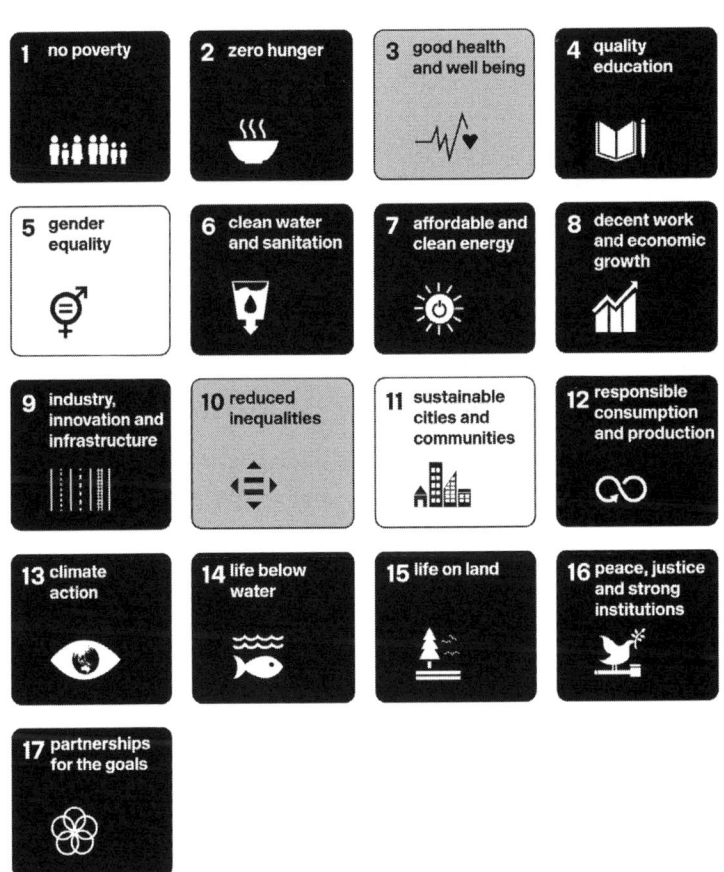

FIGURE 1.1 The book focuses on four of the sustainable development goals. Adapted from the United Nations (2015).

guidance of esteemed professionals internationally, the UN authorizes a clear framework for achieving women and girls' equality in cities across the global north and south. Using the *2030 Agenda for Sustainable Development* as a blueprint, this book is focused on empowering all women and girls (goal 5) and addresses the need to make cities inclusive and safe (goal 11). Through developing strategies to progress goals 5 and 11, this book makes secondary contributions to women's good health and wellbeing (goal number 3) and reducing inequalities (goal number 10).

The aligned UN report, *New Urban Agenda*, also recognizes the importance of women and girls, noting the ways that the urban systems of cities are "the source of solutions" and envisioning a future where "all people have equal rights and access to the benefits and opportunities that cities can offer" (UN 2017: iv). This alignment with women and girls' rights is reflected in this book but so comprises approaches which sit in direct contrast to the recent actions of some countries, where there has been a conscientious move to neutralize women's presence in the language of policy and design and—in doing so—to make women less visible. The UN could not be clearer in its authorization of "women and girls"—actively and repeatedly calling out for their rights, with explicit aims to:

> Achieve gender equality and empower all women and girls by ensuring women's full and effective participation and equal rights in all fields and in leadership at all levels of decision making, by ensuring decent work and equal pay for equal work, or work of equal value, for all women and by preventing and eliminating all forms of discrimination, violence and harassment against women and girls in private and public spaces.
>
> 2017: 5

Following the UN's vision for a "safe, healthy, inclusive and secure environment," this book puts the lives of women and girls—their family, work, education, and participation in urban life—at the center, and demands that they be free from sexism, discrimination and violence. The book notes that, while significant developmental gains may have transformed the lives of many people, a chasm remains between men and women. These inequalities have foundations in women's exclusion from public life and the different social expectations between men and women.

Research into masculinities (conducted elsewhere and by other scholars) is vital for addressing inequity and the inclusion of men will contribute to cohesive social transformation. And while generalizations about men and women's urban experiences ignores specific imbalances with social groups (for example, the privileges and barriers, or age or class), women are disproportionately and negatively impacted by: uneven access to education; their caring responsibilities and a lack of autonomy over their bodies; a lack of access to work and discrimination in the workplace; and intersectional factors such as age, disability, ethnicity, geographic location, income, indigeneity, migratory status, race, religion, and sexuality. Indeed, biological sex and gender are central and define social life in fundamental ways (Daneshpour 2023: 9). For women, it is a context where discrimination prevails and where "laws, government regulations, cultural attitudes, informal practices, and lack of awareness by professionals have created conditions which reflect and reinforce women's second-class status" (Weisman 1981: 6) and highlights that women's equity cannot be treated individualistically. This focus acknowledges that public spaces are also made up of sites of transgression, with opportunities for women to safely express themselves, but there are resistances in cities that reproduce entrenched power relations and impact women in particular ways. To understand how women *as a class* are negatively impacted by prejudice provides the conditions to foreground how women can be *positively impacted* by strategies, policies and actions that progress their freedom, rights and safety in cities and communities.

Public Space, Private Hell

Women's perceptions of risk and vulnerability are a recurring theme in this book. And for good reason. The impact of men's violence against women dominates women's lives, is an enduring public health issue, and is devastatingly and disproportionately perpetrated by men against women. Some will counter that "woman are also perpetrators" and while this statement may be true, the statistics that make any claim for parity are nothing short of ridiculous.[2] Political theorist and feminist Carole Sheffield wrote about "sexual terrorism" over thirty years ago, and in a recent updated edition of the same book, she maintains that the issues are as relevant as ever. Sheffield suggests that in the face of cultural change, and despite greater understanding of men's violence against women and girls, her position on sexual terrorism "has proven to be remarkably adaptable and sustainable" (2020: 191). Importantly, whether women are direct victims of violence or not, the mere *threat* of violence is a form of social control that impacts *all* women in cities. As Sheffield writes, "The difference between men's and women's experiences of fear underscores the fact that women's lives are bounded by both the reality of the pervasive danger of men's violence and the fear that reality engenders" (2020: 192). Similarly, Dora Epstein (1997: 134) writes about fear and the burden of staying safe in urban space. She states:

> There is a story to this fearing, this fearing that maps the cityscapes into places I will go and places I will not. As speaking subjects, sentient members of urban terrains, we can narrate our cartographies of avoidance, our fearing, far better than we can narrate how the fearing came to be. We know, can articulate, what we have deemed "unsafe"—the strange, the unfamiliar, the supposedly violent "other" against which we have insulated and barricaded ourselves—and what we have deemed as "safe"— the lit, the populated, the orderly, or seemingly controlled to which we have clung. We felt justified when violence occurred in the realm of our "unsafe"; felt shock when it occurred in our "safe."

These insights serve to demonstrate how women's fear of men's violence can be defined by "sensed risk, concern, anxiety, worry, and fear" and as such is held by women in subjective ways that defy definition and result in "many sub-constructs, each with large variations" (Struyf 2020: 348). As such, management of the fear of men's violence zaps energy from women and girls and decreases their participation in public life, and will almost certainly negatively impact their social, economic and educational outcomes (World Bank 2020). The degree of that impact will be markedly increased if a woman's experience includes additional intersectional factors and systemic disadvantage.

> **WOMEN'S EXPERIENCES OF VIOLENCE GLOBALLY: A SNAPSHOT FROM THE WORLD HEALTH ORGANIZATION (WHO)**
>
> Based on data collected between 2010 and 2018 (note that eighty-two countries were surveyed in 2010 and 161 countries were surveyed in 2018), women were asked if they had experienced:
>
> - physical and/or sexual violence from any current or former husband or male intimate partner
> - sexual violence from a non-partner (for example, strangers, acquaintances, friends, peers, teachers, neighbors, family members)
> - both of these forms of violence combined at least once in their lifetime (since the age of 15).
>
> The results indicate that 1 in 3 women globally experience violence, with younger women most at risk (WHO 2018: 1). These estimates confirm that physical and sexual intimate partner violence and non-partner sexual violence remain pervasive in the lives of women and adolescent girls across the globe.

The nuances of men's violence against women reveal a range of behaviors that are both physical and non-physical (Fig. 1.2) and occur in a range of complex social settings. Family violence (also referred to as domestic violence) is increasingly well-recognized; it is violence perpetrated against women and children in the context of a significant relationship, for example, with a current or former partner. Violence perpetrated against women and children in the context of a significant relationship, for example, a current or former partner, is also increasingly played out in the public realm—and indeed, family violence is more significant and newsworthy *when* it is played out in the public realm. Similarly, forms of family

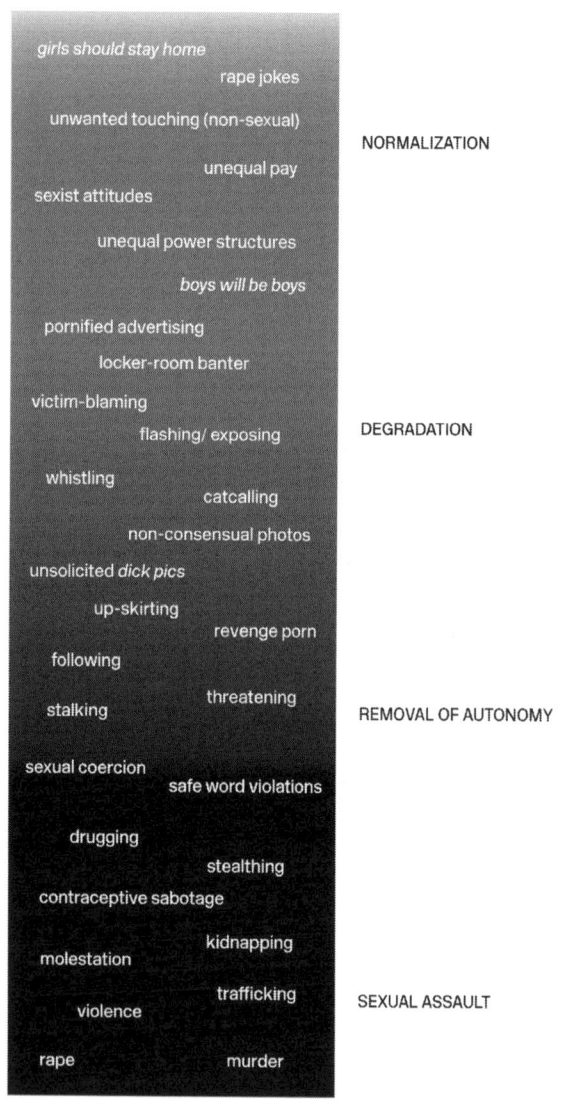

FIGURE 1.2 Continuum of violence diagram. Adapted from Liz Kelly, (1996), "Continuum of sexual violence," in Marianne Hester, Liz Kelly and Jill Radford (eds), *Women, Violence, and Male Power*, Buckingham, UK: Open University Press. Diagram further adapted by Dr. Gill Matthewson (2021) and Isabella Webb (2022), Monash University XYX Lab.

violence may include partner surveillance, where tracking technology and monitoring of women by their intimate or former partners is used. Through their interdependence, these forms of violence maintain the patriarchal social structures that keep women and girls "in their place" both in public and domestic space (Dawson 2021: para 4). This suggests that there are ways that family violence intersects with public violence and may indicate that "private and public violence complement and reinforce one another" (Ibid.).

The differentiation between the private and the public ignores how violence operates on a continuum (Fig. 1.2) and accumulates across the course of a woman's life. It is often quoted that women are most unsafe in their own home (UNODOC 2018: 17)—an unnerving and terrifying fact that speaks to women's persistent vulnerability and is frequently evoked to minimize or counteract the vulnerability that women feel in public space. The complexity increases because, while it is accurate that sexual assault more commonly occurs in domestic spaces by men known to women, women are more concerned about public spaces, and "typically consider attack is more likely at certain times, in certain places, and from strangers" (Matthewson et al. 2021: 56).

From a disciplinary perspective, architecture, planning and design have traditionally viewed public space in opposition to the spaces of the domestic realm with many of the issues arising from the dichotomy of public and private space in the discipline of planning (Greed 1994: 173). As geographer Tovi Fenster suggests: "analysis of women and men's narratives show [sic] that the right to public spaces is closely linked to the right of private spaces, especially from a gendered perspective, and the analysis of the two cannot be separated" (2005: 219). In many cases the right to the city is indeed denied by patriarchal power relations either at the home scale or at the city scale (ibid. 220). The increased blurring of technology, space and politics have challenged this separation, making urgent the need to understand the continuum of women's vulnerability across public spaces through to semi-public spaces and from semi-private spaces to the private sphere. Men's violence against women is neither rare nor episodic (Kolysh 2021: 15; Kelly 1987: 46) but is part of the background of women's everyday lives (Sheffield 2020: 192), so women's constant attention is needed to manage the threat of violence across a range of spaces and media.

> **Gender-based violence versus male violence against women**
>
> Gender-based violence is supposedly a neutral term. It suggests that the violence has a kind of equivalence between people—men, women, gender diverse—and leaves out the central fact that women are overwhelmingly the victims and men are overwhelmingly the perpetrators. Therefore, the phrase "male violence against women" is appropriate for this book.

Researchers and activists Sara Ortiz Escalante and Blanca Gutiérrez Valdivia rightly argue that bodies are the connection between the public–private realm and that to suggest their separation is a "false division" that "prevents planners from being able to effectively respond to and prevent gender violence" (2015: 115; 2010: 2143). This reflects the call of feminists from the 1960s, 1970s and 1980s for more attention to the ways that women's personal experiences impact the politics of space and the need for making connections to the structural oppression that limits women's freedom in cities. Tracing the connections, fragmentation and segregation of the public and private spheres requires more interrogation and attention to the continuum between the home and family life of women and girls, and how this aligns acutely with their perceived public vulnerability.

Not Neutral

The modes and methods to challenge women's inequity need to address an increasingly generalist (and often well-meaning) "neutral" approach to cities—where gender neutral is a buzzword that has come to dominate policy, planning and practice. While neutrality is useful when trying to unpick harmful and limiting gender stereotypes (like, for example, the gender stereotypes in children's literature, their films, or toys), the move to make neutral strategies, policies and actions in an urban design and planning context overlooks the specificity of women and girl's needs. Ortiz Escalante et al. state that the general belief that urban planning needs to be neutral has not led to greater inclusion, and that "this 'neutrality' umbrella ... has ignored women's everyday lives in its design" (2015: 115). Design researchers Maryam Heidaripour and Laura Forlano (2018: para 2) suggest that the methods and processes used by designers are often deployed to "objectively" guide solutions and resist bias, resulting in designers that are disengaged with the "ethical and political values" of design. Writer and activist Caroline Criado Perez has further popularized this perspective stating: "failing to include the perspectives of women is a huge driver of unintended male bias that attempts (often in good faith) to pass itself off as 'gender neutral' and is a form of discrimination against women" (2019: xiii). In fact, in the disciplinary context of urban design, architecture and planning, "gender-neutral design" is rarely—if ever—neutral at all.

The misuse and misinterpretation of neutral approaches in the urban design and planning of cities serves to highlight how practitioners' decisions may, unintentionally, negatively impact communities. This can set many ethically focused practitioners adrift as they try to navigate a new gendered territory. For these professionals terms like sex and gender—particularly in relation to cities—may seem outside their remit or viewed as complex, changeable and even treacherous territories. And it easy to see why. This moment in time—as feminist sociologist Rosalind Gill states—"must rank as one of the most bewildering in the history of sexual politics. The more one looks, listens, and learns, the more complicated it seems" (2016: 613).

Sex and gender

This book uses both terms, sex and gender. The word sex describes the biological characteristics that constitute female or male, for example, XX and XY chromosomes and reproductive system. The word gender refers to the social constructions of maleness and femaleness that are forced onto an individual's biology. Gender, or sex-role stereotypes, usually means the behaviors and social roles and expectations placed on people because of their sex; for example, females are expected to be feminine, males to be masculine. Gender is a hierarchical system of power that values males/masculinity and denigrates females/femininity.

The complexity resides in the heavily debated and now critical social issue of sex and gender. Where one person may argue that sex is the biological framework and believe that gender is the social construction and experience of masculinity and femininity, another person may contest the concept of female or male altogether. Some people may have an awareness of the political or ideological push toward gender and difference rather than of women and feminism. A smaller few would understand the fact that there are risks and consequences in this shift. For example, the terminology has shifted, so gender theory now replaces feminism, and/or women's studies means that issues that relate to women have been depoliticized to the point where the pursuit of women's concerns may be viewed as insensitive to complex gender constructs and pervasive identity politics.

There are waves of support for broader and more inclusive terminology related to identity that supposes greater empathy within notions of differences (Rendell et al. 2000: 7). For example, "woman" and/or "women and girls" (in this book, but also anywhere) is now considered a contentious and contended term by some people who advocate for individualized identity politics. They see use of terms like "women" as an endorsement of biological determinism—a concept that is completely in opposition to the aims of this book and a false binary that undermines the importance of gender nonconformity. While gender neutrality may be a way for organizations to reconcile the complexity of gender identity, assignation, expression and appearance, "abandoning orthodox biology-based understandings of 'woman,' 'man,' 'girl' and 'boy'," is deeply concerning and means that there will be missed opportunities to engage with "valuable tools to analyse and explain the material and social world" (Stock 2022: 27). Furthermore, the depoliticization of women's inequity—especially when there is an avalanche of oppression and violence against of women and girls—sit in contrast to the recommendations of the UN.

What these examples of tension and differences convey is that it is not possible to address the diverse perspectives of all people or all communities all the time. Planners, policymakers and designers—like many professionals—will be increasingly expected to understand and accommodate the politics of social justice and likely be required to juggle conflicting perspectives as part of their job. Many designers have—of their own accord—"become more aware of the ethics, values, responsibilities and social impacts of their work" (Heidaripour et al. 2018: para 1). And even though an understanding of sex and gender may be varied and subjective, what can generally be agreed, and what this book supports, is that the reduction of people to simplified and conservative stereotypes of masculine and feminine and the requirement for people to uphold these stereotypes is unacceptable. By returning to UN recommendations and emphasis, and by engaging with evidence-based research, the decision-making processes of practitioners can be clear and confident.

On Intersectionality

Women's diversity is revealed (among other things) in their age, disability, ethnicity, gender, geographic location, income, indigeneity, migratory status, race, religion, and sexuality. While the focus of the strategies, policies and actions discussed in this book is on women and girls, this does not imply a one-size-fits-all approach, but aims to elevate women and their divergent needs and perspectives. As a social research method, an intersectional lens can be applied in policy, planning and practice to recognize the current and historical contexts surrounding an urban issue. Prioritizing the ways to respond to the needs of women in communities, especially those living with multiple oppressions, must become central to designing cities for women. In the same way that women are not a homogenous group, so Black, Brown, Asian, White and Indigenous women across the globe are not homogeneous either. The work of designing cities for women and girls will necessarily include examining systematic racism, discrimination, bias and intersectional inequities, all of which must be negotiated, and led by women and girls to surface minoritized voices.

> **Intersectionality**
>
> Intersectionality as conceived by scholar and civil rights advocate Kimberlé Crenshaw outlines how discrimination sits alongside more than just a singular axis of race or gender, which means that these oppressions *intersect*, and lead to different experiences of oppression and create new forms of oppression (1995). In an intersectional approach, social identities include but are not limited

> to: Indigenous identity; ethnicity; race; sex; sexuality; gender identity; parent or carer status; disability; mental health; religion; migrant and/or refugee status and experience; age; socio-economic status and background; cultural background; educational and community background. It is important to note that some intersectional criteria *change over time*, which means that a woman's identity, needs and priorities may change across her life course.

Despite women's divergent needs and perspectives, and despite their various intersecting oppressions, differences, and inequalities that exist between individual women, "sexism is institutional, infused and perpetuated by dominant social groups" (Benbrahim 2021, 108), and women's oppression is experienced through their shared burden of enduring discrimination. All women suffer oppression and discrimination because of their sex, with men occupying the dominant position in the gender hierarchy that enables them to extract resources from women for men's social, political and economic benefit (MacKinnon 1991: 15; Megarry 2020: 49). It is essential to recognize that oppression of women and girls—that is, their systematic mistreatment because of sexism, coercive heteronormativity and the threat of male violence—occurs to them as a class and that this shared experience of discrimination can be useful when considering their rights, needs and fears in cities. As Catharine MacKinnon states: "Feminism sees women as a group and seeks to define and pursue women's interest" (1989: 38). It is therefore useful to center women as a group, or class, because they are oppressed by men as a group simply because they are women (Dworkin 1983: 221; Mackay 2015: 126). When designing cities, the consideration of women's shared oppressions and the feminist method and practice of consciousness raising can recognize collective experience (Mackinnon 1989: 84) and identify "structural issues that only surface when large groups are examined" (Matthewson et al. 2021: 54–55).

Intersectionality, therefore, is discussed throughout the book, with the caveat that there is a tendency to equate intersectionality "with an individual sense of identity and a vague sense of inclusion" and that this is a misinterpretation of Kimberlé Crenshaw's position (Tyler 2021). There's a risk that, without structural analysis, intersectionality becomes a "buzzword" focused on the individual and "weaponised to silence women of colour" (Hamad and Liddle, cited in Tyler 2021). As political scientist, sociologist and expert in gender inequality Meagan Tyler states: "'identity' has moved from a politically and sociologically informed understanding of power and social categories, to a more psychologized, individual understanding of a freely-chosen sense of self" (Hamad and Liddle, cited in Tyler 2021: para 11). Tyler correctly notes the consequences that this has for feminist activism as well as for the conceptualization of feminism; she continues: "Instead of talking about the material realities of women's oppression, and feminism as a social movement for the liberation of all women, mainstream representations have become stuck on feminism as the expression of an individual identity" (Hamad and Liddle, cited in Tyler 2021: para 12.). For this reason, the focus here is on the class-based analysis and prioritization of women and girls, which will have the most impact on addressing women's oppression in cities. Indeed, if implemented with the understanding that feminism and women's intersectional experience are compatible feminist frameworks will celebrate women's diversity. As Grosser et al. explain: "Naming women as a class does not mean homogenizing the experiences of women, or denying power differences among groups of women, rather, naming women as a class is understood to be a unifying strategy" (2022: 222) and will catalyze change across geographic location and socio-economic status to leverage the strengths of all women in cities and communities.

Equality versus equity

Equality is based on the premise that people are equal and should therefore be provided with equal opportunity, e.g., in education and the workforce. Equality takes a white, able-bodied, heterosexual man as the standard to which others should be treated, regardless of gender, race, class, etc. In terms of gender equality, a feminist perspective does not argue that men and women are identical in terms of behavior, preferences and capabilities. Gender equality can benefit some women in some circumstances, such as obtaining equal pay for equal work or obtaining an executive level position. However, treating men and women the same will disadvantage many more women because it

> ignores their different needs, resources, and experiences due to sex. For example, women who do not act like men, i.e., take maternity leave, have caring responsibilities, etc., may suffer career consequences. Equity acknowledges that people are not equal, due to intersecting oppressions such as, age, disability, ethnicity, gender, geographic location, income, indigeneity, migratory status, race, religion, biological sex and sexuality. Regarding sex and gender, an approach toward equity recognizes the existing systems, structures and institutions as inherently inequitable (made to serve white, able-bodied, heterosexual men). Instead of treating everyone equally, an equity approach recognizes differences between people and aims to address the barriers that prevent access to the same opportunities, for instance, through policies to protect women's jobs if they take maternity leave, anti-discrimination laws to protect minorities, etc.

Somewhere Only We Know: Bias and the Built Environment

Gender bias perpetuates inequity and occurs when sex-role stereotypes and behaviors give rise to prejudiced actions or thoughts where one gender can be favored over another. This prejudice is often based on the belief that women are not equal to men. Gender bias interacts with male violence against women where the violence and the environment also produce and reinforce gender inequality (Matthewson et al. 2021: 55).

The combined and reinforcing impact of gender bias, gender inequity and male violence against women serves to "legitimize systems of subjugation" by communicating that women's access to public spaces is conditional and always comes at a cost (Kalms 2017: 5). That cost could be the emotional time expended on weighing up the risks, or being vigilant about going out: Where is safe? What is the safest way to get there? When is the best time of the day? Or it could be having to manage physical and non-physical sexist harassment. It may also mean the financial cost of using a private vehicle to ensure greater personal safety. The cost may be to a woman's mental and/or physical health because of being stalked, assaulted, raped or worse. When factoring in the intersectional aspects of age, disability, ethnicity, gender, geographic location, income, indigeneity, migratory status, race, religion and sexuality, the risk and effort to both feel safe and stay safe will be increased.

A central theme for this work is safety and the eradication of violence against women, which has become the focus of women's organizations, NGOs and institutions across cultures and countries. Cities play a role in the cycle of violence—shaping power relations, access and interconnectedness in favor of men. This requires communities to question how social spaces endorse heteronormativity alongside a commitment to developing alternative modes to the stereotypical, sexist, biased and prejudiced measures that dominate urban life. Men and women who work in planning, policy and design can support the disestablishment of gender hierarchy to accelerate the liberation of women and girls in cities and they can interrogate their resistance to releasing power and advantage within institutions. Men within organizations can help other male colleagues to see that some aspects of their privilege will be lost as society moves toward women's liberation. They can also spread the word that there is much to be gained—not least being men's own liberation from harmful gender stereotypes, improved health and relationships (Flood 2018).

It is incumbent on men to reflect on their own socialization and step forward to implement the evidence-based strategies, practices and policies that support cities for women. A common belief is that a woman on the design team is a shortcut to ensuring that a project will meet the needs of women and girls. The assumption that women's experiences can be approximated to represent all women is incorrect and needs to be swiftly dismissed. There is value in setting targets and expanding education that provides men (and women) with directions that reinforce the value systems of organizations, institutions and society more broadly, but these can be viewed as tokenism within organizations (Flood 2019: 2387). Often this form of "checkbox" diversity and inclusion speaks more to disingenuous attempts to wrangle gender disparity within organizations and less to the needs of the people and communities who should presumably benefit from greater equity, diversity and inclusion. Practitioners must strive to remember the people cities are designed for. Practicing more authentic, impactful and evidence-based "inclusion and diversity" urgently needs to occur across policy, practice and communities.

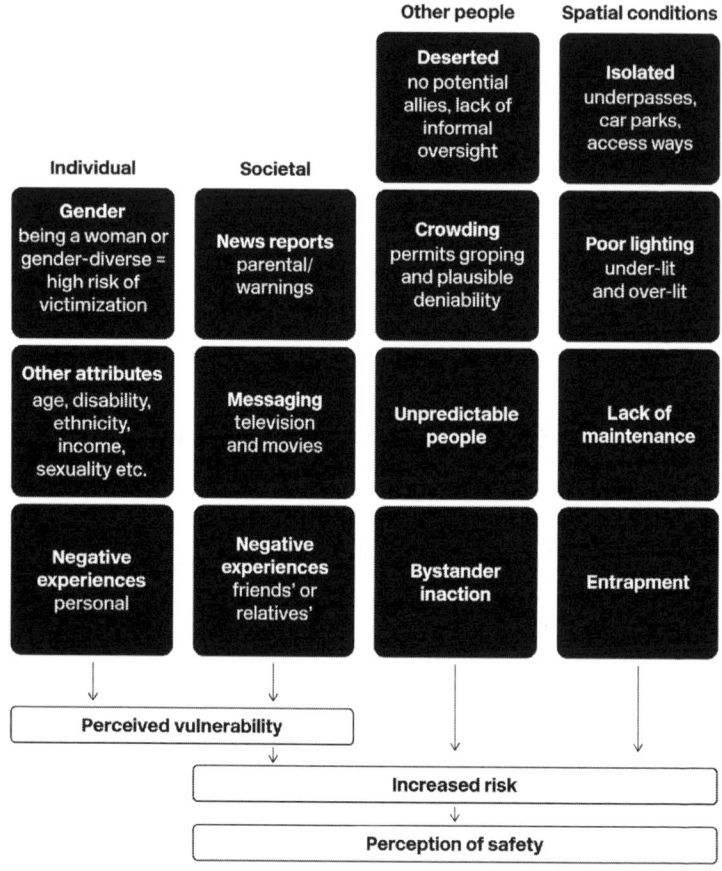

FIGURE 1.3 Perception of safety. Adapted and expanded by Gill Matthewson, Monash University XYX Lab from Yavuz and Welch 2010.

Women as Experts: Designing With, Not For

Many of the strategies examined in this book have foundations in the feminist politics of the 1960s, 1970s and 1980s. This period provided the basis for longitudinal exemplars in Northern European countries, where the support of progressive governments has seen gender equity flourish. Other cities have since followed their lead by testing elements of feminist-focused strategies at various times, but with varying degrees of success due to a less than supportive political context.

Activist and grass roots approaches have been successfully developed by women and organizations in the global south, with significant impact on communities of women often existing in difficult—if not impossible—circumstances. The United Nations Sustainable Development Goals (UN 2015) continue to acknowledge and reinforce the importance of "North-South, South-South and triangular regional and international cooperation," and many feminist-informed initiatives focus on co-designing solutions with women and have traversed the world. By creating an exchange between developed and developing countries, and by complementing and extending women-centered approaches, new directions have been forged and global connections made through urban design set within a feminist framework.

Translating the activism of the women's movement into the more formal processes of making cities *with* women requires extraordinary commitment. Even if there is social awareness of and empathy with the issues faced by women in cities, it is likely that policymakers, planners and designers will be challenged when implementing change. Many suggest that smaller shifts are more realistic and that things must be incremental if required to negotiate the patriarchal system. This suggests a sequence of "minor" revisions rather than a direct challenge to prevailing systems (Sandberg et al. 2016: 1759). While the aim is to transform existing cities—and not to start again (Greed 1994: 186)—change will be slow if there is a continued resistance in policy and planning.

Primary prevention of violence against women and urban planning

Primary prevention of violence in the context of urban planning and design does not focus on the actions of perpetrators but looks at the whole environment and the systems in the built environment that allow violence to happen.

To address men's violence against women requires the disestablishment of gender hierarchies and radical forms of primary prevention. There is a need to assertively speak back to the persistent focus on the socialization of women and girls to "keep themselves safe" and the ways that women and girls manage fear and vulnerability. In the context of inaction from authorities and a broad systemic failure to understand women's sense of vulnerability and risk when using public space, marginalized women internalize the violence, abuse, harassment, racism, heterosexism and ableism they encounter in public spaces. Many of these women may go on to avoid public spaces and, in turn, be denied access to education, health care, and other public services.

Addressing issues of safety may be viewed a defensive, victim-focused response, which overlooks the structural change that is required. Abolition of violence is the goal, where the problem is male violence, not women's vulnerability.[3] While urban places may not be able to directly challenge the gender hierarchies and the various stereotypes that are the root cause of violence against women and girls, in the short term, the built environment can work against the expression of power structures in cities and illuminate alternatives that challenge bias and stereotypes.

How to Use This Book

This book provides an overview of current perspectives and strategies to consider how feminist frameworks—with women's participation at the center—can challenge inequity in cities today. Rather than reviewing a theoretical investigation of feminist spatial practice (for example, through a triangulating feminist theory, feminist politic and spatial theory) the book aims to map out designs' vast sphere of influence in the world today to locate the arenas where designers can practically exert influence toward creating a more equitable world for women and girls. It is, therefore, a resource for architects, urban designers, planners and engineers, as well as a plethora of built environment specialists and research students who contribute to making cities and communities. These are professions which are striving to resolve complex social issues by adapting and re-working centuries of urban innovation in a system designed—and still dominated—by men.

Some of the principles and practices in this book may fit well with the culture of one institution, organization or community but only align in part with the culture of another. This reflects both the limitation of books generally and the fact that policy and practices in design materialize in particular places and in specific ways. What each chapter hopes to develop is attention to the patterns, evidence-based and impact of centering women in cities.

Each chapter summarizes a critical issue related to women in cities and discusses feminist-focused approaches for urban change within that subject area. The book is designed so that chapters are stand-alone and can be read individually, and thus the key themes are reinforced and re-problematized in each chapter thematic. A matrix (Fig. 1.4) provides a chapter overview and illustration of the potential relationship of each topic to specialist disciplinary areas. It simultaneously conveys which actors are involved in initiating and/or maintaining a holistic, aggregated and integrated approach across government, practice and communities for maximum benefit to women and girls.

Following this introduction, which sets out the context for the book and outlines the foundations, themes and approaches, the larger structure of this book has three sections. Each section has three chapters that include diagrams, definitions, tips, deep dives and stories from women's lived experience. These components work together to be both explicit and directive when considering how city stakeholders can progress the needs of women and girls through design strategy, policy and action. Each chapter establishes the ways that women's participation through co-design set within a feminist framework is central to urban transformation. A synopsis of the three sections follows.

In **Part I: Resisting sexist cities** explores the ways urban space impacts, shapes and contextualizes women's lives in cities. It seeks to understand how urban design is implicated in gendered power relations by foregrounding women's experiences of sexism and bias across the course of their lives. **Chapter 2** examines how sexist street harassment underpins heterosexism in cities and explores the impact on women's equity and participation in city life. **Chapter 3** reviews the current state of hypersexualized advertising in cities and the ways that the proliferation of sexist advertising and media reinforces women's systemic inequality. It looks at public communication campaigns and the role of communication media in addressing

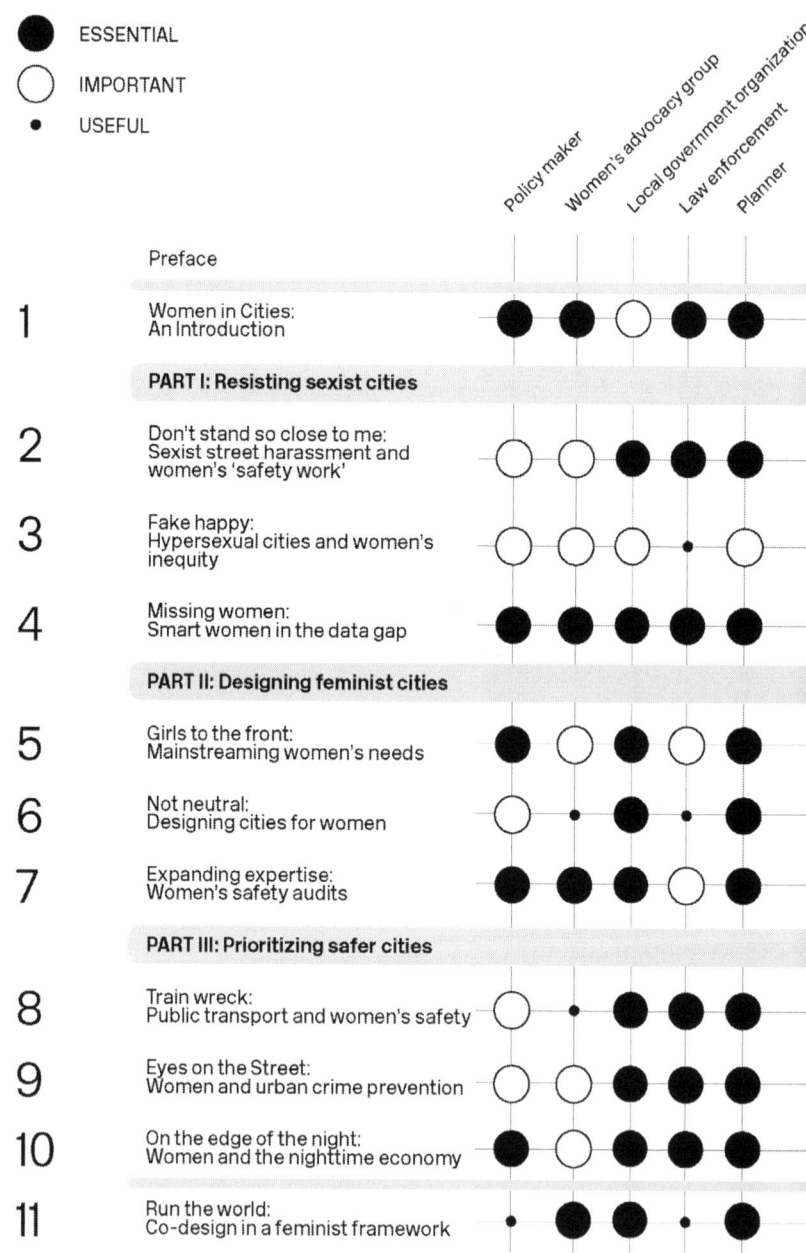

FIGURE 1.4 Chapter matrix and discipline reference.

WOMEN IN CITIES

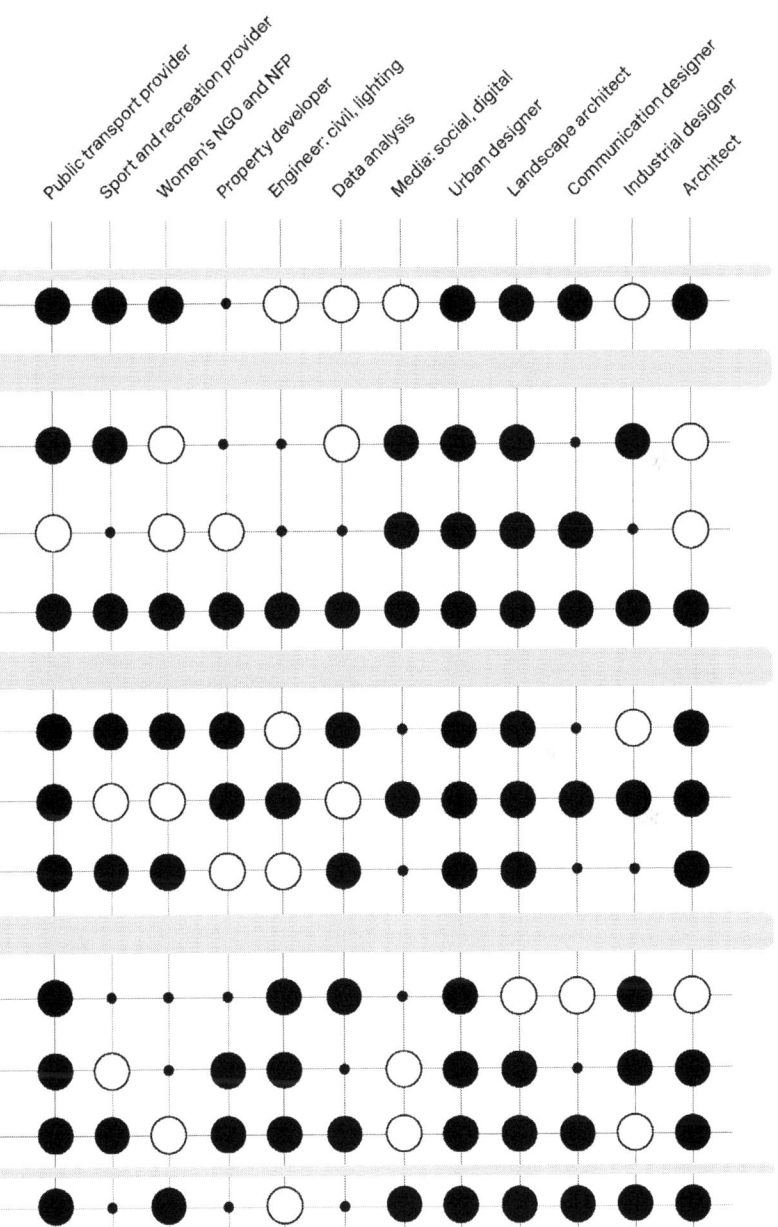

discrimination, violence and inequity using diverse, realistic and respectful gender portrayals. **Chapter 4** presents a case for sex- and gender-disaggregated data as vital for designing better cities and urban places. It asks how data about women can benefit policy, practice and communities, and discusses the emergence of alternative data collection methods to give voice to marginalized women and girls. This section shows how cities that challenge and legislate against hetero/sexist attitudes, gender stereotypes and neutrality construct places that demand respect and dignity for women and girls.

Part II: Designing feminist cities investigates how feminist-focused policies and practices accommodate the diverse needs of women. **Chapter 5** argues the pros and cons of gender mainstreaming by looking at the relationship between theoretical feminist frameworks and the practicable implementation of feminist policy. **Chapter 6** argues for the implementation of gender-sensitive design to challenge larger systems of women's oppression in cities and looks at the key tenets of gender-sensitive urban placemaking. **Chapter 7** focuses on the use of women's safety audits and the ways that communities can partner with women in the bottom-up process for women-centered communities. This section examines how feminist policy and practice can address women's inequity in the built environment.

Part III: Prioritizing safer cities examines how understanding the impact of male violence against women is central to altering women's access to civic spaces and public life. **Chapter 8** interrogates women's safe access to public transport and the issue of women's restricted mobility. It outlines how equitable access to public transport is a human right that is presently denied to women and girls across the globe and plots the evidence-based strategies that can be used to address it. **Chapter 9** critiques the gender-neutral approaches used in situated crime prevention and makes a case for urgently adopting women-centered crime prevention approaches to enable more equitable cities. **Chapter 10** presents an overview of women's participation (or lack thereof) in cities after dark, including new insights and opportunities for lighting technology. Women's oppression takes many forms, and this section discusses how architecture, planning and urban design impact men's violence against women and how the built environment can be a positive contributing factor to women's sense of inclusion and ownership of public space.

Chapter 11 is the concluding chapter that develops and reiterates the process of participatory co-design as a feminist method and the role of women-as-experts in the design process to facilitate new forms of engagement. This concluding chapter looks to the future of women-centered cities and speculates on the use of feminist praxis as an innovative mode for urban analysis and practice.

Throughout the book, the role of feminist design and activism is explored as a mode to challenge the status quo in the disciplinary areas of architecture, planning and urbanism. At the beginning of each chapter is a table titled "principles, practice, and participation." The table reviews:

Principles
Priorities for governance and legislation based on the chapter theme

Practice
Directives, methods and approaches for practitioners who are working with the chapter themes and are committed to avoiding gender bias, gender stereotyping and discrimination in their role

Participation
Opportunities for communities and local user groups to challenge barriers to women's participation in cities

There are highlighted definitions to describe the use of key (sometimes contested) terms:

Definitions

Definition boxes provide simple explanations for disciplinary-specific and technical terms.

Recognizing that there is no single, stand-alone solution that will make cities more equitable for women means that multiple strategies may be required or related. When additional information is also located in another section, a "TIP" will indicate where further or aligned information can be found:

> **TIP**
>
> Tips are extra bits of information and connections to other sections in this book that may be useful.

The lived experience of women is included throughout to support/challenge approaches and to include women's voices:

> **WOMEN'S STORIES**
>
> Women's stories are present through the book (sometimes with very minor edits) to narrate the experiences of women. These stories are selected from over 25,000 women internationally who have shared their stories across various research projects undertaken by Monash University XYX Lab. These women are from Delhi, Kampala, Lima, Madrid, Melbourne and Sydney. Sometimes these are composites from women living in the same city, where a selection of "representative elements from the data set" is constructed to compose a "new original" (Markham 2012: 342). This protects anonymity and allows for a full exploration of the complex context for women in cities.

Case studies and additional resources throughout the book highlight a deeper dive into a useful applied example:

> **DEEPER DIVE**
>
> Special topics and/or case study aim to provide extra, in-depth information and direction to other resources which are outside the scope of this book.

The material city is a representation of social and shared values, and as such, its capacity to communicate shared and diverse values is powerful. Feminist-focused policies, practices and planning strategies—while complex and imperfect—offer models for change that can be radically transformative. It is hoped that this book will provide direction to practitioners and research students and the confidence to accelerate new directions for women-centered cities.

PART ONE

Resisting Sexist Cities

CHAPTER TWO

Don't Stand So Close to Me

Sexist Street Harassment and Women's Safety Work

Principles
- Create legislation against sexist street harassment acknowledging how racism and homophobia impact women and girls' experiences
- Proactively address attitudes and behaviors, which are the root cause of violence against women and girls
- Publicly communicate definitions of sexist street harassment
- Mandate training for frontline staff about how to respond to the needs of women and girls who experience sexist street harassment

Practice
- Understand the key typologies and/or hotspots where sexist street harassment occurs and/or emboldens perpetrators
- Progress urban design that mitigates against sexist street harassment using gender-sensitive strategies to minimize occurrences

Participation
- Engage all genders in evidence-based bystander intervention training
- Engage with alternative mode for collecting sex- and gender-disaggregated data to understand how sexist street harassment impacts women and girls

Sexist Street Harassment and Women's "Safety Work"

Regardless of where they live or their socio-economic status, it is estimated that up to 90 percent of women and girls will experience sexist street harassment—perpetrated by men—in their lifetime (Fileborn 2017b: 188; Macmillan et al. 2000: 318; Lenton et al. 1999).[1] As the name suggests, sexist street harassment occurs "on the street" and in public spaces. While often described as "sexual" harassment (as opposed to *sexist* harassment), the behavior is not at all sexual, but is wholly defined by men exerting power over women and girls. This supports the fact that when men harass women and girls on the street, it is not a sexual interaction but a way to assert male heteronormative power. Professor of Cultural Studies Debbie Epstein suggests that "sexual harassment" be replaced with "hetero/sexist harassment"—a frame that may be more useful to those "on the receiving end" and includes a critique of the ways that harassment is institutionalized in heterosexuality (1997: 154–68).

The universalizing impact of sexist street harassment on women across all cultures, ages, ethnicities, religions and disabilities means that it has been a focus of feminist analysis over many decades, with a recent resurgence of attention because of feminist activism internationally. Contrary to a range of myths that construct it as innocuous behavior (minimized with phrases such as "boys will be boys" and "just harmless fun") and compartmentalized by the view that sexist street harassment happens infrequently or mostly after dark, feminist research identifies something far more concerning. Sexist street harassment can and does occur at any time, with many perpetrators emboldened to act "in broad daylight," exacerbating the shock, surprise and discombobulation for women and girls.[2] It is, therefore, far from an aberrant or rare event, but is ubiquitous, often derogatory, frightening and threatening to women (Kissling 1991: 455).

Sexist street harassment defines women's experiences of cities, revealing that urban space is not "simply the structural design of spaces" but also constructed from "feelings, fears, and anxieties" (Green et al. 2006: 866–867). This is supported by scholarship undertaken with women and girls where, through analyzing perceptions of urban safety, researchers have time and again confirmed the complexity of women's fear (Pain 2001: 910), particularly the fear of becoming victims of men's violent crime as well as the ways that heterosexuality is maintained on the street through "... regulatory regimes" (Valentine 1996: 148). For women and girls *all forms* of sexist street harassment have the potential to escalate to more violent forms of sexual assault.

WOMEN'S STORIES

I am tired of seeing sexist advertising on the streets where I live. It makes me uncomfortable and it sends a bad message to everyone in our community about how women should be valued.

While there has been an increase in social awareness of the pervasiveness of sexist street harassment in cities, the ways that it shapes the experiences of women and girls are neither well-understood nor taken seriously by policymakers, practitioners and communities. Women everywhere have adapted to the lack of address from authorities, and it is notable that many countries do not have legislation against sexist street harassment and do not even record data on the topic, which prevents any meaningful engagement with women's and girls' concerns.

Sexist street harassment (also called sexual harassment, street harassment, public harassment and eve-teasing)

Sexist street harassment is any form of unwanted sexual behavior that causes offense, humiliation, or intimidation, regardless of the intent. It occurs in public and semi-public spaces and intersects with racist, transphobic, homophobic, ableist, sizeist and/or classist harassment (Coy et al. 2021: 50; Kearl 2010: 5). With almost all incidents, men are the perpetrators and women are the victims (Herzog 2007: 580; Macmillan et al. 2000: 307). For the purposes of this book, the emphasis and inclusion of the word

> "street" is vital for communicating the impact of this behavior on cities and communities. Sexist harassment can be subtle or explicit, verbal, non-verbal and/or physical (see Fig. 2.1). It can be a single or repeated occurrence. Considered a form of sex discrimination and the result of gender inequality, sexist street harassment is also a form of violence against women.

The reasons given for the phenomenon of sexist street harassment plot a concerning history of urban violence perpetrated against women and girls. In *Behaviour in Public Places*, sociologist and social psychologist Erwin Goffman suggests that women are "open persons" and suffer from having no right to privacy (1963: 128). In "Wolf Whistles and Warnings," activist Pam McAllister suggests that street harassment reinforces the boundaries of public space which limit women in the public sphere and that this "needs to be exposed as the manipulative expression of power that it ultimately is" (1978: 37). Fatma El Nahry states that "it is not harmless" but "a direct reaction by men to women" and an "institutionalized system of violence" that is not about "how women behave in the public sphere" but "that they have chosen to enter the public sphere at all" (cited in Scholten et al 2019: 56). There is a strong consensus that sexist street harassment is a form of male backlash in response to women's increased participation in public life and the subsequent loss of men's perceived status (di Leonardo 1981: 52; Coy et al. 2021: 54; Kalms 2017: 77). Some researchers have also noted that men's harassment of women and girls is often perpetrated in groups, where men themselves view it as a form of bonding (Wesselmann et al 2010: x; Plan International 2019: 9); in this masculine mindset, the sexist street harassment associated with "girl watching" is an "officially sanctioned and widely publicized male pastime" (Hubbard 2008: 649). Sexist street harassment is therefore a way that men maintain power in cities, and in doing so, actively produce a space and culture of sexual terrorism for women and girls (Sheffield 2020: 200; Kissling et al 1991: 76).

The lack of intervention by those who have the power to stop the behavior authorizes men to continue to harass women on the streets without repercussions. The continued trivialization of women's concerns about sexist street harassment is well documented, as is the significant impact on women's lives (Vera-Gray 2018; West

2013; Tuerkheimer 1997). For example, Canadian research found that women may be negatively impacted "for days, months, and, in some cases, years" after an event of sexist sexual harassment, "illustrating the substantial and long-term effects this behaviour can have" (Lenton et al. 1999: 517–540) and the ways the impact can accumulate over time (Fileborn et al. 2017: 214). To minimize experiences of sexist street harassment as merely "harmless fun,"

Verbal or "catcalling"	Non-verbal
making comments that have a sexual meaning asking for sex or sexual favors cracking sexual jokes and comments unwanted comments demands for sex animal noises slut-shaming homophobic comment including compulsory heterosexuality comment gender policing	leering, staring and ogling shouting remarks stalking displaying rude and offensive material making sexual gestures, vulgarity public masturbation suggestive body movements towards you wolf-whistling lewd gestures car-honking curb-crawling (harassment from a car or vehicle)
Physical (with contact)	Continuum of sexist street harassment to violent crime and sexual assault
touching groping grabbing pinching slapping unwanted touching contact without consent slut-bashing	assault rape (including date rape, drug rape, gang rape) murder
Digital (in person)	Digital (remote)
showing /watching porn internet-facilitated stranger assault/rape cyber-flashing obscene phone calls	cyberstalking revenge porn

FIGURE 2.1 Sexual harassment is defined by a range of behaviors across verbal, non-verbal, physical and digital, and may escalate to violent crime and sexual assault.

"compliments" and/or "verbal banter" is to obscure the continuum of violence that women and girls must manage in cities. Importantly, naming the oppression that women suffer in relation to men's violence and "outlining structures of dominance" does not mean that women are powerless or lack agency (Grosser et al. 2021: 221); it is the naming that will allow women to challenge the existing order (Grosser et al. 2021: 222).

Managing the Risk of Men's Violence in Cities

The urban lives of many women and girls are centered around managing men's behavior. Most women carry cumulative experiences of sexist street harassment, which they perceive as "intimidating, harassing and violent" (Stanko 1985: 18) and as linked with a generalized fear of crime and victimization. This means women expend time and energy managing these intense feelings of fear and vulnerability as they anticipate incidents of sexist street harassment in their everyday lives. While this oppression is pervasive, for many women their vulnerability "does not equate to being powerless" (Benbrahim 2021: 109) and they deploy multiple "workarounds" to mitigate risk and increase their confidence in public space. Many women and girls consciously and unconsciously organize their movement through cities to avoid an incident of sexist street harassment. Equally, when sexist street harassment does occur, they focus on preventing the incident from escalating into something more serious, since "most women" are afraid of being a victim of rape and other crime most of the time (Kissling et al 1991: 84; Gordon et al. 1989; Stanko 1985). They understand that "managed poorly," an increase in verbal abuse can be followed by physical and/or sexual assault and even rape (see Fig. 2.1). Research confirms that "verbal abuse is often a prelude to physical assault" (Valentine 1993: 294) and there is a continuum of violence, such that what may be perceived as mundane rapidly moves to fatal (Kelly 1988: 97–137; Sheffield 2020: 197). It is entirely understandable, then, that women learn quickly that if they "speak back" and reject men's advances, violence may escalate into more serious forms of aggression and assault (Stanko 1985: 137) and when women minimize the event of sexist street harassment by saying, "nothing really happened," Kelly et al. suggest that "they are making a statement about how much worse it could have been" (1990: 51).

WOMEN'S STORIES

I have had multiple men try to approach me even after I've made it clear their advances were unwelcome. I have had people try to follow me into my apartment building. I have to wait for my rental contract to expire, then I won't be back again.

5pm on a Saturday night was followed by a group of teen boys making threats.

Managing these risks means that some women and girls will self-regulate and/or self-exclude from public life and this is, for them, a logical way to stay safe, as it means avoiding potential violence (Gordon et al. 1989; Vera-Gray 2018: 12–13). If incidents are regular, concerning, inescapable and/or terrifying, some women and girls will change jobs, move house, buy a car, or leave school as a result of the ongoing impact (Plan International 2018: 18).

When they are unable to avoid certain places or times of day, women carry the burden of managing sexist street harassment and use urban survival strategies to limit their vulnerability (Fig. 2.2). Even women who assert that they are not concerned about sexist street harassment will in fact describe some precautions they take to avoid being raped (Gordon et al. 1989: 3). These precautionary measures are constant and have been the subject of original research by sociologist Fiona Vera-Gray, who describes women's behavior as a form of "safety work." The term (originally coined by sociologist Liz Kelly), describes the "thinking process, decision-making, and embodied watchfulness" women use; in short, the energy that women spend planning, amending and strategizing their access to public spaces to prevent violence happening (Vera-Gray 2018: 12, 82).

carry a phone	run with a dog	ignore verbal harassment	wear reflective material if you're running at night	decide if the cost of a taxi is worth it
don't run at night	share your location with family or friends	stand up for yourself	don't speak back, it might provoke them	use multiple tracking apps or features
avoid car parks	check your backseat before getting in	don't draw attention	don't use public toilets	don't wear headphones
hold keys between your fingers	own a dog for protection	fake a phone call	pretend to wave to someone	know the opening hours of the businesses on your route
avoid eye contact with passers by	avoid unlit areas, especially at night	only have one earphone in	point your face at every CCTV camera just in case	take a photo of the driver's id
don't wear reflective gear, it might draw attention	tell someone how long you will be	don't wear headphones	stay safe	walk slowly around the corner, then run
walk clear of parked cars or bushes	don't wear something too revealing	change your route regularly to avoid being followed	text the number plate of your taxi	always carry money for a cab or Uber
leave school or work early so it's not too dark	don't wear shoes you can't run in	have 000 dialed in your phone just in case	cross the road to ensure no one is following	never leave a night out alone, even to go home early

FIGURE 2.2 An inventory of things that some women and girls to do to stay safe when out in public. Image Isabella Webb, Monash University XYX Lab, 2022.

> **DEEPER DIVE**
>
> For a comprehensive overview of women's "safety work" refer to *The Right Amount of Panic* by Fiona Vera-Gray, 2018.

By drawing attention to the restriction women place on their activities and the adaptations they make in order to negotiate public space, Vera-Gray is able to illuminate how safety work is acculturated into the lives of women and girls from an early age and becomes a habitual and often unconscious daily practice. Vera-Gray suggests that society has insufficient measurements for quantifying safety, yet the ways that women and girls "trade freedom for safety" require deeper consideration (Vera-Gray 2018). Vera-Gray makes a case for the ways that women's safety work successfully reduces the amount of sexist street harassment and, as such, is a form of "invisible labor" (2018: 17).

No amount of behavior modification will prevent the violence perpetrated by some men against women, and so, when safety work isn't successful, many women blame themselves (Vera-Gray 2018: 82). Paradoxically, and despite women's efforts, it is not possible for them to successfully avoid sexist street harassment all the time, but they may come to believe it is their responsibility to keep themselves safe and that managing sexism and men's violence against women is just part of negotiating urban life. Rather than centralizing the perpetrator's behavior as the source of their vulnerability, women may internalize the issue and conclude that it is their own fault.

Intersectional Experiences of Sexist Street Harassment

Women and girls of color as well as women and girls from lower socio-economic status are more at risk of being victimized in public (Pain 2001: 900). A variety of differences result from the cultures of different cities and communities (Kissling 1991: 452). For example, research has shown that in some cultural contexts, sexist street harassment can infringe on a young girl's right to education where girls will change or leave school as a result of the sexist street harassment they experience (Plan International 2018: 17). In this way, sexist street harassment intersects with gender, race, class and other forms of oppression (Pain 2001; Crenshaw 1991). For women who may already lack a sense of belonging in their communities because of their age, disability, ethnicity, gender, income, indigeneity, migratory status, race, religion and sexuality, sexist street harassment can amplify this disconnection and expose a chasm of inequality and discrimination.

WOMEN'S STORIES

A man, as I was walking to school, yelled out "fucking chink-loving bitch" and then muttered "suck my dick"—he was sitting at the public seats in the outdoor shopping area. It was really horrible and I immediately walked quickly away—felt targeted because I was a schoolgirl and I obviously thought he would never have said that to a male.

Street harassment and violence have negative impacts on men and boys too. While women are more fearful in public spaces, women's experience is not "counted" or viewed as "criminal"; paradoxically, crime statistics suggest that men are more likely to be the victims of crime (Vera-Gray 2018: 16). Certainly, minoritized men, in particular, express "situational fears of other men's violence" which is likely "based on their race or actual perceived sexuality/gender identity" (Sheffield 2020: 191). While worthy of deeper investigation, these specific and situated complexities are outside the scope of this book.

WOMEN'S STORIES

My mother and father observed the bad environment. Because this happens to me, my mother took me and my sister out of school

- **Sexist Street Harassment and Women with Disabilities:** Women are more at risk of experiencing disability than men (Yon et al. 2017: 34). While public spaces provide access to able-bodied people, urban planning is unlikely to consider women with disabilities or the ways that sexist street harassment may impact their experiences moving through cities. For women with disabilities, the issue of being physically excluded is compounded with the risk of sexist harassment when navigating public spaces.

  Women with disabilities will have limited access to safe spaces, especially when trying to flee violent situations. Inadequate support leads to social isolation with injustice for women, "manifest[ing] in barriers to their right to the city and thus reduced citizenship" (Yon et al. 2017: 34).

  Any assistance given to women with disabilities—often without their consent—as well as the fact that many women may rely on some form of physical support when navigating inadequate public transport systems, can leave women with disabilities vulnerable to perpetrators. Women with disabilities therefore incur exponential disadvantage because of the intersection of gender and disability with violence.

- **Sexist Street Harassment and Lesbian, Gay & Bisexual Women:** Lesbian, gay and bisexual women suffer not just sexist street harassment but *heterosexist* street harassment (Valentine 1993: 293–294; Kolysh 2021: 79–104). Lesbian, gay and bisexual women as well as gender diverse people may suffer increased, discriminatory, sexist street harassment, under the assumption that heterosexuality is the "normal" sexual orientation and privileged over other sexualities. Lesbian, gay, bisexual women are less likely to report to authorities. Women who are perceived as lesbian are more at risk of victimization and likely to experience "corrective heterosexism" (Kolysh 2021: 84) if they do not adhere to normative heterosexual expectations (and therefore breach multiple heterosexist, hypersexualized and stereotyped attitudes of men and boys); they are punished for deviating from normative heterosexuality (Epstein 1997: 203).

  Public displays of affection between lesbian and gay women in heterosexist urban spaces may also be subject to harassment and will be exacerbated by race where—for interracial lesbian couples—their displays of affection disrupt both the heterosexual/heterosexist space *and* discriminatory beliefs that people should couple with their own race (Steinbugler 2005: 433; Kolysh 2021: 91).

> **Heteronormativity**
>
> The concept that heterosexuality is the preferred, natural or normal mode of sexual orientation is universal. Sexual geographer Phil Hubbard suggests that "heterosexual norms are constructed and reproduced spatially" (2008: 640) and are "associated with certain material privileges as well as political rights" (Hubbard 2008: 643). Hubbard emphasizes the importance of "documenting how different spaces enable or constrain different heterosexual performances" (Hubbard 2008: 643).

Feminist scholar Simone Kolysh suggests the complexities of public aggression and the embedded heteronormativity of public spaces mean it is possible for heterosexual people (women included) to be aggressive toward lesbian, gay women and gender diverse people and that there are "different types of power ... in tension, all of which require an intersectional understanding" (Kolysh 2021: 7). Kolysh suggests that street harassment is heterosexist and a way for heterosexual men to enforce compulsory heterosexuality and heteronormativity.

> **DEEPER DIVE**
>
> For a fuller discussion of gender diverse and transgender experiences of street harassment, see Simone Kolysh's book, *Everyday violence: The public harassment of women and LGBTQ people* (2021).

Understanding Typologies and Hotspots for Sexist Street Harassment

Research has shown that there is a relationship between the types of urban spaces and where the perpetration of sexist street harassment occurs. The urban conditions of cities therefore "offer opportunities for offending as well as victimization" (Madan et al. 2016: 82) and should be a focus for policymakers, practitioners and communities when designing cities for women.

Understanding the complex geographic zones which shape women's daily mobility is central to the problem. It is a system which is highly gendered, as a greater proportion of women than men walk in cities, thus increasing their vulnerability to sexist street harassment (Fig. 2.3). Focusing on improving the walkability of streets and cities—including access, comfort, safety and active frontages—will encourage women to feel part of public spaces and increase their presence and feelings of safety.

By addressing the environmental and spatial factors that can embolden sexist street harassment, public policy, strategy and design can deter offenders and reduce uncivil behavior. Identified hotspots and areas of concern can be flagged for more intensive investment and priority intervention. The following typologies provide an overview of spaces where sexist street harassment proliferates.

- **Parks, Trails, Waterfronts and Recreation Facilities:** For women, recreational spaces are rarely entirely safe or entirely unsafe; they are complex physical environments that women choose to negotiate by managing their risk. Often defined by a lack of oversight and a space of reflection and repose, the common understanding of the park as sanctuary or space of respite from urban life also means that they are places that many women avoid, particularly at night. Walking is the most common recreational activity for women in most cities, and depending on socio-economic privilege, some women will view parks as safe and value the natural environment, while others will see them as unsafe and risky places due to the lack of visibility and isolation. Incidents that involve sexual harassment in parks, trails and waterfronts will receive media attention and shift the behaviors of women as a result. While some women and girls will benefit from the social networks and connections that they are able to forge when recreating in recreational spaces others, such as homeless women sleeping rough, will be at increased risk of violence.

City	Country	Region	Walking (%) Female	Male
Accra	Ghana	Africa	60.6	56.4
Kisumu	Kenya	Africa	50.5	38.3
Cape Town	South Africa	Africa	30.2	29.2
Delhi	India	Asia	66.2	39.9
Melbourne	Australia	Australia	17.0	16.3
London	England	Europe	33.7	29.3
Berlin	Germany	Europe	26.8	24.1
Cologne	Germany	Europe	26.0	22.9
Hamburg	Germany	Europe	26.9	23.1
Munich	Germany	Europe	23.4	21.6
Zurich	Switzerland	Europe	37.1	32.1
Buenos Aires	Argentina	Latin America	32.1	22.3
Sao Paulo	Brazil	Latin America	34.8	28.1
Santiago	Chile	Latin America	33.9	24.0
Bogota	Colombia	Latin America	41.0	29.1
Mexico City	Mexico	Latin America	40.3	23.3
Chicago	USA	North America	11.1	10.3
Los Angeles	USA	North America	13.2	12.0
New York City	USA	North America	31.8	30.2

FIGURE 2.3 The daily mobility of women with a comparison to men. Adapted from Rahul Goel, Oyinlola Oyebode, Louise Foley, Lambed Tatah, Christopher Millett, and James Woodcock (2022).

> **WOMEN'S STORIES**

I used to walk here regularly, but then I had a "minor" encounter with a creepy man. Realized that for long stretches of the path, there's no easy escape route if you're being harassed, and no easy way to access nearby residences to seek help, as there would be on a suburban street. Started limiting my walks here to busy times on weekend days only.

- **On the Street:** The street, unsurprisingly, is the most likely place for women to experience sexist harassment. It is the place where women move through frequently as they seek out education, work and socialize with friends. Women are more likely to use the streets and public spaces and for a wider variety of purposes than men (UN-HABITAT 2016: 20). For young girls in particular, the street is a complex space, as it represents a space of anonymity, freedom and self-expression. Many feel that the public space is more private than home or school, where there may be supervision by parents and teachers (Kern 2020: 66). The interactions and dynamics with men in cars are also concerning, where women and girls are "curb crawled" and harassed and/or threatened with assault or kidnapping by men (or groups of men) in cars.

- **Shopping Malls, Marketplaces or Highstreets:** While shopping malls with good passive surveillance and/or security may be places of relative safety, the surrounding areas where there may be a lack of "eyes on the street" hold safety issues for women and girls. Informal marketplaces are often overcrowded and threatening spaces where groping, pinching and other unwanted touching can occur.

> **WOMEN'S STORIES**

This street always feels abandoned, the shops are always closed, they don't look out on the street, there's nowhere to sit. It's just a bloody fast walk past a bunch of half-empty buildings hoping you won't get hassled. Everyone is skeevy, lots of old assholes hanging around . . . no women.

- **Public Transport:** Public transport is one of the most universally problematic spaces for women and girls managing sexist harassment and personal safety is the key barrier to increasing women's use of public transport. Transport networks and the intermediary spaces of train stations, bus stops and larger interconnecting hubs (including car parks, subways and overpasses) are sites where perpetrators have significant and assured access to women and girls. The over-crowdedness, anonymity and easy "getaway" is often a cover for emboldened perpetrators. For women, there are often spaces of entrapment in carriages, but also in the circulation systems of transport hubs; there may be a lack of multiple exit points and many women are "transit captives" in that they must use public transport for work or caring roles, with schoolgirls commuting at guaranteed times.

> **TIP**
>
> Further details about women's experiences of male violence in public transport spaces can be found in **Chapter 8—*Train wreck: Public transport and women's safety*.**

Pedestrian spaces which are the result of the dominance of cars, such as underpasses and overpasses, are designed to ensure the cars are moving safely, but these spaces are concerning and entrapping infrastructures for women and girls to navigate—often lacking surveillance and adequate lighting.

WOMEN'S STORIES

I was followed by a man from the train station to this spot after a scheduled class. It wasn't yet dark and there was no one around. I avoid this spot at all costs, day or night, and there never seems to be people around to help despite the train station being so close.

Hard to navigate if you're not used to the area. The underpass is incredibly dark. Not easy to escape if you're being followed. Right on the road so it's not safe to run. I avoid this stop unless it is daytime.

Reporting, Under-reporting and Counter-reporting

Like other forms of sexual violence, there are significant failures to address sexist street harassment and women can experience further harm through dismissal and re-traumatization when trying to seek justice (Fileborn 2017a: 1482). As Kelly et al. state:

> The law plays the central role in constructing 'what counts' as crime, and in the case of sexual violence (unlike, for example, public order offenses) it focusses almost entirely on extremes, thereby discounting many women's experiences. Thus, only a proportion of women's complaints are seen as legitimate, according to the law – legitimacy here defined in terms of the actions, behaviour and relationships of the male assailant and the female he victimises. Thus, the law suggests that clear distinctions can be made between violence and not violence, and thereby between abusive and 'normal' men.
>
> 1990: 41

These barriers to reporting sexist street harassment reflect broader issues for police and other authorities that have a poor track record in addressing violence against women. Many women and girls, for example, find that if they do seek out support from authorities, they are seen as lacking credibility, and that they themselves may be blamed or their experience will be diminished by the reporting process. For most women, whether to make a formal report will depend on both the type of sexist street harassment experienced and the legal jurisdiction in which it occurred. For younger women and girls, incidents may be so regular that it is entirely impractical to report each event. When victims do report, it is not uncommon for them to experience disbelief, trivialization, normalization, abdication from responsibility, as well as victim

Disbelief
Women lack credibility; they exaggerate and can't be believed. There are many highly publicized cases of this failure to believe.

Trivialization
There is no problem. No harm done. It's a low impact 'crime', if indeed it is a crime. Is there a risk of criminalizing generally accepted behaviour'?

Normalization
It's pointless to fight the inevitable. Boys will be boys, it's normal behaviour – we can't stop that.

Abdication
It's not my job (it's cultural, nothing to do with designers, planners)

Victim-blaming and stigmatization
Women should protect themselves, it's their fault. Women experience shame and blame if something happens to them (What was she wearing? What was she doing there? What was she thinking?)

FIGURE 2.4 Typical responses to sexual harassment reporting. Adapted from Gwen Kash (2019) and Anna Gekoski, Jacqueline M. Gray, Miranda A.H. Horvath, Sarah Edwards, Aliye Emirali & Joanna R. Adler, (2017). Collated by Dr. Gill Matthewson and Isabella Webb, Monash University XYX Lab.

blaming and stigmatization from authorities (see Fig. 2.4). It is unsurprising that researchers express concern about the under-reporting of incidents that occur in public and semi-public spaces (Vera-Gray 2016: 14; Macmillan 2000: 309). It is also unsurprising that, if women and girls do report incidents to authorities, the chances of action being taken are small; international research suggests that less than a third of the reports are formally followed up (Plan International 2019: 7). In research undertaken across five continents only 10 percent of young women reported incidents of sexist street harassment to authorities (Tanner et al 2020: 120).

WOMEN'S STORIES

I used to do morning personal training here; for months this guy would sit in his car and watch us group of women exercise in the morning. When our personal trainer reported his loitering to police they laughed at her and refused to check on him.

Under-reporting and access to accurate data on the prevalence of sexist street harassment is therefore a key challenge for policymakers, practitioners and communities. The cycle is a vicious one: as women and girls feel stigmatized by the unsatisfactory processes available to them, they suffer further indignation. They learn quickly that reporting sexist street harassment to authorities will likely result in a disappointing encounter (Plan International 2018: 19). These experiences and women's awareness of reporting issues contribute to further under-reporting, making the true extent of violence against women invisible.

It is not an easy task for authorities either. The anonymity of perpetrators can make an investigation difficult, therefore the offense of sexist street harassment is hard to regulate (Vera-Gray 2016: 11), identify or prosecute. The fleeting nature of the incident coupled with the fact that women and girls may not have a lot of information to share with authorities (e.g., appearance, car make and model, number plates) can make "it difficult to ascertain details about the offender" meaning that reporting can seem futile (Plan International 2019: 7). As the first occurrence of sexist street harassment often occurs before the onset of adolescence, there may be challenges to articulating the nuances of what has occurred alongside the existing challenge of having her report taken seriously.

Raising Women's Voices: Alternative Modes of Reporting

Since the mid-1990s, alternative modes of capturing sexist street harassment have provided an important way for women and girls to share their experiences in ways that traditional reporting or justice systems cannot (or will not). The #MeToo movement attests to a lack of progress on sexual harassment and gender equality more broadly (Grosser et al. 2021: 229). The "outrage economy" (Phipps 2018) has meant that in public discussion of the perpetration of harassment, there has been a rise in the use of media and technology to name unsafe places in cities (Kalms 2018: 162). These modes are critical to understanding women's experiences in cities and opening up "new possibilities for transnational or worldwide activism, and for sharing stories" (Wånggren 2016: 403). Right to Be (an activist organization originally named Hollaback!), for example, is one of the early movements to end harassment. Originating in the UK, the organization does not see each individual women's story as a singular incident but part of a larger issue that is worldwide and, when understood together, an expression of women's oppression as a sex class. Right to Be therefore extends the long feminist history of women sharing experiences in collectives and communities; this practice has transformed, using digital technology and social media, to develop new forms of feminist resistance and alternative forms of justice (Fileborn 2017a).

The capacity for technology to capture the collective voice of women and girls has transformed social awareness of sexist street harassment and is critical to uncovering the reality of women's sexist and violent experiences in cities. Alternative modes of reporting should contribute to more formal research from scholars or "authorized"—albeit inadequate—research by police and other authorities. Using research from alternative modes of reporting the tendencies, hotspots and intersectional oppressions of women and girls can inform wider urban interventions. Policymakers, planners and designers should not underestimate the role that data and technology can play to engage women in new ways of co-designing better outcomes for women in cities. Together, and when considering the typologies where women and girls manage sexist street harassment, the continuum of their vulnerability is significant.

TIP

For more information on digital storytelling and crowd mapping see **Chapter 4—*Missing women: Women and the data gap***

The Role of Policy, Practice and Communities

Because sexist attitudes and behaviors will take many generations to shift, policymakers, planners and designers are central to making cities safer for women and girls. Any urban action, intervention or activity to address sexist street harassment must sit within strong leadership and aligned legislation. The "mayors, managers and planners" need awareness of the issues to ensure that they engage with women and girls to support the implementation of gender-sensitive urban infrastructure and public space (Plan International 2018: 28). By creating thoughtful, gender-sensitive urban places, design can be deployed to mitigate women's risk of experiencing harassment and fearing violence. This involves what may appear to be small changes, but the reality is that most women will feel visible and welcome in public spaces as a result. When more women occupy public spaces then, increasingly, more women feel safer. And—better yet—while these changes will improve women's security, they will also help improve cities' accessibility and belonging for everyone.

- **Legislation:** The importance of governments, municipal bodies and local communities prioritizing the prevention of sexist street harassment and furthering existing public awareness is vital for the successful implementation of legislation. Effective on-the-ground response needs to support legislative initiative, whereby trauma-informed law enforcement officers and gender-sensitive surveillance can work alongside communication campaigns and education for primary prevention.

While laws against sexist street harassment are becoming more common—for example, at present, laws exist in Belgium, Portugal, Peru, New Zealand, Buenos Aires, Argentina, Quito, Ecuador, France and the UK (Plan International 2018: 30–32)—in most cities, there is less recognition and few established laws, if any. Some aspects of street harassment may be illegal (flashing for example) but most sexist street harassment is not considered a crime, as it is perceived as "too ambiguous to legislate" (Vera-Gray 2018: 7). The constraints around the enforceability of the crime are a hurdle, but policymakers should not underestimate their power to communicate the unacceptability of sexist street harassment. Legislation (whether

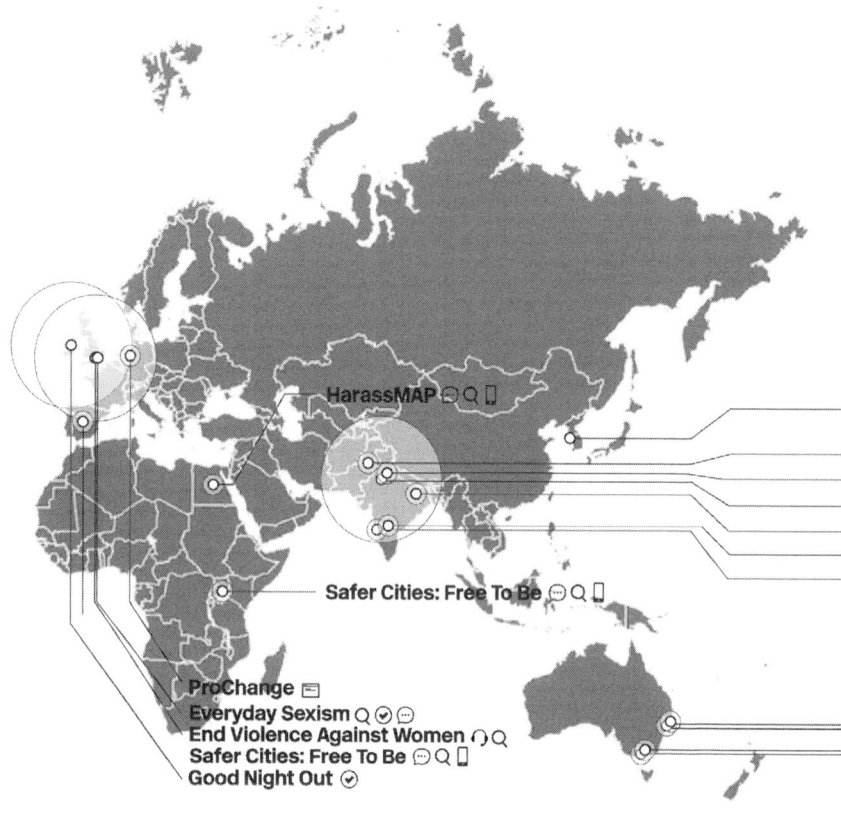

FIGURE 2.5 Alternative forums for collective action against sexist street harassment have been developed internationally with various modes for gathering women's experiences of sexist harassment. Note: crowd mapping and geo-locative data collection with women and girls is discussed in Chapter 4. Image Isabella Webb, Monash University XYX Lab.

DON'T STAND SO CLOSE TO ME

People Unite against Street Harassment (PUSH) 🗐
Safer Cities: Free To Be 💬 Q 📱
Why Loiter? 🗐
Safetipin 💬 Q 📱
Sayfty 🗐 ✓
Blank Noise 🗐 ✓
Why Loiter? 🗐

Right To Be Q ✓ 📱
Stop Street Harassment 💬 ✓

Cat Call's: Called Out 🗐
Safer Cities: Free To Be 💬 Q 📱
Safer Cities: Free To Be 💬 Q 📱
It's Not A Compliment ✓ ⌒

Safer Cities: Free To Be 💬 Q 📱

Observatory Against Street Harassment Q ✓

INITIATIVE TYPE
💬 Story telling
📱 App
⌒ Hotline/ support
🗐 Online / social media
✓ Training / education
Q Research

NUMBER OF LOCATIONS

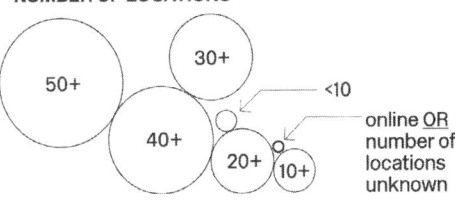

50+
30+
40+
20+
10+
<10
online OR number of locations unknown

criminal or civil) has a role to play in addressing sexist street harassment and is crucial for addressing this pervasive issue.

> **DEEPER DIVE: FRANCE: LAWS AGAINST SEXIST STREET HARASSMENT**
>
> In France, on-the-spot fines for "degrading or humiliating comments or hostile and offensive sexual or sexist behavior toward a person in a public place" (Chrisafis 2018: para 5) are enforced by an additional 10,000 police officers recruited to enforce the law and trained in identifying street harassment. Along with fines, offenders are requested to complete courses focused on sexual violence (at their own expense). The symbolic value of the French law and larger commitment also serves to act as a deterrent to perpetrators.
>
> Note: Any jurisdictions considering adopting such anti-sexist street harassment legislation must consider the consequences regarding the stigmatization of already vulnerable groups.

- **Training for Frontline Staff and Accreditation for Licensed Venues:** To respond to the needs of women and girls, frontline staff working in the public realm need to undergo evidence-based training in their responses to and management of sexist street harassment and reporting to support women and girls. They need to understand how built environment typologies contribute to sexist street harassment. For police, transport staff, security personnel, and other representatives working with members of the public, training would include being well-versed in the nuances of physical and non-physical sexist harassment and sexual assault. Research indicates that education of male police officers that emphasizes sensitive and empathic policing can challenge sexist views (Gekoski et al 2015).

Frontline staff would need to understand and recognize the intersectional aspects of sexist street harassment and violence against women. Competency in assisting women to report (if they want to) and an understanding of the barriers to reporting and any alternative modes are required too, as is the capability to respond in a trauma-informed manner. The staff of public service providers and venues (especially where alcohol is served) need to have awareness training in an effective reporting process (if it exists) to ensure that they can support and inform victims of the protocols for managing the sexism and violence of perpetrators. Frontline staff need to understand the local legislation and be committed to protecting the rights of women and girls.

- **Communication Campaigns to Combat Sexist Street Harassment:** Communication campaigns are used internationally and may include posters, print and online media, digital and social media, including video-based communication.[3] When designed with gender-sensitive messages—and often through engagement with women and girls—communication campaigns can target specific audiences with the aim to change behavior. Campaigns against violence toward women are deployed in cities all over the world; they include strategies to combat various forms of violence against women, including sexist harassment in cities, on public transport, at live events and on the street. As such, communication campaigns can "play a major role in activating and shifting community attitudes and behaviours to social issues" (TramLab 2020: 13).

WOMEN'S STORIES

On public transport I have experienced a lot of sexual harassment; I feel very unsafe when getting off a train in places where there are very few other people around at night. Especially when travelling to get home. I think some ideas to improve feeling safe on public transport are helplines to report sexual harassment and having advertisements on trains to say that sexually harassing behavior is unacceptable.

While the long-term efficacy of communication campaigns to combat sexist street harassment is limited, there is support from women and girls for the ways that public messages can create a public dialogue around issues that have historically been minimized or overlooked. For example, communication campaigns supported by mechanisms for reporting can result in an increase of women feeling empowered to use formal processes to report sexist harassment. There is also agreement that communication campaigns

FIGURE 2.6 Illustration of sexual harassment campaign, "Respect women 'Call it Out' 2018, Australia." Illustration Isabella Webb, Monash University XYX Lab 2022.

can communicate the public "codes" and expectations about attitudes and a sense that this contributes to longer-term change (TramLab 2020: 14). Successful strategies are informed by diverse community voices and aim to build momentum for attitudinal and behavioral change that will reduce violence against women.

DEEPER DIVE: RESPECT VICTORIA COMMUNICATION CAMPAIGN

Respect Victoria, established in 2018 as part of the Safe and Strong strategy, developed and implemented three campaigns designed at changing the social norms, behaviors and attitudes that allow all forms of family violence and violence against women to occur; these include: Respect Women: Call It Out (Fig. 2.6). Consumer research undertaken in 2018 indicated that those who had seen one of the campaigns had more positive attitudes toward gender equality, the police, and the government's response to family violence and violence against women (Respect Victoria 2020). Respect Victoria is currently undertaking and commissioning research to better understand the drivers of violence against women.

- **Training for Bystanders:** For women to feel safe, they need to be visible to other people who are connected to public space and are able to notice signs of stress and distress. Evidence about techniques for intervention in sexist street harassment is ongoing and is viewed as a method to manage the prevalence of sexist street harassment and provide informal surveillance when more formal surveillance (like police, security guards or bouncers) may not be present.

  It is increasingly common for organizations to "address the importance of being a bystander, how to identify harassment and safe, practical strategies for intervening" (Fileborn 2022: 107). De-escalation techniques seem to be useful, but the ways that bystanders intervene are wide-ranging, different across cultures and may or may not be effective. Criminologist Bianca Fileborn's research has examined a range of direct and indirect bystander actions and/or interventions. These included: verbal intervention directed at perpetrator; ejecting perpetrator from the spaces; making physical space between the victim and perpetrator; "checking in" verbally with the victim; contacting police about a concerning incident; intervention by a male partner; and support from the physical presence of bystanders (2017b: 192–195). While bystander intervention tools are promoted as ways to assist with de-escalation of sexist street harassment, further evidence is required to "inform safe and effective intervention" (Fileborn 2022: 107).

- **Co-design:** Crucial to the gender-sensitive design of cities and communities is engagement with women and girls in a process of co-design, which should also include their involvement in the post-occupancy and monitoring of public space, infrastructure and public services. While more professional women at the decision-making levels of urban planning will provide impact, it is also necessary to involve those who will benefit from the public spaces, which requires local investment and relationship building with diverse communities of women.

- **Safe Spaces:** A "safe space" is a feminist term developed during the consciousness raising circles in the 1970s and has become a contested idea in feminist politics (Lewis et al. 2015: 1). While the term has continued to be defined and re-defined by women's groups over the last thirty years, women's-only safe spaces have been called into question within the broader discourse and politics of gender diversity. In the contemporary context, some businesses, communities, music events and transport service providers support women through well publicized forms of safe space. Research by Plan International with young women and girls found that safe spaces in cities (particularly in transport and entertainment hubs) were a priority (2018: 31). Crucially, the safe space would require "specially trained staff, where girls can go, both to report harassment and to escape from it" (Ibid.). From the perspective of women and girls, safe spaces are designated zones but are also symbolic places that validate their concerns about sexist sexual harassment—that it is taken seriously and is made visible.

- **Lighting Strategies:** Many streets are lit to accommodate vehicular transport and neglect the needs of pedestrians. This can create areas of shadow, glare and inconsistency with large contrasts between the illuminated and non-illuminated areas of the footpath and passageways. Being able to distinguish shapes and colors also helps to create a sense of safety (Merchant 2019) as does being able to distinguish a passer-by—and gage potential risk.

WOMEN'S STORIES

Very poor lighting, close to train line, have been approached by men around this spot and worried about being followed home.

Personal safety risks are greater after dark, when poor lighting (or lighting that is not maintained or subject to vandalism) creates opportunities for sexual harassment and assault to occur, especially in the entertainment district, where alcohol consumption is also a factor. Improved lighting increases feelings of safety and encourages more women into public spaces which, in turn, means there is more oversight of people and their behaviors. Research with young women reveals a sensitivity to cool white light, with warmer light promoting feelings of safety (Kalms 2019). Urban spaces should work with warmer color temperatures to make women-focused places.

> **TIP**
>
> Further details about violence against women and safety can be found in **Chapter 9 — *Eyes on the street: Women and urban crime prevention***

Unburdening Women and Girls

The fear, anger and distress generated by managing the threat of sexist street harassment can dominate women's and girls' lives in cities. Women's vulnerability to sexist street harassment and the threat of escalation of violence limit their capacity to access and participate fully in public life. It is unfortunate that many of those who have the power to change approaches to violence against women—in all its forms—continue to ignore women's right to safely access cities. Many follow the narratives of neoliberalism, which serve to keep women's stories invisible and cloaked in a false rhetoric of neutral policy that ignores the rights of women and girls.

It must be widely acknowledged that sexist street harassment is part of a larger system of violence against women, all of which are strategies to control women through sexual terrorism (Kissling 1991: 455). The culture of minimization, victim blaming and normalization contributes to under-reporting, with women and girls internalizing the issue.

The challenges and opportunities for addressing sexist street harassment issues in policy, planning and design of cities are paradoxical. The goal is to challenge gender stereotypes and to change men's attitudes toward women and girls, and—through primary prevention—prevent violence against women altogether. Equally, there needs to be balance, with understanding that behavior change is slow and, at best, several generations away. In this sense, the built environment, planning and design have a key role to play.

This cannot be underestimated by policymakers, planners and designers. Women's experiences of sexist street harassment need to be taken seriously and governments need to prioritize effective legislation that criminalizes all forms of men's violence against women and girls. The role of planning and design is to recognize that participatory co-design with women and girls can ensure that the implementation of communication campaigns, safe spaces, lighting and other urban strategies can free women from the burden of sexist street harassment. When women develop stronger ties to their communities and enjoy their right to occupy and shape public places, then progress is made.

CHAPTER THREE

Fake Happy

Hypersexual Cities and Women's Inequity

Principles

- Use feminist definitions of sexist advertising
- Follow standards from international best practice to manage gender discriminatory advertising in urban places
- Consider legislation to counteract sexist and gendered stereotyping in urban advertising
- Instate gender-sensitive processes in approvals for urban advertising
- Penalize advertisers who breach standards by suspending distribution and applying a financial penalty
- Monitor and assess breaches. Refer to higher authority if necessary
- Regulate the location/placement of some advertisements
- Support research into the increase of personalized digital/tech-based advertising and their potential to cause harm
- Contextualized action against sexist advertising and media as part of a range of interventions to change sexist attitudes and behaviors
- Provide clear and well-communicated avenues for public complaint

Practice

- Embed gender-sensitive design education in tertiary curricula for architecture, urban planning, media and communication design students
- Increase the representation of women practitioners in regulatory positions and processes
- When designing urban places consider the placement of advertising infrastructure and the ways it may interact with the community and context
- Re-consider the specification of public infrastructure that allows for advertising to be embedded in the asset

Participation

- Increasing community awareness and complaints process
- Raise awareness of sexist and pornified advertising via social media platforms
- Join online petitions and campaigns
- Boycott products and services by advertisers that breach standards or legislation
- Provide media awareness and literacy training in schools and public libraries

Sexism, Pornographication and Women's Oppression

Over the past century, the built environment has been transformed by capitalist and neoliberal advertising media. In the context of "sexual liberation" sexist images have flourished in the public realm. As the passive, mute advertising images of women produced in the 1950s (Gill 2008: 42) have evolved, the relaxation of censorship in the 1960s and 1970s, and the impact of an increase in men's access to prostitution and pornography, has supported a concerning transformation of advertising images encountered in public spaces where women are routinely objectified through sexist representations (Kalms 2017: 94).

Heteronormative and heterosexist representation now dominate socio-cultural life, with the proliferation of gender stereotypes that reinforce and regulate sexist attitudes toward women and girls. While lifting of stigma associated with sex and gender is welcomed and mostly viewed as a positive social step in the context of the "sexual revolution" (Jeffreys 2015: 61), the last two decades have seen a marked shift in urban media and outdoor advertising, where sexualized, sexist and pornographically-styled images are now ubiquitous and are propelled by the normalization of hardcore pornography available via the internet (Kalms 2017). A pro-sex viewpoint may take the position that if these images are readily available on any computer or smart phone, then regulating sexist images in public space is inconsequential. Some researchers have argued that sexualized advertising images that circulate in the contemporary city are unproblematic and can be understood as evidence of women's personal freedom (McNair 2002). Certainly, the hardcore, violent, racist and paedophilic pornography available via online pornography can make "soft-core" or sexist representation in urban advertising seem mundane, but this belies the ways the private and public consumption of sexist and pornographic images reinforce male violence against women.

Research consistently shows negative effects of sexist advertising on women and girls; furthermore, when unavoidably displayed in public space, these images and messages serve to frame women as sex objects and reinforce gender stereotypes. Researcher and commentator Lauren Rosewarne argues that the perpetual display of women's bodies creates urban environments that are "complicit" in women's social exclusion, sexual harassment and fear for their safety (2007a: 137). The Task Force on the Sexualisation of Girls Report links sexualization with "impaired cognitive performance in college-aged women" as well as a "raft of other body, eating and mental health disorders" (APA 2007: 23). Frequent exposure to media images that sexualize girls and women affects how girls conceptualize femininity and sexuality. In addition, sexist advertising impacts the physical and mental health of the women and girls and undermines attempts to influence men's violence against women (Papadopoulos 2010: 25; Women's Health Victoria 2019: 2) and gender inequality more broadly.

> **Sexist advertising**
>
> Sexist advertising is markedly different to advertising that shows healthy relationships and positive sexuality (Drenten et al. 2020: 45). Advertising is considered sexist when it portrays sexualizing, objectifying and/or degrading images of women and stereotyped representations of masculinity and femininity that reinforce harmful gender norms. Sexist advertising has a cumulative effect on shaping societal beliefs, attitudes and behaviors. Sexually objectifying images of women in advertising negatively impact the health and wellbeing of women and girls, in particular. Sexist advertising may include images and depictions that:
>
> - Degrade women
> - Affect human dignity
> - Promote discrimination based on sex, gender and/or sexual orientation
> - Endanger public sexual health or safety through unhealthy body ideals
> - Show nudity that denigrates based on sex or gender
> - Show one sex or gender as socially, financially, or culturally subordinate/superior to the other sex or gender
> - Portray one sex or gender with negative personal characteristics
> - Are offensive or derogatory appraisals of women, men or gender diverse people
> - Show violence against women and girls
> - Discriminate based on sex or gender (but also race, age, ethnicity, religion, indigeneity and disability).

Pornographication, Porno-chic, Raunch Culture, Hypersexualization . . . You Know It When You See It[1]

Some feminists have argued that the use of the word "sexualization" is misleading and problematic (Coy et al. 2021: 50). They suggest that the problem is two-fold: first, it mistakenly implies that there is a "neutral" connection between the image and sex, which does "not adequately or accurately name what is happening as being fundamentally linked to the pornography industry and to the sexual inequality of women" (Tyler et al 2016: 8). Second, it is often used in the context of the sexualization of children (which is an appropriate and justified concern) which problematically distracts—if not obscures—the issue of feminist criticism, namely, the impact of the mainstreaming of pornography on *adult* women (Tyler et al 2016: 10).

> **Pornographication**
>
> The term "pornographication" can be used to describe the mainstreaming of pornographically-styled images and an increasing "accessibility" and "acceptability" of pornographic imagery in non-pornographic forms of popular culture (Coy et al. 2021: 50).

Feminists who take a more critical approach to sexist and sexualized advertising choose to use a range of terms to define their shared concern. Gender researcher Anette Sørensen describes "porn chic" as the "cultural process by which pornography slips into our everyday lives as a commonly accepted and often idealized cultural element" (2005: 2). Sociologist Gail Dines exposes links between the sex industry and the mainstreaming and normalization of porn-styled images using the term "hypersexualized media" (2010)—a term widely used to describe the uptake of the aesthetic of stripping and pornography within popular culture—including the built environment with the expansion of pornography into urban spaces in unforeseen and concerning ways (Kalms 2017). More recently, gender and consumption academic Lauren Gurrieri uses the term "patriarchal marketing" to describe how advertising operates within a male-dominated power structure that oppresses and exploits women (2021: 364). Researchers Meagan Tyler and Maddy Coy argue that the "pornographication" of urban spaces highlights the male's sex rights and creates hostile spaces for women (2021: 56–57). These researchers highlight that the term "sexualization" obscures the greater harm of pornographication and the ways that the public objectification of women connects to

FIGURE 3.1 Example of type of pornographication in public space infrastructure. Illustration Isabella Webb, Monash University XYX Lab 2022.

pornography. It also obscures how the proliferation of pornified images of *some* women results in *all women* expecting to be objectified, commodified, and required to subjugate themselves to men's desires.

Feminist researchers and activists call for greater understanding of the ways that advertising draws on representational qualities in the pornography industry (Kalms 2017; Tyler et al. 2016). They are rightly concerned that when the discussion is "lightened," there is a risk that policymakers, planners, designers and society more broadly will lack a critical understanding of how pornography is a cultural influence on the built environment and its impacts on women's inequality. Decision-makers may overlook the ways that pornified advertising exists within a continuum of men's violence against women (Fig. 3.2) and miss the fact that accepting the circulations of pornified advertising images in public space also accepts women's oppression in cities. In her discussion of the convergence of fashion photography and pornography in the 1990s, scholar of political science and feminist Sheila Jeffreys suggests that the distinction between the two is narrow and they both "popularize" the sex industry (2015: 68). Jeffreys' argument correctly positions pornified advertising in the context of larger systems of violence against women and in the context of women's degradation (see Chapter 1, Fig. 1.2). This is supported by a meta-analysis of published research in peer-reviewed English-language journals between 1995 and 2015 which found that exposure to pornified content results in a "diminished view of women's competence, morality, and humanity" (Ward 2016: 570) as well as by scholarship by Crabbe et al. who argue that the content of pornography and sexual media "influences children and young people's attitudes, behaviors, and sexual scripts" (2021: 4).

Types of Representations of Women and Girls

Pornographically-styled advertising and media include a range of images of women that all frame women's identity as one requiring continual regulation (Kalms 2017: 22). These images rely on the fact that sexuality in mass culture is attention-catching (Sørensen 2005: 2).

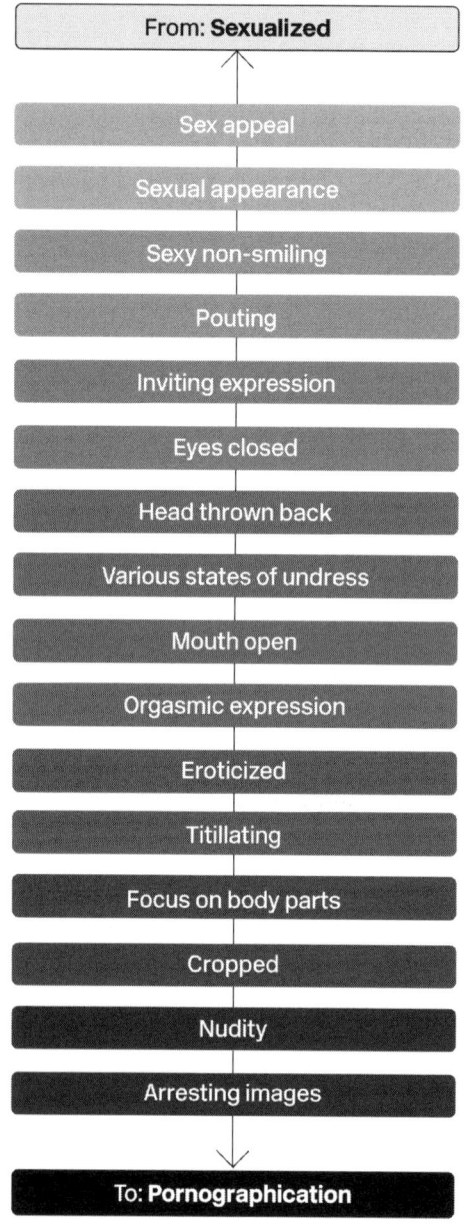

FIGURE 3.2 Types of representations of women and girls. Adapted from Nicole Kalms (2017); Lauren Rosewarne (2007a); Leena–Maija Rossi (2007).

Intersecting with the issue of pornographication is the young age of the women and girls and the invisibility of women over forty (Gurrieri 2021: 366). The dominance of women with white skin also means that analysis of other power systems require exploration. Research suggests that the representations of marginalized and/or multiracial communities feature stereotypical portrayals. For example, in 2022, the Advertising Standards Authority (ASA) in the UK looked at the advertising representation of Black, Asian and minority ethnic groups to understand how "stereotypes associated with race and ethnicity" create offense and/or harm from the perspective of members of the minority groups depicted. They found that advertising "that sexualised and/or objectified ethnic groups" is harmful, noting the fetishization and eroticization of Asian women (ASA 2022). This reflects the position of researchers Harrison et al. who suggest that the sociopolitical context is often missing from multiracial representations in advertising, where "multiracial representations are used as a form of cultural currency and mythologize mixed-race bodies as the new beauty standard and as representing a racial bridge, physically and culturally tailored to ameliorate perceived racial divides" (2017: 503). These examples serve to look beyond the pornographication through sex and gender, to suggest how advertising creates dual oppressions through age, disability, ethnicity, geographic location, income, indigeneity, migratory status, race, and religion.

> **TIP**
>
> For insights into advertising, diversity and inclusion refer to: *Promoting diversity and inclusion in advertising: A UNICEF playbook* (2021).

Overexposure

Pornographically-styled images in the public realm cannot be "dodged or ignored" (Kalms 2017: 50; Rossi 2007: 129) and encountering them in public space is guaranteed. Unlike images and media explored on a personal device or in the privacy of one's own home, the pornographically-styled images situated in the public realm cannot be turned off (Kalms 2017). In the 1970s, it was estimated that the average North American was exposed to around 500 ads per day; by 2000, that estimate had climbed to 3,000 advertising messages a day and by 2006, the estimate was 5,000 a day. Today it is estimated to be up to 10,000 a day (Bloor 2020), although potentially much more, given the number of platforms and the "blurring—if not the complete breakdown—of the boundaries between advertising and other media" (Kohrs and Gill 2021: 529). With approximately 20 percent of ads containing sexual content (Sorrow 2012), this raises question about the ways audiences are held captive advertising images which circulate in public space.

Pornographically-styled images can contribute to or induce hostile built environments (Coy et al. 2021; Kalms 2017; Rosewarne 2007a; 2007b), where the portrayal of women in gender-stereotyped and heteronormative ways reinforce heteronormative behavior and "attitudes that favour opposite-sex sexuality and relationship," which in turn "endorse heterosexuality as the normal and preferred sexual orientation" (Kalms 2017: 5–6). This hostility may be increased for lesbian, gay and bisexual women where heteronormative representations of women in the public realm reflect a form of compulsory heterosexuality (Rich 1980). This may ostracize women who do not conform to an ideal of femininity.

Understanding Infrastructures of Advertising Media in Cities

The urban spaces of cities—particularly those focused on retail, entertainment and transport infrastructure—are the landscapes where contemporary advertising often presents pornified advertising images. In recent decades, the sponsorship (and provision of urban infrastructure by advertising companies) has further complexified once public and ad-free infrastructure. Visible surfaces are viewed as an opportunity for a vast range of traditional and innovative outdoor advertising formats, from billboards and digital media to projections and geolocated pop-ups on personal devices.

Today, everything from street furniture to bus shelters, public toilets, rubbish bins, buses and scooters may be the site of commercial messages in a mostly unregulated context. Women observe that when sexist and sexualized advertising and media are in a public context (for example, transport spaces like bus stops,

Mobile spaces and non-places (Auge 1992)

Transport networks	Billboard
Mobile advertising: Buses, scooter, vehicle, train, tram, ferry	Advertising wrap
Transport Infrasructure: Bus & tram shelters, train stations,	Corporate sponsored urban infrastructure
Freeways	Civic branding
On the street	Street furniture
Airports	Bus shelters
	Rubbish bins
	Interactive screens
	Multi modal
	Spectaculars
	Brandscapes

'Middle zones' (Clara Greed 1994) and spaces of 'Public Intimacy' (Brian McNair 2002)

Shopping precincts	Billboard
Entertainment areas	Advertising wrap
Sex districts	Corporate sponsored urban infrastructure
Public toilets	Civic branding
	Street furniture
	Rubbish bins
	Interactive screens
	Multi modal
	Spectaculars
	Brandscapes

FIGURE 3.3 Sites of urban media infrastructure in cities.

stations, and especially in spaces where they may be waiting), a confluence occurs. For example, sexist advertising may increase feelings of vulnerability; research suggests that sexualized content can cancel out positive messages in public space (TramLab 2020: 14). In this sense, advertising does not exist as a standalone visual or ineffective wallpaper, but is affected and altered by competing messages, the media infrastructure and local context, as well as the people and density within that context.

Normalization of Violence Against Women

When pornified images of women and girls proliferate in public space, social interaction is impacted. The harm occurs both to the women "performing" in the images and to women as a class, through the "increasing normalization of the sex industry and its broader cultural influence" (Coy et al. 2021: 55). Not only are sexist attitudes normalized, so too are the violence, victimization and exploitation represented in the images. As advertising as a technique aims to persuade a public response, to change opinions and promote ideas, then it makes sense that some men's expectations of women will be shaped by these images. Indeed, the demand for and popularity of these kinds of images means that "some areas of porn have become more and more extreme in the violence directed at women" with the result that other forms of pornography become normalized and move seamlessly into other respectable arenas (Jeffreys 2015: 63). Some women will be impacted and may rehearse the pornified tropes in advertising images to meet social expectations of "beauty," "value" and "sexiness." The effects can and do reinforce male violence against women (Kalms 2017).

> **TIP**
>
> Some of the discussion about advertising media is extended by the discussion of sexist street harassment in **Chapter 2**. For example, the pornification of public space can not only make women feel unsafe but should also "be considered a form of sexual harassment" (Coy et al. 2021: 57) and becomes a landscape of sexual harassment and social exclusion (Rosewarne 2007a: 137).

The violence of pornographication in cities needs to be contextualized within a spectrum of sexism, sexualization and abuse, including sexual harassment and assault, coercion, prostitution, and the trafficking of women and girls (See Fig. 1.3 showing the continuum of gender-based violence). Coy et al., for example, argue that the expansion of pornographication normalizes "various forms of the sex industry," recreating women's inequality

(2021: 56) and reinforces women's subjugation within other systems of exploitation (Kalms 2017: 231).

Urban Advertising and the Role of Policy and Activism

While some may argue that advertising and media images are just a "backdrop" with little impact on behavior and relationships, feminist scholars argue otherwise to outline that hypersexualized advertising and media reflects and maintains male authority in public space (Coy et al. 2021; Kalms 2017; Rosewarne 2007a). Communication analysts support this concern and suggest it is naive to underestimate the impact of sexist and pornified images in the urban environment. Neuroscientist Cordelia Fine points out that the "cultural realities and beliefs" about men and women are represented "in commercials, in conversations, in the minds, expectations or behaviors of others; or primed in our own minds by the environment" (2011: 95). As cities are now the context for constructing and rehearsing gender stereotypes, policymakers, practitioners and communities alike need to understand how media and advertising intersect with the built environment, sexism and inequity. This requires city stakeholders to consider urban space from an expanded perspective, to recognize how various disciplinary areas overlap and the social–cultural interactions which take place because of this context and connection. There are four main areas to consider in terms of sexist and pornified images: legislation, co- or self-regulation, media literacy training and community advocacy.

WOMEN'S STORIES

A ban on sexist advertising would contribute to less physical, sexual harassment in the same spaces.

- **Legislation:** Legislative models can be an effective way to change attitudes through the alignment of public commitment to gender equality and the images and messages of public advertising. Legislation "sets a clear standard for advertisers and the community about what is acceptable" and can provide opportunities for active monitoring (Women's Health Victoria 2019: 4). Some countries have progressed legislation and others have yet to enact laws pertaining to sexist advertising (often citing the primacy of free speech). Some cities have gender equality legislation that prohibits sexist advertising, but the scope of the legislation differs, and some countries may have more generic laws related to human rights and dignity (PILPG 2015: 48). This diverse context poses several challenges for progressing equity for women and girls in cities where cityscapes may be dominated by heterosexist and stereotyped media.

For example, at the time of writing this book, seven countries have in place a form of legislation that prohibits gender discrimination in advertising in general terms (Belgium, France, Finland, Greece, Hungary, Ireland, UK), while two countries (Norway and Spain) have in place legislation that specifically addresses the portrayal of gender in advertising (Women's Health Victoria 2019: 13).

France, for example, has a legislative framework that includes a broad range of protections that restrict practices of sexist advertising bolstered by "pre-existing requirements to monitor 'human dignity' and discrimination in the media" (Gurrieri et al. 2019: 18). The 2014 Law for Real Equality between Women and Men drives the focus on how women are represented in the media. Two regulatory bodies, the High Authority for Audiovisual Media (Conseil Supérieur de l'Audiovisuel, CSA) and the Authority for Self-Regulation of Advertising (Autorité de Régulation Professionnelle de la Publicité, ARPP), play a role in monitoring compliance of audio-visual broadcast content and posters and billboards respectively (see Gurrieri et al. 2019: 18–19 for detailed outline of roles).

Outdoor advertising highlights a gap in the French legislative framework between the remit of the CSA (audio-visual media) and the ARPP (posters and billboards). Gurrieri et al. summarize the strengths and weaknesses of France's approach when they state:

> The French system demonstrates the power of clear legislative instruments, offering government regulators the capacity to remove offending content and sanction advertisers. However, in

articulating these requirements in a narrow manner the state has limited the capacity of regulators to address the breadth of sexist advertising. Further, by separating both the legislation and its regulatory administrator from the industry and its mechanisms of self-regulation, a disconnect is created regarding the appropriate bounds of advertising as well as potential confusion over the mechanisms of responsibility and regulation.

2019: 19

DEEPER DIVE: FRANCE

An ARPP ruling against fashion brand Yves Saint Laurent led to the introduction of municipal bans regulating outdoor advertising in Paris.

During Paris Fashion Week 2017, Yves Saint Laurent's "porno chic" ad campaign displayed on the city's outdoor advertising sites featured "very thin, fishnet-clad women in stiletto roller skates, splay-legged and draped over furniture" (Lampen 2017). The ad campaign was criticized as "incitement to rape" by viewers and prompted more than 200 complaints to the French advertising watchdog.[2] Raphaëlle Rémy-Leleu, spokesperson for French feminist group *Osez le Feminisme!* (Dare to Be Feminist!) said the campaign subtext was extremely violent and sexist and that the women are shown in submissive positions and are objectified and hypersexualized.[3]

In response, the Council of Paris (the body responsible for governing the city) voted for a new contract for outdoor advertising controlled by the municipal government. Effective January 1, 2018, outdoor advertising that propagates sexist, homophobic, ageist, ethnic and religious discrimination, along with "degrading" or "dehumanizing" depictions of people and "images that adversely affect human dignity" are prohibited (Rath 2017). It is too soon to assess the effectiveness of these measures; however, this example demonstrates the potential of strong legislative constraints on advertising.

Research by the UN Women and Unstereotype Alliance in a study across twenty countries shows attitudes toward gender roles have deteriorated and that the media portrays women's and men's gender-stereotyped roles. For example, 68 percent of respondents believe that the "media portrays women in traditional female roles, such as wives, mothers, or caregivers" (up 14 percentage points since 2018) and 72 percent of respondents believe the "media represents men in conventional male roles, including as providers for the family, as leaders, or as businessmen" (up 20 percentage points since 2018) (UN Women 2022: 62–64).

Some South American countries have their own anti-sexist advertising legislation, such as the Brazil state law against sexist advertising in Rio de Janeiro.[4] Additionally, many countries in this region have self-regulatory and co-regulatory frameworks. For example, in October 2019, the *Buenos Aires Declaration for Progressive Advertising* was launched by the World Federation of Advertisers (WFA), and the national advertiser associations of Argentina, Brazil, Colombia, Chile and Paraguay at the WFA's annual Latin American Regional Meeting.

The WFA is a global organization representing the common interests of marketers. It is a not-for-profit organization that represents client-side marketers, not agencies, media owners or vendors. WFA's aim is to champion responsible and effective marketing communications worldwide.

The *Buenos Aires Declaration* signatories are committed to:

- Promoting the development of progressive content that doesn't objectify but instead depicts people as empowered actors, in all their different forms.

- Promoting a progressive work culture, which offers a place for people, in all their diversity, to flourish and grow.

- Promoting measurement tools and reporting mechanisms to ensure accountability and to help accelerate progress.[5]

This declaration builds on efforts already taken at a global and market level by WFA and its members, including national advertiser associations in Brazil, Chile, Colombia and Paraguay, as well as in Belgium, France, Turkey and the US, where #SeeHer has become a flagship movement led by the Association of National Advertisers (ANA).

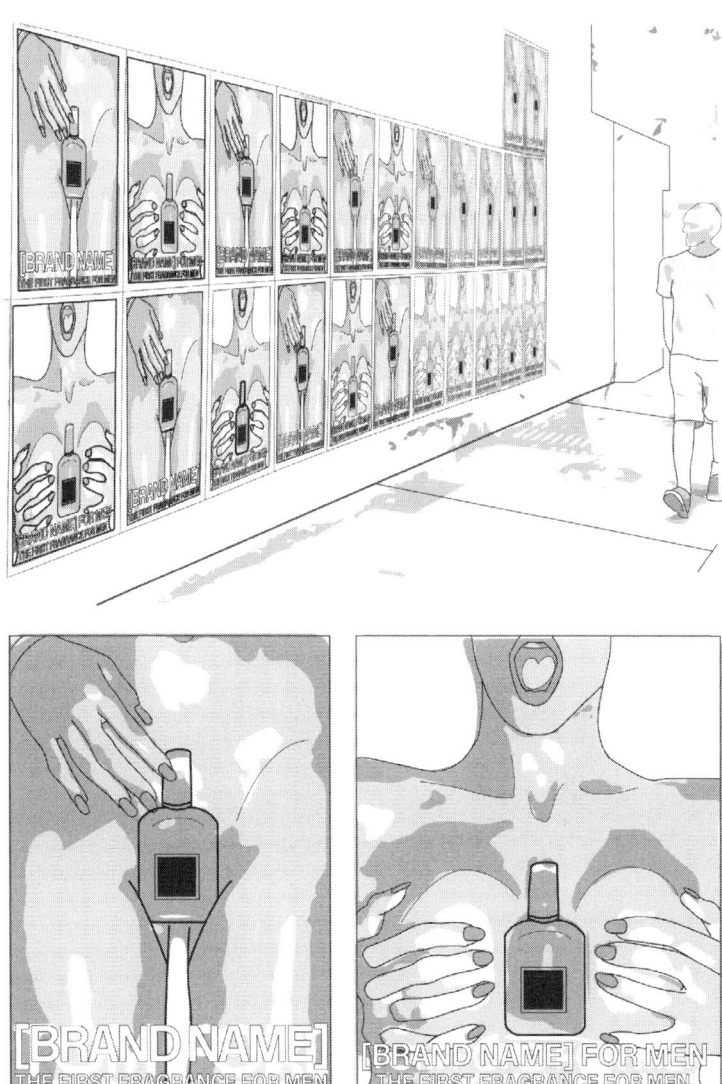

FIGURE 3.4 Example of type of pornographication and iteration in public space. Illustration Isabella Webb, Monash University XYX Lab 2022.

#SeeHer was launched in June 2016 as a partnership between the ANA's subcommittee, the Alliance for Family Entertainment (AFE) and The Female Quotient (TFQ). The #SeeHer mission is to achieve a 20 percent rise in accurate portrayals of women and girls in advertising and media by 2020.[6]

- **Co-regulation (Versus Self-regulation)**: The context is also important for managing the complaints process—one advertisement may cause widespread offense when placed in an area of the city or community, whereas it causes no issue when placed in another.

Self-regulation presents a range of issues, particularly the fact that the regulatory body is generally assembled from people working in the industry and with the intent ensure that the industry is financially viable and therefore is biased by a primary aim to protect its own interests.

The WFA and the *Buenos Aires Declaration for Progressive Advertising* are co- and self-regulatory mechanisms, rather than legislative frameworks:

- In Brazil, the Advertisers' Association (ABA) facilitated the launch of Unstereotype Alliance Brazil, an alliance between UN Women and industry representatives including Unilever, Grupo Boticário, Heads and Mastercard.

- In Colombia, the Advertisers' Association is working on a guide for a better representation of gender in advertising, which will be released in November 2019 and was inspired by WFA's own guide.

- In Chile, the Advertisers' Association launched a *Best Practice Guide: The Representation of Women in Advertising*, which highlights areas of improvement toward eliminating harmful and narrow stereotypes about women.

- In Paraguay since 2016, the Advertisers' Chamber has been running the program "Empresarias CAP," which looks to promote a better representation of women in marketing—both in organizations and in advertising, through activities such as mentoring programs, best practice sharing and bespoke magazine columns.[7]

- **Community Education and Media Literacy:** Rosewarne (2007a: 57) and Gurrieri et al. (2019: 28) suggest that media literacy will assist with exposing the damage and concerns regarding sexist advertising. Some sex education programs may address sexist content and representations in advertising, which can assist girls to navigate contradictory messages and differences between the portrayal of men and women (Jackson & Vares 2015).

- **Community Advocacy and Complaints:** Regardless of whether there is legislation and regulation in place, there needs to be a process for members of the community to voice concerns and complaints about sexist and pornified advertising and media. Usually, this process would happen through a board convened to review complaints, who liaise with the advertiser where necessary to make them aware of the complaint and to resolve the issue. If the process is insufficient or inadequate, then "community silence" on sexist and pornified advertising and media is "read by advertisers as agreement, if not *encouragement*" (original emphasis) and "tacit approval" or "acceptance" (Rosewarne 2010: 73).

> ### DEEPER DIVE: GRASSROOTS FEMINISM AND PORNOGRAPHICATION
>
> Grassroots organizations across the world may offer guidelines and education resources for activism about the pornographication of women and girls. They may engage in petitions, assistance with enforcing regulations and dealing with regular offenders against the guidelines. For further information refer to the websites at Collective Shout (Aus) and Culture Reframed (USA)

Get Serious

There has been a radical shift in the relationship between the built environment, advertising, and media. With the rise of smart cities and the integration of interactive technology into everyday life, there is an increase in access to pornographic images, making women's objectification and exploitation an unavoidable part of urban life. Some suggest that urban architecture and media can no longer be differentiated, and a reconceptualization of public space, where media is at once multimodal, mobile and inescapable, is required (McQuire 2008; Kalms 2017: 24). While legislation, regulation and industry initiatives may exist in varying degrees from city to city, sexist media, pornographication and objectifying messages can be unrelenting.

While the most obvious sites of pornographically-styled images of women and girls will occur in urban advertising media (for example, billboards and other forms of outdoor and mobile media) personal devices have an increasingly "powerful and pervasive influence on sexual culture" in cities (Kalms 2017: 7) and are now used as a weapon of violence against women (watching pornography in public space is discussed in **Chapter 1**). Networks in the built environment may, for example, trigger notifications on smart phones related to the user's digital profile. Smart devices may be used to perpetrate sexual harassment in public spaces. Social media and advertising will continue to complexify and interact with the built environment in ways that objectify and oppress women and girls.

Scholars reasonably assert that there is a link between normalization of pornography traditionally used for private use (for example via the internet) and the normalization of pornographically-styled images in public places, with research highlighting that links to the sex industry and larger systems of violence against women and girls are deeply concerning (Dines et al. 1998; Kalms 2017; Jeffreys 2015; Flood 2018; Tyler et al. 2016). Interestingly, the consumption of pornographically-styled images in public spaces (for example, people openly watching pornography on public transport) has increased, with research now established in the area of digital publics. The prevalence of pornographication and the present digital blurring of public space and pornographic content must be taken seriously and highlights the direct connections between the gender inequality faced by women and girls and the built environment. Restrictions on contents that legitimize sexism and heterosexism and authorize larger systems of violence against women is the first and important step to preventing this.

CHAPTER FOUR

Missing Women
Smart Women in the Data Gap

Principles

- Set policy frameworks for minimum data collection with consistent definition for sex and gender fields across all governance of /city/policing/public transport/communities
- Disaggregation by biological sex alone is paramount but insufficient. Additional indicators should reflect the community-specific priorities and might include age, disability, ethnicity, gender, geographic location, income, indigeneity, migratory status, race, religion and sexuality
- Develop protocols for data sharing across government and communities
- Support a web portal for sex- and gender-disaggregated data with intersectional indicators
- Prioritize women-centered (rather than result-focused) approaches to data collection, including innovative/alternative methods
- Measure factors over time with the understanding that intersectional oppression changes across a woman's life

Practice

- Ensure that quality assurance practices are followed when using data
- Access relevant gender data at the beginning of each project
- Gather additional data from diverse groups of women and girls
- Ensure post-occupancy surveys with women and girls are undertaken, evaluated and results integrated into practice learnings

Participation

- Activate women's voices through the collection of alternative and innovative data gathering initiatives

Sex and the Data Gap

The collection of timely, quality and accurate data about women and girls is critical for making equitable cities and allowing policymakers, planners and designers to respond to the diverse needs of women and girls in their communities. When data are gathered using sex- and gender-disaggregated indicators, organizations and communities are better placed to address issues impacting women and girls and to counter concerns with solutions that can make women's experiences in cities safer, more enjoyable and more productive. Quality data (and the evidence-based insights that it produces) build awareness, assesses the costs of women's oppression, and lobbies for adequate resources to counter the gender bias. The lack of comprehensive sex- and gender-disaggregated data is a critical gap in the goal to achieve equality in cities (Data2x 2022).

Overwhelmingly, the data about women and girls' experiences in cities are missing or incomplete. Women have been overwhelmingly "left out of technological history as inventors, as producers and, as user" (Rothschild 1995: 100). This gap is significant in the dynamic relationship that exists between the digital online world and the "offline" world, with the evaporation of any separation between the two (Clements 2020: 577). With this "infosphere" and the insights that are developed in the digital spaces of cities, bias is well documented. The everyday data systems is a complex problem that creates a risk when those who create the data products are from a dominant group—meaning that datasets may be "bias[ed] or unrepresentative" or that some data may "never get collected at all" (D'Ignazio et al. 2020: 28, 33). This has consequences for gender policy, urban development, and monitoring women's equity in cities. This silences the ways that women and girls can participate in society and contribute to urban development.

> ### WOMEN'S STORIES
>
> *I actually tried to report an incident. The policeman told me "don't worry, he's forgotten about you by now", and just left it at that. It just reminded me why I don't report the majority of incidents.*
>
> *I went for a run, was cat called—three times and then followed home by some 45-year-old guy! I reported it to my parents who did nothing.*

As there is a disproportionate number of men who are working with data—whether in the creation of research methods or developing the algorithms and systems to code and gather insights—the analysis and insights are subject to gender bias. In this sense the pattern of bias is inherent and pervasive.

The objective of collecting and operationalizing data about women and girls in cities is to quantify their experiences, to measure changes and to compare and track trends in urban interventions over time and within urban typologies. Without the collection and dissemination of representative data that include sex and gender disaggregation, it is not possible to reveal how women are advantaged or disadvantaged. Equally, it is impossible to know how they may be further advantaged or disadvantaged because of intersectional markers and differences.

The obstacles that many policymakers, planners and practitioners face when trying to access sex- and gender-disaggregated data can be addressed by statutes around the standardization of data collection. At present, most data lacks clarity and consistency about sex and gender indicators, and most omit the many intersecting oppressions, such as age, disability, ethnicity, geographic location, income, indigeneity, migratory status, race, religion and sexuality that will give data greater depth. These indicators are key to evidence-based implementation and monitoring and evaluating of initiatives and will also detect intersectional systems of oppression and disadvantage. Given that sex- and gender-disaggregated data's influence on policy and practices is a key factor in positively impacting women's urban experiences, the need to operationalize statistical information on women and girls is urgent.

In some countries, sex-disaggregated data is not regularly collected at all.[1] One of the unfortunate legacies of the information age is the way that data tend toward prejudice and biased algorithms and are dominated by the perspectives of men. Criado Perez notes a fatal problem, where supposedly "objective" research (an assumption which dominates rhetoric around data) fails to account for the needs and experiences of women and girls. She suggests that the data gap is a form of "silencing" which is "the cause and a consequence of the type of unthinking that conceives of humanity as almost exclusively male" (2019: xv). Criado Perez reflects on earlier observations by Pierre Bourdieu (1977) to discuss how the positions of "whiteness" and "male-ness" are so pervasive that the bias is rarely even noted or vocalized (Criado Perez 2019: 23).

Sex/gender-disaggregated data

Sex-disaggregated data relates to female and male data sets to measure the differences between women and men on various social and economic dimensions. UN Women suggest the data is "collected by sex as a primary and overall classification" (UN Women 2021: 12). Gender-disaggregated data can extend the sex disaggregation to capture gender statistics, including gender roles, relations, and other intersectional inequalities.

Combined sex- and gender-disaggregated data assist in the development of an appropriate gender-sensitive and evidence-based policy responses. Data disaggregated by sex/gender ensure a more accurate measure and representation of the realities and experiences of the lives of women, men and people of different genders.

Data About Women in Cities

When seeking out data about women's experiences in cities, it is vital to understand that most of the existing data are partial and are inherently designed to reduce complexity rather than embody it. When considering how best to use data, organizations must review what (if any) data are already available about women's experiences and investigate whether the data contain sex and gender fields.

Household surveys, for example, can be biased, as they may only look at outcomes from the perspective of the person completing the form, and may therefore overlook some issues. In particular, this occurs with those related to men's violence against women and girls, and/or the health and wellbeing of women and girls which may have negative impacts if unreported (Data2X 2017). As such, data collected directly from women and girls is best.

Existing data sources need to be reviewed for the limitations of the data set, for example, date and relevance—especially if the data are not recent. Data may be shaped by the intended audience, or the population being surveyed. Definitions should be reviewed for clarity and existing surveys may or may not have a uniform collection method. Some areas with sensitivities (for example, research into violence against women or research about minoritized communities) will have protocols, and without these, the data may be invalidated. With some digital platforms, it will be necessary to seek expert assistance in utilizing tools and data technology to understand the indicators and synthesis.

When there is a need to use or combine various digital data sources for urban insights, they should be reviewed in terms of comparability across spatial or thematic areas and time periods covered, and assessed as to whether the data is suitable to evaluate the area/thematic/context proposed. Many organizations have websites and online platforms that can collate women's experiences in cities—from travel and mobility patterns to transaction patterns and social media/consumer behavior. When accessing women's data using digital technology, understand that some women are unable to contribute due to lack of access to the internet (UN 2017) and that any insights will need to address this shortcoming.

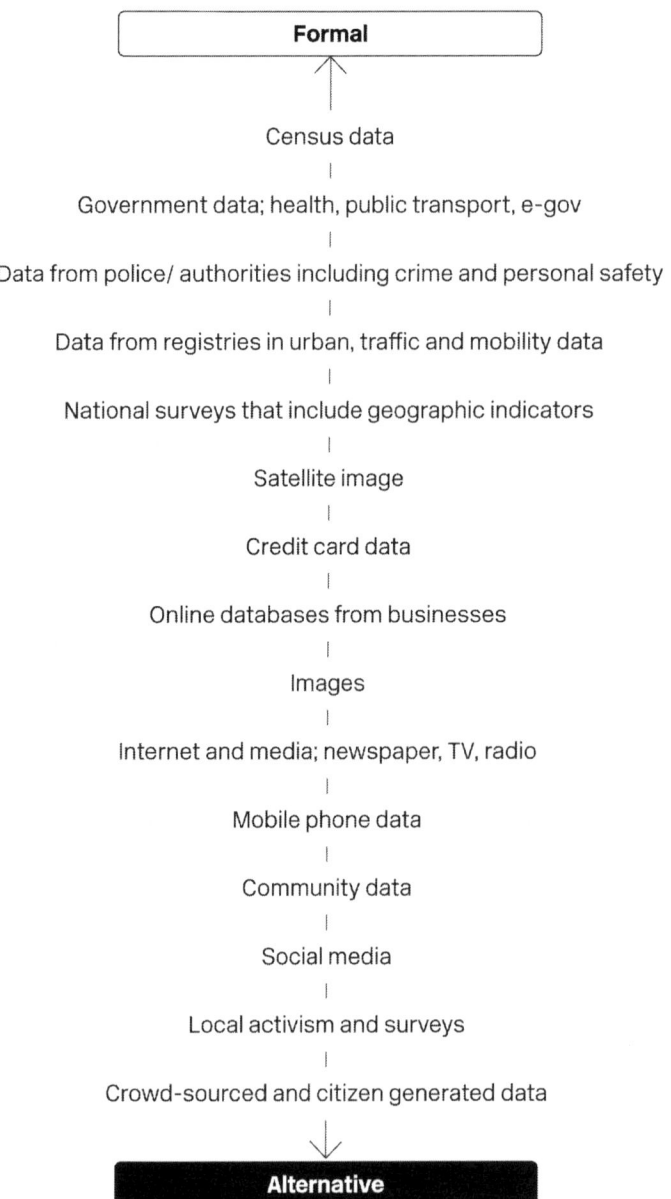

FIGURE 4.1 Data sources that may provide sex- and gender-disaggregated indicators.

Monitoring data is key to understanding progress toward tackling the barriers faced by women in cities. One-off surveys are limited and will only show a moment in time. As some intersectional oppression may change across a woman's life, where possible, women should be able to update or amend data.

> **TIP**
>
> ### DATA *ABOUT* WOMEN VERSUS WOMEN *DESIGNING* DATA
>
> There are two ways to think about data and women. First is to consider how data are biased and how to gather more representative data *about* women. The second is to consider how women can influence both the collection of data and what is deemed "data" (and the radical, alternative possibilities for forms of *feminist* data).

- **Data, Biological Sex and Gender Identity:** The foundational data should cover the biological aspects of male and female, ideally with an additional option to self-describe. The terms male and female should only be used when referring to biological aspects. Gender describes the expression or perception of a person's identity, noting that the variabilities may change across time, culture and communities. Gender may not align with the sex assigned at birth, nor gender expression align with gender identity, and may be irrelevant for some people who do not identify with any gender identity. As transgender people's identity differs from the one assigned at birth, a direct question can be asked about this, if relevant. For example: "Is your gender different from the sex you were assigned at birth?" There are, therefore, multiple ways to capture this, including free text for participants to self-describe and options where participants may check a defined box (note that this should also include a free-text option for people to self-describe). The contested nature of some terms and phrases is also changeable, so it is recommended to discuss terminology with an expert in gender analysis of survey methods at the time of engagement.

Sexuality data can be collected to capture information about the proportion of women who are same-sex attracted, attracted to the opposite sex or different gender, both sexes or several genders. In some countries, lesbian women as well as gender diverse people may be stigmatized, or it may not be possible to collect (or for women to safely share) identity information.

> **DEEPER DIVE**
>
> For a comprehensive overview of data relating to LGB and TQ lives, refer to Kevin Guyan's *Queer data: Using gender sex and sexuality data for action*, 2022.

• **A Fundamentally Biased System?:** International comparisons looking at women's and girls' use of tech show that women and girls remain scarce in key digital access areas, hampering policies to narrow gender inequalities as well as to monitor several gender-related targets under the Sustainable Development Goals (Global Partnership for Sustainable Development 2017). The methods and categorization (and more recently, the digital platforms in which data are gathered and reside) raise fundamental questions about whether data systems and digital data collection mechanisms are inherently discriminatory when underacknowledged bias in the system can shape the outcomes. For example, men are usually the creators of digital platforms and may dominate the system in which women are sharing their experiences (smart phones, laptops and other digital devices); coders may lack understanding of the bias in algorithms, and analysts and visualizers may lack training in how to analyse qualitative data.

With the digital transformation of cities and the proliferation of artificial intelligence (AI), there is a risk that automated decision making and innovations will omit gender-sensitive methods and continue to generate systems that reinforce stereotypes and oppression. The risk of not approaching AI with a gender lens is that bias is reinforced and the inequity of cities is further cemented by this technology.

- **Being Counted?:** While there are benefits in being counted, heard, and made visible, consequences and risks are present too. Some stories won't be gathered, some women will be left out, and some may feel misrepresented. In the worst-case scenario, it is possible that some women's discrimination may be deepened while other women benefit. This paradox is captured by scholar in gender and postcolonial studies Koen Leurs, who problematizes the politics of data which may be simultaneously viewed as objective and "omnipotent" at the same time as being viewed as a strict form of "data fundamentalism" (2017: 115). The benefits and risks need to be evaluated and risk mitigated by gathering diverse experiences and perspectives.

- **Aggregated Data Sources:** If there is a lack of deliberate investment in synthesizing the intersectional aspects of discrimination, then assumptions will be made which may create further harm. Quality data are data where each datum is individual and can be clearly defined and separable. Quality data can be aggregated and built or combined into categories or with other datasets. It may also be useful to look at the comparison between women—for example, differences across geographical location, wealth, age and ability.

- **Using Data About Women in Cities:** Ideally, when the data is gathered using a feminist framework, insights can identify inequalities, barriers and gaps. When compared to men's data, the divergent experiences can be highlighted and addressed with target intervention. The issues faced by women in the public realm can be better monitored and tendencies or patterns will determine hotspots. This can provide a deeper understanding of overlapping factors, including health, crime, mobility and exclusion. The collection of data without action will not advance equity for women and girls. Understanding how data may increase and decrease over periods of time and tracking and comparing data across generations can provide insights into longitudinal issues and changes in gender equity.

> **Datafication**
>
> Datafication refers to the collective establishment of tools, technologies and processes for organizations to use data-driven insights to transform business practices.

- **Big Data:** Although not well defined, "big data" comprises of "internet traffic, data from online social networking websites, remote sensing data, and data from mobile phone operators" (Data2X 2017). Big data can be described by three characteristics—volume, velocity and variety which together are "information assets that demand cost-effective, innovative forms of information processing that enable enhanced insight, decision making, and process automation" (Gartner n.d). The social dynamics of big data are increasingly providing insights into individuals' perceptions, behavior, and behavior modification in public spaces; although research into the ways this capture women's perspectives is still evolving, there is agreement that when "combined with traditional data sources" big data "can shed light on the lives of women and girls" (UN Women 2018: 23).

Big data can assist to fill gaps when some information may not exist, which is common in some of the issues pertaining to women and girls.

Female Data/Feminist Data

The ways that data is collected, the tools, technologies and methodologies used to extract insights, can shape critical information and decision making. The collection of data from or about women and girls—as well as the datafication of the collected information—needs to adopt a feminist framework (some call this data justice or data feminism). Female data is about establishing categories that can be used by policymakers, practitioners and communities to establish priorities and protocols. *Feminist* data requires a framework that looks beyond merely collecting sex- and gender-disaggregated data in a cohesive and ethical way, and goes further to critically consider the methods and approaches to data

> **DEEPER DIVE**
>
> For a fuller discussion of feminist methods and data, see *Data Feminism*, by Catherine D'Ignazio and Lauren F. Klein, 2020.

collection, with the aims of challenging "unequal power structures and working toward justice" (D'Ignazio et al. 2020: 49).

A feminist approach to data may also collect and examine data in a way that resists disembodiment (Perera 2022: 46); that is, it looks at the ways in which access to technology (in this case, in relation to data technology) may be both empowering and disempowering for women. For women, their capacity and agency to share data may come at a cost within the patriarchal systems. For example, a consequence of sharing data may be that their material realities are minimized or made invisible through the process, or that the storage and extraction of data may be less than ethical, or that information is manipulated. It is through transparency and accountability that data can be used to understand the issues faced by women and girls in cities. Data feminism must look to develop diverse forms of knowledge that challenge hierarchies and include feminist approaches to consent, protection and sovereignty.

Feminist data can tell the stories of women and girls in their own way and often outside of traditional data collection methods. Scholars argue that the activism of feminist data in the context of digital technologies can transform women's lives, whereby testimonials are a way to give voice to women's experiences and provide a way to be "seen, heard and validated" (Mendes et al. 2019: 176). This gives them the opportunity to feel part of a community where the perspective is shared, and to see how their experiences may sit in the context of the diversity of other women. The data is able to be compared to information provided by men and can catalyse action through women's demands and desire to see their rights enacted and the transformation of cities.

- **Smart(er) Cities for Women and Girls:** Technological forms of data collection have proven useful for understanding and comparing the international experiences of women and girls in cities. While the real-time and "live" modes for women and girls to report incidents, especially of violence and sexual harassment, has the potential to help communities uncover hotspots of crime and the behavior of perpetrators as it relates to the built environment, the reports require live monitoring and for them to be beneficial for women in cities (UN Women 2021: 12). When there is no response to women's request for support, then the system is undermined and ultimately useless.

Less a live "reporting" and more a way to gather impressions of urban spaces, the use of crowd-mapping has been used internationally as a method for deepening an understanding of the urban experiences of women and girls. Recognizing that women and girls have been historically excluded from urban discourse, the opportunities provided by crowd-sourced media have amplified the voice of women and girls and accelerated change in the built environment internationally. With a view to harnessing crowd-mapped voices, and to extending socio-cultural understanding of cities, the possibility of more inclusive cities is revealed. As a bottom-up process, crowd-mapping can impact on democratic processes by identifying issues and challenging dominant perspectives to draw out issues specific to women and girls' experiences.

By using crowd-mapping, women and girls push back against stereotypes and oppression and discover new ways to assert their voice. Mobile technology has become a medium of "collective wisdom" (Stephens 2013: 981) which enables users to connect and collaborate, as well as to monitor and moderate experiences and behaviors in cities. They anonymously pool to forge an invisible urban network of feminist imagination.

Alongside other international (but non-locative) activist campaigns on Twitter and Facebook, networked technology encourages women and girls who have experienced or fear sexual harassment to disclose the location and context of their experience "in their own words, without the restrictions on narrative form associated with the traditional justice system" (Fileborn 2014: 45). #MeToo is a more recent example of consciousness-raising feminism striving to use alternate methods.

HARASSMAP AND SAFETIPIN

HarassMap (since 2010) is a Cairo-based interactive online map used for anonymous reporting of incidents of sexual harassment in real time. Safetipin (since 2013) is an innovative mobile app originally used in Delhi, India that collects data about women's safety. HarassMap and Safetipin are both examples of crowd-maps that aim to combat sex crimes in public spaces. Both campaigns focus on the ways that "large-scale data collection can lead to change" with the desire for "more people [to] become engaged in the issue" (Viswanath et al. 2015: 45). The geolocative methods in HarassMap and Safetipin address "the problem of gendered human security through a series of technological interventions" with a desire to bring attention to where women are targeted (Grove 2015: 347). These same objectives are taken up in cities where innovative crowd-mapping surveys aim to extend other social media activism (Rabie 2013; Kalms 2018).

These tools have been designed to advocate for awareness and leveraged to prioritize areas for intervention. They have allowed communities to understand what kinds of experiences women and girls are having, but also how communities might make spaces more gender sensitive, and the kinds of things women and girls need in those spaces to ensure they feel safe and a sense of belonging.

Of course, while online activism can offer many opportunities for feminist participation, it may also exclude people not using new media. It is not a cure-all. If those who have the capacity to provide knowledge in user-generated forums about urban spaces are the ones that then have the means to re-shape communities then it follows that the use of feminist crowd-mapping can only challenge the contributions made by certain races, classes and genders. And these users may be disproportionate. Therefore, it is a tool that is not without bias, and its application needs testing and refining.

"Digital bodyguards" are available through mobile phone apps and are designed to allow women to tell friends or family members that they are safe when they travel alone at night. Digital bodyguards are being increasingly used by partners and family members, to monitor women and girls' movements through cities and to maintain synchronistic communication while women are going about their day-to-day lives. This dangerously mimics the ways that women have "historically been monitored and may mirror the controlling behaviour of perpetrators" (Kalms 2018: 130). The apps may give a sense of false security, as a digital tool cannot stop the perpetration of violence against women in city spaces and may even remove agency from women and girls in cities (Kalms 2018). Indeed, they may even "serve to control and prohibit women's full participation in city life" and "reinforce that safety is women's responsibility" (ibid. 131).

Data and the Role of Policy, Practice and Communities

For too long, policymakers, practitioners and communities have overlooked the importance of ensuring data indicators include sex- and gender-disaggregated fields as well as additional intersectional indicators. When these indicators are included, then oppression and disadvantage can be made visible and addressed. As data provide a foundation for influencing policy and process, monitoring data for both consistency and variability is a way to advocate for addressing the barriers faced by women.

- **Gathering Your Own:** Collection of sex- and gender-disaggregated data must ensure that it centers on the experiences of women, with the aim to understand and make sense of their perspectives. Some may view sharing their experience as an opportunity to be heard, while for others, this could be challenging and invasive. Understanding the harms and consequences for women in sharing information and the ethical considerations is mandatory for those gathering new data. Ensuring that a statement is provided to explain collection of information and how it will be used, including data protection measures, is useful and should be accessed in the women's first language group, where possible. Human rights issues in relation to privacy, consent, data collection and data use is a huge concern to women and girls and can be costly if overlooked; therefore, permissions and consent should be secured from participants in the first instance.

Data can be both passively and actively collected. Quantitative data collected about women's experiences in cities will consist of numeric records, usually related to the need for statistical analysis like averages and comparisons. This will result in reductive, often abstract and fixed category insights. This kind of data requires a significant number of participants for sound results. Qualitative data, on the other hand, are not focused on numbers and may take the form of text, narratives, stories or transcripts; it may include images and recordings and is a method used to "tease out and build up meaning and understanding" (Kitchin 2014: 5). Qualitative and quantitative methods may be used together, where qualitative data may be exported into a quantitative dataset.

The emergence of artificial and constructed technology that collects data from the environment, synthesizes the data and looks for patterns to deliver outputs—all without the need for human input—make the disaggregated element of data more critical. With any tech, the investment in the services of skilled data scientists will ensure quality data are obtained, analysed and well communicated. There is a vast array of technology emerging around women-centered campaigns that can be productively aligned with data, reporting, and monitoring, especially when the process of reporting is an ethically developed, user-friendly web browser, reporting platform or app.

TIP

For protocols on gathering, comparing and assessing quantitative data and qualitative data, see various sources from the UN, World Bank and OECD, including:

- UN Women, Women Count, *Counted & Visible Toolkit*, 2021
- United Nations Foundation, Data2x and Open data Watch, *Solutions to Close Gender Data Gaps*, 2022.
- UN Women, Gender Equality and Big Data, 2018.

- **Methodological Considerations:** The method of collection should be appropriate to the demographic. Communication and participation may require that materials are translated into other language groups and the responses translated and checked to ensure the nuances of women's experiences are related. When working with personal data, it is necessary to ensure that it is not possible to infer information about individuals. While most formal research data is anonymized, the alternative forms may not be or may have handles or identifying factors that then need to be addressed and/or redacted. Assessment and reduction of any risk to women providing data is imperative, as is understanding data protection, whereby characteristics such as religion and beliefs, sexual orientation and disabilities are considered sensitive data and are subject to data protection rules.

    Issues pertaining to data sovereignty and women (where information in digital form is subject to the laws of the country in which it is located) have emerged through "debates on the development, implementation, and adjustment of new data-driven technologies and their infrastructures" (Hummel et al. 2021: 1). The capacity for data to negatively impact women's human rights as subjects needs deep interrogation. Furthermore, the concerns of "data colonialism" (where governments, non-governmental organizations and corporations claim ownership of and privatize the data that is produced by their users and citizens) need to be assessed for the possibility of exploitation (Mumford 2021).

- **Representation and Visualization:** Data visualization may accompany reports in the forms of graphs, tables, infographics, maps, etc. If statistics are not communicated, it is almost as if they did not exist (UN Women 2021: 75), so the distribution of data is paramount to the process. The audience should be considered to ensure the communication is user friendly. Stereotypical colors or images should be avoided. The appropriate medium for dissemination is vital and most likely will extend beyond traditional fora to include news articles, data narratives, fact sheets, animated infographics, and a variety of accessible social media content. Some data findings will benefit from a press release, media launch or public presentation. Cultural sensitivities should be noted when using visuals or infographics, with key definitions, terms and indicators selected for suitability to the context and intended audience/s.

Amplifying Voices

Sex- and gender-disaggregated data can enable gender equity through monitoring progress and ensuring that priorities are evidence based. Data about women in cities needs to be activated, as it is the advocacy that is "critical for putting the spotlight on inequality and underscoring the need to realize the rights of poor and marginalized women and girls who are left behind and whose rights are not always prioritized in policy-making processes" (UN Women 2021: 11). Policymakers, practitioners, communities, and women themselves need to understand the indicators to ensure evidence-based evaluation across a range of urban factors, including prioritizing policy, assessing the impact of placemaking and providing adequate amenity. The urban spaces of cities and communities increasingly blur the "boundaries between the online and offline worlds" where "perpetual connectivity and interactivity" dominate environments (Clements 2020: 581). A quality evidence base can ensure quality strategies are implemented, that awareness raising and advocacy are based on real-world issues, and that their prioritization of resources and intended impact is well-founded.

Some governments, organizations and communities are better than others at seeking out data shared by women. A developed policy framework that outlines the common principles of data collection for women and girls should reflect the best practice planning for progressing gender equity. There needs to be standardization of the ways to collect sex- and gender-disaggregated data that is supportive of women and sensitively captures the perspectives of lesbian, gay and bisexual women as well as other intersectional criteria that may reveal needs, wants and/or desires.

While the sharing of data (and protocols to ethically support this) can be a sensitive area, this practice will allow the stakeholders of public space (including policymakers, planners, architects and designers) to support and improve experiences for women in cities. In some cases, the sharing of data can be a preventative measure or improve response rates, especially to the issue of violence experienced by women in cities.

PART TWO

Designing Feminist Cities

CHAPTER FIVE

Girls to the Front

Mainstreaming Women's Needs

Principles

- Acknowledge that the inequity in the built environment is a pervasive problem and makes women visible in policy documents with a focus on power imbalances
- Revise policy frameworks so that women and girls can benefit equitably
- Ensure compliance and quality assurance with gender mainstreaming initiatives
- Provide financial support to organizations for additional administrative load to meet gender mainstreaming actions
- Consider multiple frameworks that invite complexity and include wider demographics such as age, disability, ethnicity, geographic location, income, indigeneity, migratory status, race, religion and sexuality as well as biological sex and gender
- Ensure that evidence captures the resultant change to avoid stigmatization

Practice

- Examine decisions and analyse the impact on women and men, girls and boys through a gender lens
- Deploy gender budgeting alongside gender audits (see also **Chapter 7**), gender-sensitive design (see also **Chapter 6**) and the collection and synthesis of sex- and gender-disaggregated data (see also **Chapter 4**)

- Consider how women's oppression is linked to material and programmatic aspects of designing cities
- Undertake further training in gender-inclusive placemaking and intersectionality
- Check for self-interest, bias, and subjective interpretations of gender frameworks
- Commit to connecting with the lived experiences of those who will be the beneficiaries of design projects and planning strategies

Participation

- Include women and minoritized users of public spaces in community processes so they are empowered to co-create actions/solutions
- Consider that women may suffer multiple oppressions in various combinations, such as age, disability, ethnicity, geographic location, income, indigeneity, migratory status, race, religion and sexuality as well as biological sex and gender
- Ensure that any language barriers and socio-cultural factors are overcome to ensure diverse participation

Who Gets What, Where, How and Why (and Who Decides)[1]

Over the past three decades, powerful organizations such as the European Union, the United Nations and the World Bank have required policymakers, planners and designers to accept that women's inequity is a pervasive problem that impacts men and women differently. Precipitated by the early activism of feminists in the 1960s and 1970s, the concept that women's equity should be progressed in policy development ruptured grass roots women's organizations, as they were displaced by the formalization of gender mainstreaming strategies in systems of global governance (Scala et al. 2018: 210). This has been described as the "NGO-ization" of the women's movements, where the "gender agenda" transformed into a "box to be ticked" and feminism was co-opted into fundable and manageable projects. In this context, some NGOs are required to manage the fallout of neoliberalism in an environment where they must compete for philanthropic funding while attempting to support minoritized women. Cultural theorist Angela McRobbie argues that this requires gender mainstreaming to "play on the international stage" and suggests that this is "feminism 'made-over' for approval by global governance" (2009: 154).

> ### Gender mainstreaming[2]
>
> Gender mainstreaming refers to policymaking that reorganizes, improves, develops and evaluates policy processes, so that "a gender equality perspective is incorporated into all policies at all levels at all stages, by the actors normally involved in policy making" (Council of Europe 1998: 12). It is an approach that integrates a gender perspective at all stages of government and is best understood as a process or strategy (or "a conceptual guide and practical toolkit," Scala et al. 2018: 209) rather than a goal (Lomazzi et al. 2019: 146).

Despite tensions, the broad acknowledgment of women's inequity has helped to advance gender mainstreaming (Sánchez de Madariaga 2016: 327). As a "meta policy" capable of drawing out the ways that gender intersects with multiple frames and structures (Cavaghan 2017: 33), it ideally ensures diverse perspectives are addressed and progresses "instruments for strategic action" (Huning et al. 2019: 2) through a "frame of analysis" (Daly 2005: 448). Yet critique has continually exposed tensions in gender mainstreaming implementation. Some view it as a reforming process of neoliberal politics, while others prefer to critique it from the perspective of the radical feminist roots held within the original social project. Certainly, gender mainstreaming has "fallen short of its goals" because of poor compliance with non-binding policies, box-ticking and self-assessed performance benchmarks (Scala et al. 2018: 208–12). The array of guidelines, checklists, and criteria places additional strain on the organization, with pressure on financial resources that results in a lack of enforcement and accountability.

These problems are set within a system where responsibility for implementation, processes and analysis rests predominantly with public servants (Scala et al. 2018: 211). The act of "doing" gender, therefore, becomes part of an "audit culture" emphasizing the measurement of performance and quality control. Its efficacy is tied to issues of procedural consistency across the implementation of policy, programs, processes and projects (Greed 2005: 268). Given the "soft incentives" it is unsurprising that this results in a "variable" and "generally disappointing pattern of implementation" that lacks consistent outcomes (Pollack et al. 2010: 308).

It seems the translation from feminist grass roots action to government-led policy has resulted in a fuzzy, often poorly defined remit, where gender mainstreaming tries to address "all areas of policy" and often with a version somewhat diluted from the original feminist intent (Cavaghan 2017: 19, 32). While Davids et al. optimistically describe the "promise" of gender mainstreaming and the theoretical approach as producing a "slow revolution" (2014: 396), most critics are less patient, preferring to focus on gender mainstreaming's "litany of failures" (Milward et al. 2015: 75; Brouwers 2013).

Human geographer Martin Zebracki (2014) is interested, however, in the political context that seems to shape the implementation and impact of gender mainstreaming. In countries like Sweden, with a democratic tradition of egalitarian planning and policymaking, outcomes and impact are much stronger. The policies in the Scandinavian context address work and caring roles, mobility, and the provision of safe pedestrian access, adequate public transport and the consideration of car use. The success in this instance most likely relates to the explicitly "feminist government"[3] and the equal (or near-equal) representation of women in politics. Zebracki reflects on the comparative success of gender mainstreaming in Sweden and suggests that in countries where there is a low level of women participating in politics, there will be a "paucity of gender awareness" and "ad hoc" gender mainstreaming policies (Zebracki 2014: 60).

Uptake of Gender Mainstreaming by Design and Planning Practitioners

When it comes to overcoming "cultural and attitudinal bias toward women in the planning system" (Greed 2006: 276) a gender mainstreaming framework can support planners and designers to radically transform "neutral" approaches. The methodology, when implemented correctly, should intercept all stages of the design process to account for gendered power structures, including: applying a gender lens to operational mechanisms; analysis of urban design methods and tasks; the formulation of goals and gender budget allocation; the use of sex- and gender-disaggregated data; the implementation of gender-informed interventions; and the evaluation and measurement of the impact of the interventions, all with the aim of specifying gender-sensitive approaches to land use, development, and the design of city spaces.

Working across academia, government, non-profit, and the private sector, urban planner and researcher Carolyn Whitzman has championed gender mainstreaming, providing a welcome platform for discussions about the prioritization of gender equality at a policy and urban planning level. She examines a wide range of sectors, including health, housing, childcare and transport (Whitzman 2013: 145). Similarly, urban planning scholar Clara Greed considers the sex-based biological pressures in the built environment that impact women in different ways to men (Greed 2005: 268).

Greed's research provides critique about the productive links between gender mainstreaming and planning practice and suggests that effective gender mainstreaming would result in links to the social considerations and physical planning of space which, in turn, should lead to changes in policy direction (Greed 2000: 191–192). From a feminist perspective, the aim is not for gender mainstreaming

1	2	3
Preparatory Phase	**Implementation Phase**	**Evaluation**
• Employ gender specialist • Identify initiatives • Seek out gender perspectives • Policy review • Clarify methodology • Set goals • Anticipate evaluation technique • Undertake gender sensitive training • Partnership development advisory panel	• Review policy, sex- and gender-disaggregated data • Conduct gender analysis across relevant projects, organisations • Stakeholder meeting • Audit analysis including engagement with diverse women from the community • Co-design/develop decisions with diverse women from the community	• Establish indicators • Program regular monitoring and synthesis • Deliver progress reports

FIGURE 5.1 Phases of gender mainstreaming in urban planning.

to be a niche skill set within planning and design, but a framework that is integrated into practice, where the needs of different users of public space are taken seriously. One set of needs should not dominate another. Given the built environment is uniquely positioned at the nexus of theoretical and practical knowledge, the uptake of gender mainstreaming should, in principle, excel. And yet there are challenges, complacency, and a lack of will.

Like other women-centered initiatives in planning and design, a fundamental hurdle for gender mainstreaming is that it may be implemented by practitioners who have little or no understanding of feminist issues. The opportunity, therefore, for gender mainstreaming to positively impact planning and design practice is often not met. The recommendations have not resulted in transformative change, where "attempts to reshape aspects of entire cities" are not forthcoming; instead, all that can be found are smaller examples (Greed 2006: 276). This reflects the legacy and priorities of a profession that is preoccupied—even if unintentionally—with public space provision and land-use policy. In this scenario, the needs of women and girls continue to come toward the end of the queue.

And so, according to policy researcher Rosalind Cavaghan (2017: 30–32) and Huning et al. (2019: 3) what remains is a *rhetorical* commitment to gender mainstreaming that—on deeper inspection—lacks action and integration. A range of red flags fly. There may be forms of "outreach" into the communities, but changes and challenges to stereotypes do not take place. Frontline staff may be biased facilitators of the policies or may be "self-interested" or "interpret policies" to protect their own agendas (Scala et al. 2018: 213). Issues may be compounded in organizations that do not value gender expertise or where women's inequity is not well-understood by professionals or their peers (Huning et al. 2019: 11).

Who, *Exactly*

Understanding the nuances of gender terminology can vary across socio-cultural contexts. Individual understanding varies; some people will be more aware than others, and the politics of gender are subject to politicization and change. The shift away from gender mainstreaming's feminist roots is contextualized by ambiguity and leaves some people wondering: *Who, exactly, is gender mainstreaming for?* The theoretical categories for "gender," "women" and recent "inclusion" frameworks have made implementation and uptake of gender mainstreaming across policy, planning and design challenging. For some, there is an assumption that "gender" mainstreaming is more accurately "women" mainstreaming. Urban planner Clara Greed, for example, writing about gender mainstreaming in the United Kingdom, notes that, while gender is not a synonym for "women," there is something about the word "gender" that has intrinsically retained gender relations specific to patriarchy (2005: 720).

Others problematize a different but similarly ambiguous route, where the term "gender" may start off as the underlying concept, but "ends, via a detour, with the category of women" and may problematically reflect the division between sex and gender as well as women and men, but also the ways that women become the "inborn fighters for gender equality" (Davids et al. 2014: 402–403).

Highlighting gender (rather than women) requires a reframing of the foundational initiatives that were once focused specifically on women. The ambiguity has resulted in a lack of traction, with practitioners noting the uncertainty around the meaning of the words "gender" and "equality" (Daly 2005). Huning et al., for example, note a problematic shift in terminology from "women's issues" to "gender relations" and "a discursive turn from feminist planning critique to gender planning" (2019: 1). Rieker et al. (2013) propose that the "unstable subject of women has become fixed and absorbed by gender mainstreaming and its institutionalization" (2013: 7). For planners, "uncertainty" reigns and creates ongoing problems for gender mainstreaming that result in confusion about what gender mainstreaming might actually "look like" or "how to do it" (Zalewski, 2010: 7, 21).

A shift in emphasis from a framework focused on women to one arguably more neutral and focused on gender *could* be a positive move and signal that women's oppression in cities should not be a burden for women only. The broadening of terminology to gender and the inclusion of men and boys potentially signals that women's rights in cities require exploration and cultural change from everyone. Equally, this can suggest that "user-orientated" and "inclusive" planning methods can supplant gender, and in the process, lose sight of the gender equality goals (Tummers et al. 2019: 90). There are tensions between the ideology and the practicalities of how best to approach women's inequity.

Davids et al. reflect on the trajectory of gender mainstreaming and the complex relationship to women with different "theoretical standpoints and debates on the origins and solutions of gender inequality" in relation to "women, gender, and change" (2014: 398). It seems that the broader definition through "gender" most likely endorses a continued lack of engagement with women's specific policy needs and the power imbalances they face. For some governments and policymakers, the interpretation of the framework means that there is "no longer a need to allocate specific funds and resources for women's issues" (Shaw et al. 2013: 5). Indeed, some city planning practitioners go a step further to emphasize gender mainstreaming as a mode to actively resist engaging with women or the feminist frameworks that underpin gender mainstreaming. This forces an acknowledgment of the implicit tension of gender mainstreaming. While it is vital to implement women-centered approaches across planning policy and the design process more broadly, some practitioners will always remain resistant to change and more equitable thinking. For example, Former Deputy Mayor of Vienna, Maria Vassilakou, announces "It's not about feminism. It's about doing things better." (Palit 2018: 4)

This kind of position fits neatly into institutional practices that value "neutrality" and "technocracy" (Scala et al. 2018: 230) and is central to the evasive ambiguity of gender mainstreaming, where to speak of women and feminism is viewed as too political. Although the words "gender" and "equality" are used, they are rendered meaningless in the process. In its present incarnation, the feminist activism and centering of women that was so present at the inception (and that led to EU support) is in question and at risk.

Women and Girls on the Ground

All these challenges set up a difficult context for gender mainstreaming and could paint it as a failed project, except for the fact that there have been—and continue to be—some stand-out successes led by policy, practice and communities. Several cities have taken up gender mainstreaming in terms of urban planning and practice with transformative results. The City of Vienna has led on the issue for more than three decades. Mainstreaming was implemented in Vienna in 1991, when a group of city planners organized a photography exhibit titled "Who Owns Public Space – Women's Everyday Life in the City." It depicted the daily routines of a diverse group of women, highlighting safety and ease of movement as a priority for all women. For the first time, women's concerns explicitly demanded a specific planning approach. Gender mainstreaming in Vienna today is well established as a central, strategic discipline of urban planning. With the objective of making sure that everyone has equal access to urban resources, Vienna's gender mainstreaming approach has reshaped the city and continues to do so (Kern 2020).

> **DEEPER DIVE**
>
> The *Manual for Gender Mainstreaming in Urban Planning and Urban Development* (2013) summarizes and disseminates the experience and results of many successful pilot processes and projects since 1991. The manual highlights the basic principles of gender-sensitive planning, and the objectives of gender mainstreaming as a comprehensive planning strategy are explained in relation to four areas: (1) master plans, concepts and visions of urban design; (2) land use and development planning; (3) public space planning; (4) housing construction and public service buildings (*The Manual* 2013: 52, 65, 73, 87). The more recent document, *Gender Mainstreaming – Made Easy* (2021) is a new update to the original. Other planning handbooks exist for a range of cities:
>
> - *Women's Public Space* (WPS) Prague uses eight simple storytelling vignettes in "How to Design a Fair Shared City?"
> - *Gender Mainstreaming in National Sustainable Development Planning in the Caribbean*
> - *Eurofem_Toolbox*, Finland
> - *Handbook for Gender-inclusive Urban Planning and Design*, The World Bank
> - *Gender Mainstreaming in Urban Development*, Berlin
> - *Localizing the Gender Equality Goals Through Urban Planning Tools in South Asia*.

- **Land Use and Development Plans:** In translating the qualities formulated in master plans, urban design concepts and visions into formal planning instruments, numerous (often competing) aspects must be considered. Stipulations in land use and development plans are a key prerequisite for the implementation of many gender-relevant and quality criteria for essential spatial–structural conditions. At the same time, excessive restrictions for design and placemaking must be prevented to avoid negatively impacting the capacity for implementation. The conditions that contextualize governance and the implementation of planning policy and project are thus critical for quality assurance and accountability.

- **Public Space:** Public space offers many aspects that tie in with the gender mainstreaming agenda. This is the place where numerous, competing forms of use often clash and diverse interests must be negotiated. In particular, during the project development and implementation phases, myriad details are decided that strongly impact the everyday life of various user groups.

WOMEN'S STORIES

The carpark is pitch black after sport when the court/field lights are turned off. Too dark for waiting for a ride home. There is a walking track but no passive surveillance. There's no changing rooms for females, only males, so it's uncomfortable to get changed in front of everyone.

- **Housing and Public Service Buildings:** The design of housing construction and public service buildings is gender-sensitive if planning and implementation take equitable account of different life phases and life realities. The needs of residents and users of public buildings and their everyday lives are at the center of all considerations. For housing projects, this means providing a wide range of typologies and layouts.

- **Intersectional Mainstreaming:** More recently, critique has turned to gender mainstreaming's lack of address and operationality in terms of intersectional practices (Tummers et al. 2019: 83) where "reclaiming any right to the city on gendered grounds must consider intersectional discrimination" (Yon et al. 2017: 38). Raising questions about the extent to which gender—as a single axis of oppression—can be truly transformative, Huning et al., argue that there is a need to invite complexity "rather than abandoning it" (2019: 10) with the inclusion of women's lives, aiming to capture the nuance and complexity of women's needs (Lacy et al. 2013: 143; Hankivsky 2005, cited in Scala et al. 2018: 211).

Similarly, geographer Leslie Kern suggests that gender, as the "primary category for equality" can inhibit the exploration of planning, whereby the "narrowly imagined . . . white, cis, able-bodied, middle class, heterosexual man" sits alongside the "married, able-bodied mother with a pink or white-collar job" (2020: 36). Some scholars assert that gender mainstreaming policy can create and sustain unequal power relations (Eveline and Bacchi 2005). Davids et al. state that mainstreaming strategies may "partly subvert and partly comply" with "steps forward, backward and sideways" (2014: 405).

WOMEN'S STORIES

One side of the footpath on this street is broken and uneven and the other side of the footpath is unable to be used due to housing developments. This makes it difficult for mothers with prams and older adults with walking frames to safely walk around this area.

Acknowledging the differences and complexities that result in varying kinds of discrimination will require the exploration of multiple frameworks rather than singular policy approaches and would also resist any tendencies to view women as a homogenous group. Simultaneously exploring age, disability, ethnicity, gender, geographic location, income, indigeneity, migratory status, race, religion and sexuality alongside biological sex and gender may better serve, for example, the aims for gender-aware, inclusive communities (Eveline and Bacchi 2005: 507; Huning et al. 2019: 211; Lacy et al. 2013). With the renewed investment in gender equality brought about by the Sustainable Development Goals (SDGs) 2030, there is optimism that a mainstreaming framework can provide greater possibilities for an intersectional lens. The SDGs remind us how cities play a vital role in the achievement of gender equality. Key tenets that an intersectional form of mainstreaming could address include access to public transport by sex, age and persons with disabilities; open space for public use for all, by sex, age and persons with disabilities; and tracking the proportion of persons who are victims of physical or sexual harassment, by sex, age, disability status and place of occurrence (UN Women 2021).

International expert in gender planning Inés Sánchez de Madariaga suggests that a "new wave, or period, of gender policy in planning might be unfolding" (2016: 326) and that this may include insights and visibility from queer and post-colonial feminist theory. In this sense, redefining gender mainstreaming through the lens of intersectionality could better develop initiatives and policies that can work with "multiple and intersecting social, physical, political and economic aspects of individual lives, not limited to gender" (Lacy et al. 2013: 143).

Intersectionality (see also definition in Chapter 1)

This critique of gender mainstreaming is influenced by the theory and activism posed by leading American scholars of race, class and gender theories, Kimberlé Crenshaw and Patricia Hill Collins. Crenshaw (1989), who developed the theory of intersectionality from the work of feminists of color, examined how different forms of marginalization (notably, she focused on sexism and racism) intersect with each another. The "matrix of domination" (Fig. 5.2), developed by Collins (1990), provides the lens for the development of an intersectional framework that challenges the systems of domination.

DEEPER DIVE

For in-depth discussion of gender-sensitive design, see **Chapter 6**. For in-depth discussion of gender audits, see **Chapter 7**.

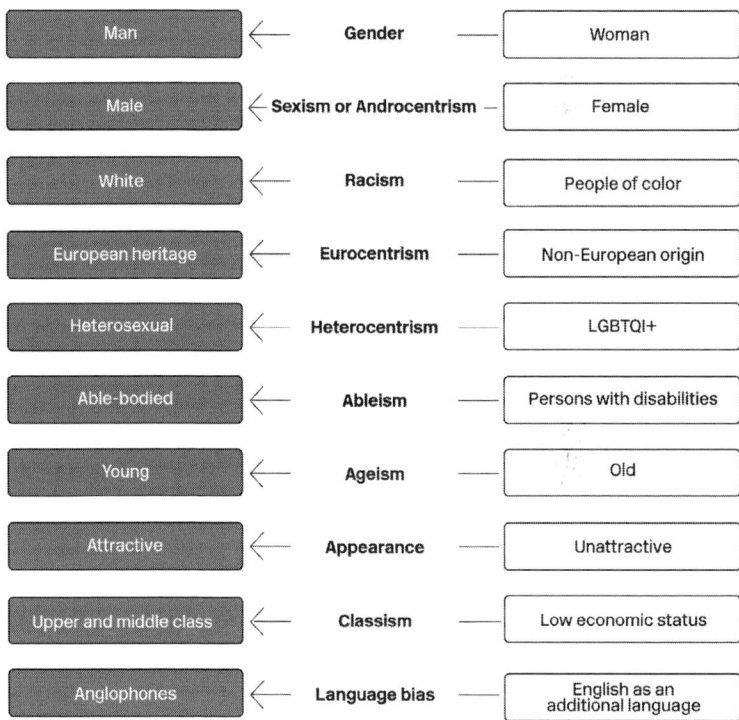

FIGURE 5.2 Domination and oppression adapted from the "matrix of domination" developed by Patricia Hill Collins. Illustration Isabella Webb, Monash University XYX Lab 2022.

What Is the Future for Gender Mainstreaming?

Some with contrary views believe that including these intersectional complexities has various implications for gender mainstreaming—making this period a critical juncture. For some, the retention of (or return to) the feminist grass roots foundation is vital. Revising the gender mainstreaming model as an intersection framework risks the disappearance of gender or, at the very least, the divestment of gender into a "wider diversity policy covering other factors of social disadvantage" (Sánchez de Madariaga 2016: 331). Within the context of gender identity politics, the change is already underway, and this may result in a vague description of individualized identity disguised in "inclusivity." This is concerning because, as Huning et al. note, diversity policies focus on integration and recognition, but "do not overcome institutional and structural questions of inclusion and exclusion" (2019: 12). One of the outcomes of prioritizing intersectional oppressions over gender is the disappearance of women. While many may see this as precisely the objective, this was never the intention of Kimberlé Crenshaw, Patricia Hill Collins and bell hooks, who originally intended that these be inextricably linked via the primary and foundation division of biological sex (Tyler 2021: np). In the same way that gender mainstreaming has become a wider diversity policy, "intersectionality" has arguably become a de-politicized, meaningless slogan. Sánchez de Madariaga states:

> Gender is a key structuring factor of society which provides the basis for the subordinate position of half of the population; it has a biological component that cannot be changed; and it has proved to be, among the many possible factors for discrimination, the most resistant to change across time and space. For at least these reasons, 'gender must stand on its own as a separate category deserving a specifically devised policy'.
>
> 2016: 330

Within these tensions, is there a workable future for gender mainstreaming? The need for equitable public spaces should—as urban geographer Kurt Iveson and anthropologist Setha Low propose—mean the "provision of more just public space …

achieved through process that seek to redistribute resources, recognise difference, foster encounter/interaction ... and ensure procedural fairness" (2022: 175). Certainly, there is a need for wider debate about the practices and implementation of gender mainstreaming, which must acknowledge the difficulties of operating in a policy context. On-the-ground implementation of gender mainstreaming from planning and design practitioners is critical. There is much to resolve about how those charged with the implementation of gender mainstreaming in planning and design will "make sense" of the policy and process (Scala et al. 2018: 230). The professional context is challenging and not to be underestimated as it poses a significant barrier and "opens the debate to a feminist argument toward the politics of difference, highlighting the extent to which access and use rights for women are denied" (Yon et al. 2017: 33).

It is worth considering whether the complexity of gender mainstreaming and the struggles with implementation mean that the arenas and institutions where gender mainstreaming is supposed to be enacted may be so enmeshed with the interests of the patriarchy that feminist intervention is ineffective. Architecture, planning and design should, theoretically, be ideal arenas for exploring gender mainstreaming as a bridge theory and practice. Some challenge the notion that "gender considerations have been integrated into every aspect of policy work" and reveal an "alternative reality" marked by women's disappearance (Milward et al. 2015: 230). A more moderate position suggests that "using the interstices left by the programmes and policies of urban governance to intertwine top-down and bottom-up structures and initiatives – and hence interlink actions – might produce the most effective results as far as gender mainstreaming in the city is concerned" (Zebracki 2014: 61).

For design and planning practitioners, the imperative is not to see women as a "special needs" group, but to understand the design process as a mode to consider the diversity of the minoritized people who can benefit from cities and communities. This is to argue for a more productive way to view gender mainstreaming as a fact-finding opportunity to uncover the processes that serve to maintain gender inequality (Cavaghan 2017: 183). Implicit in the arguments that continue to favor gender mainstreaming is that government, planning, and policy are valid and valuable foci for challenging women's oppression in cities.

CHAPTER SIX

Not Neutral

Designing Cities for Women

Principles
- Consider the particularities and differences for women navigating urban life, with the aim to eliminate inequity in cities
- Understand the nuances of gender-sensitive approaches to avoidance of condoning or accepting male violence

Practice
- Undertake training in gender-sensitive design approaches
- Engage the perspectives of women and girls
- Encourage a sense of belonging and accommodate the programmatic needs and desire of women and girls
- Design for the bodily proportions of women and girls

Participation
- Advocate for gender-sensitive approaches to public space procurement
- Form advisory groups of professional and task forces with women and girls
- Embed evaluation and monitoring in new initiatives
- Build knowledge through sharing case study examples

Designing Cities for Women

As a process and method, gender-sensitive design considers the particularities of women's lives, with the aim of eliminating inequity. Actively designing for the rights of women and girls directly challenges the rhetoric of gender-neutral policy and design. It also challenges some of the principles of "inclusive cities" that have come to dominate the urban design rhetoric. The tendency in the disciplines of planning, urban design and architecture—as well as many other design disciplines working in the public realm—has been to strive for gender-neutral design, with the idea that this will meet the middling needs of every person. The intentions are that inclusive design will address unintended male bias and meet the diverse needs of communities. The reality is that most people will design for the needs of people like themselves, including their own ideas of what is "normal" (Greed 1994, 1999, and 2005: 738). So, the well-intentioned attempts to be unbiased through gender neutral and/or inclusive design will likely result in more entrenched forms of discrimination against women and other minoritized people.

Advocating for gender-sensitive design can raise an important (and even controversial) set of foundational feminist concerns. Some may argue that to design cities with the intention that women can feel and/or be safer resists dealing with the primary prevention of men's violence, that is, understanding and addressing what encourages men's violence, or problematizing why men are violent at all.[1] Indeed, some may argue that designing to the fears and sensitivities of women frames them as deficient, or victims, and in doing so diverts the focus away from the problem which is, essentially, the threat of male violence.

Gender-sensitive design

Gender-sensitive design acknowledges that urban environments are far from gender neutral by recognizing and responding to differences, particularities and inequalities between women, men and people of all genders. Gender-sensitive design aims to reduce, rather than perpetuate, gender inequality by including diverse voices traditionally underrepresented in the planning and design process, such as those of women and girls. It aims to combat spatial inequities by drawing out the various patterns of discrimination that are often disguised in gender "neutral" points of view. A gender-sensitive approach—when applied across the whole design process—ensures that the specific needs of people of different genders and intersecting identities inform the design process.

Universal design

Pertains to the fixed attributes of an environment and aims to ensure that a space can be accessed by as many people as possible without the need for changes in behavior. An emphasis is placed on accessibility and designers will need to refer to the local specifications and/or legislation. A universal design approach can minimize retrofitting and will provide flexibility for a diverse range of users.

Inclusive design

Inclusive design is a process or methodology for design that considers the diversity of users in the design of products and objects as well as the built environment and open spaces, and which aims to include as many people as possible. While accessible and universal design also aims to include a wide range of people, these are much narrower approaches and only one of the outcomes of inclusive design. Inclusive design recognizes possible points of exclusion, taking into consideration individual factors including intersectional and socio-cultural differences, and actively aims to address them.

It is accurate that gender-sensitive design accepts the fear and risks and focuses on designing for women rather than preventing the cause of the issues. Certainly, balancing the provision of practicable design for the current needs of women in cities while keeping an eye on the distant future (when the abolition of men's violence against women has been achieved) is key. Policymakers, planners and practitioners need to understand this nuance to avoid implicitly contributing to a culture that condones or accepts male violence as a fait accompli. Unfortunately, it is estimated that it will be over 135 years before gender equality is achieved (Devlin 2021), so the elimination of male violence against women is many generations away. It is also an unfortunate fact that, in the present socio-cultural context, no amount of gender-sensitive design will prevent the random acts of male violence committed against women and girls in public spaces. In this sense, gender-sensitive approaches can offer practitioners a way to mitigate risk and encourage more women to enact their rights to be in public spaces.

As well as the impact of larger strategic decisions, designing urban spaces with the minutiae of women's preferences, practical needs and proportions in mind increases their access to public space and feelings of belonging and safety. The extent to which access to and the use of city spaces restrict women through the proportions, materials and layout of spaces and buildings is concerning. The supposedly neutral approaches to design often result in spaces being designed for the proportions of an average man, likely unaccompanied, untethered, and able-bodied. This directly results in spaces that prohibit women's access and mobility and can mean that seats, handrails and support may be too high or poorly positioned, that openings and carriageways may be too narrow for carers, and interchanges convoluted and time consuming. Without mandated redress, barriers to women's inclusion and safe access prevail.

Ideally, legislative support should be put in place to demand the equitable distribution of civic resources. Specific approaches and methods for public space design can then authorize designers to challenge fixed attitudes associated with entrenched and outdated urban design principles. These include gender-neutral design, design for crime prevention (as a "cover-all" for *all* safety issues) and the proliferation of or reliance on CCTV as well as over-lit cities. The impact on women through the implementation of these outdated approaches is enormous. Positive experiences for women in urban spaces mean that women will access and occupy cities more frequently as more women feel safe and secure and there will be an increasing solidarity between women with a sense of belonging in cities. When women increase their participation in public life, then their access (as well as their children's access) to education, work and health care is also increased.

> **TIP**
>
> To create cities that are gender-sensitive, designers, planners and policymakers need to engage with the breadth of community diversity. This would include the examination of biological sex and gender as they intersect with age, disability, ethnicity, geographic location, income, indigeneity, migratory status, race, religion and sexuality.

Setting the Scene for Gender-sensitive Design for Women

At every stage of the decision-making process, a gender lens is critical. All intervention in the built environment must encourage a sense of belonging and accommodate the needs of women and girls. Gender-sensitive responses that center women and girls in the creation of urban spaces can transform design practice and avoid the pitfalls of designing for a default or neutral user, and require adopting some foundations for engagement and accountability. Designing for women in cities means incorporating key strategies, actions and interventions from an evolving evidence-based kit of parts. The aim is to reduce, rather than reinforce, gender inequality.

- **Be Led by Women in Indigenous Communities:** The first action is to identify and engage with local women's organizations and community groups, especially local Indigenous women, whose perspectives will need to be sought and respected about the project. In many countries, placemaking takes place on land that is unceded and any project contextualized by traditional custodians will need to form and maintain good relationships to Indigenous people and culture through reciprocity and respect. The International Indigenous Design Charter (Kennedy et al. 2018) identifies and addresses these concerns across design disciplines, noting a range of protocols for implementation (Kennedy et al. 2018: 31–32).

> **DEEPER DIVE**
>
> The protocols, context and actions for Indigenous engagement are available in the "International Indigenous Design Charter: Protocols for Sharing Indigenous Knowledge in Professional Design Practice," 2018, by Russell Kennedy, Meghan Kelly, Jefa Greenaway, and Brian Martin.

- **Audit Spaces with Women:** Auditing urban spaces is participatory engagement with small groups of women from the local community. Their first-hand experiences can surface social issues that may be otherwise missed by "outsiders" or "experts" (including women). Audits take place on-site where women are asked to examine both the physical and socio-spatial aspects of the environment. The on-the-ground evaluation of local spaces may include streets, residential areas, parks, markets and public transport.

Audits may focus on the efficacy (from local women's point of view) of the physical environment and may include rating lighting, maintenance, surveillance, sightlines, visibility, and egress in terms of safety and perceived efficacy. Within this method, women should be invited to think about the socio-cultural aspects of spaces (not just the material urban environment) to identify the factors that make them feel unsafe or safe. When undertaking an audit, women may or may not be asked to offer ways to make spaces safer from their perspective.

> **TIP**
>
> See also **Chapter 7—*Expanding expertise: Women's safety audits***, for a fuller discussion about undertaking audits with women and girls.

- **Understand Discrimination and Budgeting for Equity:** Gender-sensitive budgeting "demand[s] a substantial and meaningful change" with governments, policymakers and communities prioritizing the allocation of resources, ensuring that gender equality is central (Daneshpour 2023: 91). Knowing that a gender-sensitive budget is a key expectation for public space projects can create leverage within the design program and budget allocation. A gender-sensitive budget will use a "rights-based approach" to prioritize "fairness and justice" (Daneshpour 2023: 91)to advance women and uphold their rights to access public spaces, services and amenities. A budget that analyses and meets women's needs means that resources can then be measured in terms of impact, and in turn, accountability and transparency for government and organizations are supported.

- **Synthesize Relevant Sex- and Gender-disaggregated Datasets:** As well as crime statistics and census data, access to data that relates to sex and gender is produced and/or captured through a range of media across many different issues faced by women and girls. Data, for example, may be produced by governments—for example, census, surveys and community data—or through mobile phones, social media, news media, mobility data, financial data, satellite data, and can also be self-generated by communities to drive advocacy and change. Multiple data sets can be triangulated and will require specialized gender analysis and interpretation. Data can be real-time, participatory, local or global. Ensuring that high-quality, relevant, and timely data are analysed can provide insights into the issues and opportunities for women and girls in cities. Quality data will contribute to raising awareness about women's experiences, measuring the "cost" of women's inequity.

> **TIP**
>
> For more information on how to use sex- and gender-disaggregated data or how to gather data about women in cities, see **Chapter 4—*Missing women: Smart women in the data gap***

- **Establish an Expert Panel, Working Group and/or Advisory Committee:** Expert consultation in the forms of an expert panel, working group or advisory committee will provide guidance, specialization and input from disciplinary experts. Generally, their role is to support the project team to focus on the needs of women and girls. They should provide context and currency to the policy and practices in which the project exists, facilitate introductions and access to other key people of organizations which would benefit the projects, and provide input into the design and execution of project/s. Ideally, the panel, group or committee will have equal representation of diverse women across community groups, stakeholders, community leaders, local government, design teams, client representatives, peak women's organizations and feminist activists.

- **Initiate Co-design with Women and Girls from the Local Community:** Gender-sensitive co-design involves women and girls in the decision-making, planning and design process and is a key indicator of an organization's commitment to implementing gender-sensitive design approaches. Co-design activities challenge "top-down" implementation structures and can help capture the nuances of women's and girls' concerns—particularly drawing out specific spatial typologies and socio-spatial concerns. Facilitation of the process is a critical component and drives the success of a co-design method. The facilitator requires skills in listening, a keen understanding of the power dynamics in the group (including any internal agendas) as well as expertise in the social issues that may be relevant to the participating women. Participants need to understand their role in the process—that of bringing together different stakeholders and people with different perspectives—and the intent to question power relations and perceived "expertise" within the co-design process. Women and girls should be remunerated for their time and contribution and should be recognized as active co-contributors to the design process. No progress in cities can be made without women's inclusion (Whitzman et al. 2013: 50).

> **TIP**
>
> For a more detailed understanding of undertaking a co-design process with women and girls, see **Chapter 10—*Run the world: Co-design in a feminist framework*.**

- Have Case Studies at Hand: Gender-sensitive design is a burgeoning field with some excellent case studies, including interventions, strategic programs, co-design processes, and projects across all stages of city development and social economic contexts. Developing and maintaining a reference list of case studies that are relevant to the context in which practitioners work will remind teams of the available methodologies and approaches to gender-sensitive public space design. It is important to recognize that case studies are temporal, formal or material projects and may address socio-spatial aspects of space as well as more formal architectural gestures. Often tools, methods and processes will include digital media and innovative design approaches. This will assist with access to diverse groups of women with the aim of maximizing knowledge about community needs (Andersdotter et al. 2019: 169).

> **DEEPER DIVE**
>
> For a range of international case studies and co-design projects with girls and young women, refer to the *Urban Girls Catalogue: How Cities Planned for and by Girls Work for Everyone*, Elin Fabre Andersdotter, Emelie Anneroth and Caroline Wrangsten (2019).

- Evaluation and Gender-sensitive Monitoring: Because cities are always changing the evaluation and monitoring of initiatives for women will need to assess if objectives have been met and track the impact on the women who should presumably benefit from the project. In this context, continued evaluation and monitoring of gender-sensitive initiatives will ensure that positive impacts can be leveraged for future engagement. While this process occurs at the completion of a project, it needs to be embedded into the project cycles from the very beginning (RTPI 2007: 13). Best practice projects can be disseminated more broadly, and case study examples used to extend knowledge for policymakers, planners and designers. Evaluation and monitoring also provides the foundation for advocating for new projects within the community.

The Role of Practice and Communities on the Ground

Gender-sensitive design is focused on the ways that sex and gender inform an individual's experience. There are evidence-based strategies that can be implemented on the ground by policymakers, planners and designers for a marked improvement in women's and girls' perception of safety, their sense of belonging, and mobility in public life.

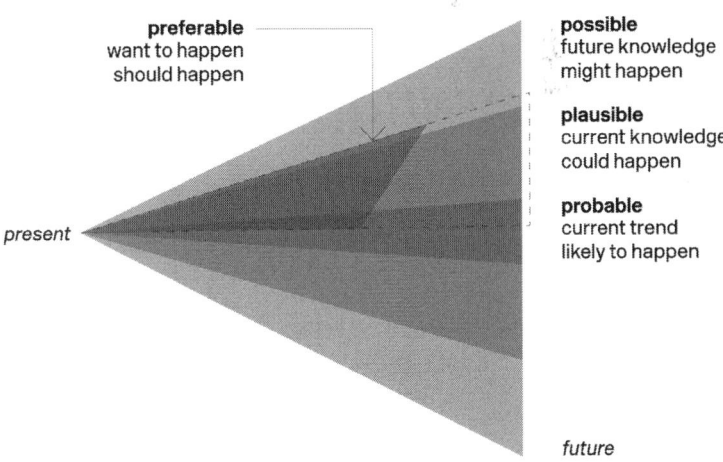

FIGURE 6.1 "Probable/Plausible/Possible/Preferable/Possibility" cone adapted from Anthony Dunne and Fiona Raby (2013).

- **Connection to the Surrounding Community:** Invest in developing interventions that increase activity with the diversity of women in the community. Consider mapping the existing communities through census data but also by examining the communities for women who differentiate themselves in groups and collectives that may be based on age, race, ethnicity, indigeneity, sexuality, caring roles, geographic location, socio-economics, and disability. Work responsively and flexibly in areas where there may be safety concerns, deploying events and strategic programming in the daytime as well as the night-time.

WOMEN'S STORIES

This playground is great for people of all ages. There are always people in this park so it makes it feel very safe. The design is lovely and there is an excellent view of the city from the top of the hill.

- **Increased Presence of Other Women and Girls:** A key safety indicator for women and girls moving through and occupying public space is the presence of other women and girls. In communities with diverse populations, seeing other people and people "like you" (for example the same race, age or sexuality) increases feelings of safety. Research suggests that women and girls benefit from areas that have a diverse population (Andersdotter et al. 2019: 171).

- **Provide Toilet and Breastfeeding Facilities for Women and their Children:** Over the last decade, the debate around all-gender public toilets has become increasingly heated. Increasingly, traditional sex-segregated public toilet facilities, originally designed to enable women's participation in public life, have been criticized for excluding gender diverse people who face barriers to accessing space that is segregated by sex. The most common solution has been to provide "gender-neutral" toilets, with many venues opting for a quick fix by simply changing the sign on the existing male (with urinal) and female (with stalls) toilet to an all-gender sign.

While some have labeled resistance to blanket gender-neutral toilets as a "moral panic," some feminists have pointed out real concerns for women that arise from desegregated public toilets and change rooms.

Women of all ages require access to toilets and sanitation, and this is crucial for women's ability to safely access and dwell in urban spaces. Sex-segregated toilets and segregated wet areas are important for women from culturally diverse backgrounds who may have specific sex-segregated needs and wants. Amenities, therefore, should include sex-segregated *and* all-gender toilets to accommodate the diverse needs of women as well as gender diverse people. All facilities should have universal access with the same attention to aesthetics and quality of fittings.

WOMEN'S STORIES

I know I'm not supposed to say this, but I miss female toilets. I feel less safe and comfortable in the new arrangements.

Baby change facilities available in all toilets, including the men's, which makes it inclusive for all parents.

Poorly maintained and very dirty, with an unsafe layout. Someone coming in can block you from leaving your cubicle.

Poor/unsafe change room facilities for girls who play here. Need to have people who make sure people guard the entrance to change rooms. Sometimes parents form a circle in the open to let girls get changed. Fix the change rooms!

Whilst I was in the wash area a male emerged from a cubicle. I feel strongly about retaining the safety and privacy of women's facilities and I don't welcome males in them. I see more and more mixed sex facilities, and I think it's leading to a loss of safe spaces for women and girls. The change I will have to make is to be more careful when using facilities, and particularly when my daughter needs to use them.

Where possible, facilities with scaled facilities for children are ideal. Designers should also consider the spatial configuration for women who may be using the facilities with several children in tow. For example, where is the pushchair stowed, and/or how are other children managed while she uses the facilities or tends to a child?

Public breastfeeding facilities for mothers and their children as well as spaces conducive to parents' needs more broadly will promote a feeling of belonging rather than a sense that the place is transient. While it is increasingly common to provide a private breastfeeding space in semi-private public buildings, creating appropriate places for public breastfeeding is less accounted for in public and urban spaces. When there is physical provision for women to breastfeed, the "emotional comfort" (Donovan et al. 2019) may be lacking. Feeling unsafe or being in a place where she may fear reproach means that women are less likely to breastfeed publicly. Urban Designer Jenny Donovan and colleagues (2019) suggest that there are several key principles for quality breastfeeding space, including: safety and physical comfort (arm rests, shade, temperate climate); accessibility (this should consider prams and buggies); consideration of their other needs and responsibilities (for example, other children); offering a high level of hygiene amenity (including access to clear water). Paramount to public and semi-public breastfeeding spaces are maintenance and regular cleaning as well as good lighting and security.[2]

- **Greater Access to Parks, Trails, Foreshores, and Recreation:** Parks and sporting facilities are dominated by the wants, needs and desires of men and boys. Most recreation areas are "made up almost entirely of skate parks and football pitches" (Make Space for Girls 2022). In contrast, many women and girls feel that parks are unsafe or restrict their recreational use of spaces at times of day (XYX Lab et al. 2021: 108–111). Skate parks are spaces where groups of men reproduce stereotypes and women are, at best, observers. Ensure the fenced areas are not entrapping and create informal areas for sitting and playing as well as places for informal ball games (Sidorova et al. 2016: 5).

- **Pros and Cons of Semi-private Public Spaces:** While some women will benefit from the added security of shopping malls, institutional centers and food courts, many others will feel excluded in places that are not free or require "know-how" to interact or participate in. The creep in corporate-owned public spaces require people to behave in a "civil way" or risk exclusion and will also place limitations on the presence of homeless people and public demonstrations.

- **Better Access and Mobility:** Many women do not own cars or have access to a car during the day. Streets and cities need to be walkable and barrier-free, with wide footpaths and infrastructure to accommodate all accessibility requirements, including wheelchairs, walking frames, mobility scooters and strollers. This includes installing ramps and elevators as alternatives to stairways. Access and mobility increase women's and girls' health and wellbeing.

- **Supporting Use of Active Transport:** Ensure that active transport (like bike riding, walking and micro-mobility) is supported by infrastructure that prioritizes the movement of people rather than cars. This should include places to safely cross roads and footpaths separated for pedestrian and bike/scooter lanes. Engage with tools that can identify the range for walkability from activity centers and various modes of public transport. Ensure traffic calming measures are applied around public buildings and transport (Sidorova et al. 2016: 21; TramLab 2020: 18). Address short-cut routes that younger groups may prefer to take (Sidorova et al. 2016: 18).

- **Provide Integrated Public Transport:** Use real-time data and technology to provide seamless connections. MaaS stands for "Mobility as a service," it is an integrated digital service that enables users to plan, book and purchase multiple types of transport services through a single portal. This is especially useful for trip-chaining, where there are multiple trips to get to a single destination, or where there are multiple destinations (for example, for work, caring, accessing services or education). This means that there is less waiting time for women and girls as well as less vulnerability and risk management (or safety work). Ensure that low visibility, lack of surveillance and/or entrapping spaces are addressed in public transport integration.

> **TIP**
>
> For a more detailed understanding of the challenges that women and girls face when using public transport, see **Chapter 7—*Train wreck: Public transport and women's safety*.**

- **Make Wayfinding a Priority:** Wayfinding and integrated directions to key sites, activity centers and various forms of public transport services are vital. This includes eliminating narrow passageways and installing mirrors if necessary to reveal who is approaching (Sidorova et al. 2016: 9). These should be incorporated into public infrastructure and align with the local community brand, providing iterative signage that includes walking times to destinations and well-lit pathways that prioritize active transport. Providing appropriate languages for mixed populations will increase safety and belonging.

WOMEN'S STORIES

No lighting, narrow path, fences on both sides so you're trapped if anything happens. Very sketchy and stopped walking along it in daytime even though it's a quicker way through.

- **Ensure "Eyes on the Street" Is Gender-sensitive:** The presence of visible authority figures and members of the community looking over the activities in public space can make some women feel safer (Andersdotter et al. 2019: 170; TramLab 2020: 19). While the presence of workers, staff and local businesses can make contributions to passive surveillance and urban oversight, there are some caveats.

Examine the adjacent activities and industries that may encourage violence against women and girls, including brothels, strip clubs and massage parlors (Kalms 2017) and places where alcohol can be purchased, or drugs consumed (Fileborn 2016). Certain locations, such as lap dancing and exotic dancing clubs make women feel threatened or uncomfortable (RTPI 2007: 9) and just because areas are populated does not mean that they are safe places for all women.

- **Re-think CCTV:** For women, surveillance is seen as potentially helpful in the event of witnessing a crime, but only if the technology is live monitored by appropriate authorities (a very costly and rare occurrence). However, the ubiquitous placement of CCTV—as a mode to document and recall urban events, if required—is unsuccessful in terms of gender -sensitive crime prevention. While it may identify suspects or function as a form of forensic examination for the identification of perpetrators and criminals it does not contribute to women's feelings of safety. This means that the ways that CCTV "frames crime and victimisation" need to be better understood in terms of women's experiences of safety (Overington 2017).

- **Address the After-dark Experience:** There is a rise in the 24-hour city and night-time economy. As such, the views of women are critical. Women feel unsafe at night to a higher degree than men (OECD 2022). Investment in improving visibility and good lighting is imperative for an equitable and gender-sensitive built environment. Good lighting will make public places less threatening after dark and impact women to a greater degree, due to their perceived vulnerability at night (Andersdotter et al. 2019: 170; Kalms 2019; Yang et al. 2022). The form and degree of the lighting needs to be considered. Foundational crowd-mapping research undertaken by Plan International, ARUP and XYX Lab in Melbourne noted that places that have high illuminance, or very *bright and over-lit* spaces, do not correlate with young women's perceptions of urban safety (Kalms 2019). To create more inclusive spaces for women and girls after dark, night-time strategies should be implemented that balance environmental concerns with the technical requirements outlined in the local community design guides and policy.

> **TIP**
>
> The importance of lighting for women after dark is outlined in Chapter 10—*On the edge of the night: Women and the night-time economy.*

- **Maintenance is Crucial:** The maintenance and cleanliness of public spaces is a factor that is underestimated in making women feel safer and more connected to urban space. Ensuring that evidence of unwelcome behavior and unpredictable people—such as drug use, homelessness and vandalism—is sensitively managed (without stigmatizing vulnerable and marginalized groups) via regular clean-ups and scheduled maintenance makes women feel at ease. Well-maintained vegetation is vital for women's comfort and belonging, but needs regular attention to ensure good sight lines and visibility.

  Landscaping and greenery are important for women and girls in terms of aesthetics and feelings of belonging. Importantly, these spaces must be well maintained and visibility after dark ensured. The physical state of an area has an effect in determining whether a place is accessible and safe, with adequate lighting, cleanliness, and the presence of good infrastructure (Plan International 2018: 20).

- **Woman-scale Design:** Following a standard ergonomics manual may mean that urban places are designed solely for the size and shape of an average man. Public spaces must also address the needs, wants and desires of women and girls of all ages and abilities. Digging deeper into the various heights, shapes, sizes and weight of populations is critical. Installing seating (with armrests), hand holds, stairs and ramps for a variety of heights will assist elderly people to stand and sit independently (Sidorova et al. 2016: 16). This will also assist more diverse groups of people to feel welcomed to a public space.

- **Encourage Intergenerational Activity:** Public spaces where women from various generations can co-exist and take the opportunity to dwell (instead of always passing through) is vital for women's sense of belonging in cities. The *Urban Girls Catalogue* (Andersdotter et al. 2019: 170) suggests that seating is the way to encourage multiple generations to come together, and that including various arrangements of seating and benches is vital, as women—due to clothing and social expectations—tend not to use city infrastructure for seating or lingering (which is more common among men in public spaces).

CHAPTER SEVEN

Expanding Expertise
Women's Safety Audits

Principles
- Place women at the center of public space assessment
- Use women's safety audits for short-, medium- and long-term planning
- Actively recruit women's diverse perspectives including those who are most vulnerable when auditing public places
- Involve key decision-makers to help leverage outcomes

Practice
- Re-think perceived professional "expert" knowledge by observing women's safety audits "in action"
- Challenge assumptions about gender-neutral design, universal access and inclusive design by commissioning women's safety audits for public space projects
- Enlist a professional facilitator to meet the needs of the organizations as well as the women participants
- Understand how the insights from women's safety audits offer a counterpoint to traditional space assessments and urban data

Participation
- Increase community engagement and strengthen women's viewpoints by encouraging women's participation in safety audits
- Identify and prioritize hotspots in the local community through regular women's safety audits and tactical walking groups

- Accept that women's expertise may sit in contrast to the crime prevention methods implemented via Crime Prevention Through Environmental Design (CPTED) or by other authorities, like the police and security services
- Install a women's taskforce to undertake women's safety audits for the local community and remunerate women accordingly for their time

Women's Safety Audits

A women's safety audit is a tool used to measure subjective experiences of safety, connection, access, and the overall "feel" of urban spaces from a woman's perspective. Developed in Canada in the late 1980s, there has been a recent resurgence in its use due to an emphasis on democratic, citizen-led participatory approaches, which have come to dominate urban space development internationally. The use of women's safety audits can increase engagement and dialogue with local communities to address urban problems and provide a counternarrative to traditional modes of decision making, including who should make decisions (Lindell et al. 2020: 480). The approach involves a group of local women who are charged with identifying local safety issues in the built environment. The audit process ideally trains women to undertake a review of the sites and to gather insights. This material encounter with the built environment also authorizes women to speculate about alternative approaches that can inform local communities and designers.

As a woman-focused approach, women's safety audits "emphasise the importance of human interactions, rather than reliance on technocratic solutions" (Beebeejaun 2009: 223), aiming to understand how women's exclusion and fear in public spaces can inform planning, urban design and architecture and thereby positively affect women's participation in the public realm. By sharing and documenting the various and multiple female perspectives, a significant contribution a women's safety audit makes is to "find/create/redefine words which reflect and record women's experiences" (Kelly et al. 1990: 40). The implementation of women's safety audits is, therefore, a move that targets the supposedly "neutral" approaches to urban design by foregrounding the emotional and experiential knowledge of women. Innovative modes for undertaking women's safety audits may also include creating "subjective maps," rating perceptions of fear and the use of personal diaries to locate specific hotspots and capture possible solutions (Lambrick et al. 2008: 15). Safety audits draw out how women may "read" the urban environment differently to men because of their concerns related to men's "violence against women and women's feelings of insecurity" (Lambrick et al. 2008: 9).

> ### Women's safety audits
>
> A women's safety audit is a place-based assessment tool undertaken from the subjective perspective of women. It is participatory form of engagement, and the tool can be analogue or digital and is modified and adapted for the specifics of each site. Women work together in small groups using the audit tool to note feelings of safety and tackle complex public space issues, examining the built environment and the social/behavioral elements of space. With the aim to promote gender equity, a women's safety audit tool is a way to understand and respond to public space needs as articulated by women and girls. The data and insights collected during a women's safety audit provide an evidence base that can be used to develop gender-sensitive strategies and to measure changes to women's perceptions of safety over time. As women's safety audits radically center women as the "experts" in the urban design process, this participatory feminist method is one of the most significant things that planning can do to address their concerns about women's personal safety (Greed 1994: 177).

Safety audits bring diverse groups of women together to physically move through community environments with the tool modified to review the specific issues for local women. For most women, this will mean walking deliberately through local areas and as such. this process can be understood as a form of tactical walking that explores the meaning of place and landscape through women-centered approaches to urban design. The qualitative data generated is informed by women's analysis of the built environment which emphasizes the importance of urban features in a way that an off-site questionnaire or more traditional interview technique would not be able to capture.

> ### Tactical walking
>
> Walking with research participants generates place-specific data; the engagement is more spatially focused, and able to engage with the features of the study area (Evans 2011: 856). It can be described as "tactical response to gendered violence in the city" (Berry 2021: 143) and it may not be a coincidence that walking is critical to feminist activism and resistance.

Defined by women's evaluation and speculation, the safety audit assesses existing spaces to identify ways to make spaces safer, reimagine a new urban space that has been designed for the needs of women, and finally, to consider what strategies might bring about their suggested changes. As women are asked to assess the quality of existing public spaces, the safety audit is a *social* research tool, where the activities are undertaken *with* women and girls rather than being undertaken for women or about them. The process is a form of co-produced research and supports the view of theorist and feminist philosopher Sandra Harding when she discusses the importance of using women's insights as a source for research and as a mode to "generate scientific problems, hypotheses, and evidence" and to "design for women and to place the researcher in the same critical plane as the research subject" (1987: 181). Harding's significant contribution of "standpoint theory" is reflected in the women's safety audit process, where marginalized groups (or "outsiders"—in this case diverse groups of women) are called upon to challenge the status quo of the "expert" knowledge.

When undertaken correctly, the audit will draw out the perspectives of diverse groups of women and actively resist a top-down approach, where a policy, planning or design professional is likely to speculate incorrectly on how women might interact with public spaces and what is best for them as they move through their communities. In this sense, women's safety audits are also a form of participatory feminist research that flips traditional approaches to urban design and requires "the establishment of new research processes that encourage the sharing of power and a redistribution of research roles" (Gervais 2018: 2).

> **TIP**
>
> Women's safety audits are a key element for progressing gender mainstreaming frameworks and gender-sensitive design approaches. For more details about how they relate, see **Chapter 5—*Girls to the Front: Mainstreaming women's needs*** and **Chapter 6—*Not-neutral: Gender-sensitive cities***.

For policymakers, planners and design practitioners, the practical observations and insights from women can prove transformational to the designer's process. They may, for example, be prompted by the women's auditing insights to consider how to better accommodate women's needs and desires in urban space. As the women working together need to discuss and critique the physical and socio-spatial environment, the process will require the designer to engage reflexively with women's responses and the ways that women are challenged by the built environment.

WOMEN'S STORIES

The streetlights are insufficient at night-time. Lots of shrubbery/trees between the footpath and the road so visibility to the public is low. There is no footpath on the opposite side of the road so you cannot cross the road if you feel unsafe.

There are many kids, families, people with dogs and elderly people that walk here that often get run down by cyclists. Not all, but a fair majority travel extremely fast. It would be better if there was a separate lane for bike riders or if pedestrians were going one way and cyclists the other way.

Walking from the station up this street makes me quite uncomfortable, it isn't lit well enough and you cannot see when you cross the road.

Good pedestrian infrastructure, good road design which separates pedestrians and drivers and cyclists.

- **How to Undertake a Women's Safety Audit:** An audit should be designed and facilitated by researchers with local community development skills as well as gender-sensitive expertise and cultural diversity skills, if required. The process relies on collaboration between a range of stakeholders and will require interacting with a range of organizations. An effective partnership will require engagement with Indigenous groups and the women within those groups. From there, partnership can be made with local community groups and trust can be built by involving women in the process from the beginning.

- **What to Audit?:** Various typologies will benefit from women's safety audits, including streets, residential areas, parks, markets and shopping centers, sporting amenities, activity centers, public toilets, community buildings, and public transport sites. Of particular interest are aspects of the physical built environment, for example: lighting, digital surveillance, cleanliness, evidence of incivility, visibility, and sightlines. While engaging in the audit, women may be asked if aspects of the built environment could be amended for improvement against a range of criteria. For example, when assessing the security of an area after dark, women may be asked for their feedback on how best to improve lighting or visibility across and through a site.

DEEPER DIVE

"Safe in Her City," developed by Casey City Council (Fig. 7.1), is a gender audit tool and analytical technique to empower women to assess their perceptions of safety. The tool extends a number of audit tools used internationally since women's safety audits were implemented in Toronto by the Metropolitan Toronto Action Committee on Violence Against Women and Children in the 1980s. Winning commendation in the 2021 Australian Urban Design Awards for *Leadership, Advocacy and Research*, the initiative highlights "issues that impact the safety, freedom and movement of women and girls, who often

> feel unsafe and can be the target of sexual harassment and violence in public space." The City of Casey recognized the need for the tool as well as the research expertise and partnered with Monash University XYX Lab to champion its development. The tool is "replicable, scalable and easily adopted by communities elsewhere."

- **Adapting an Existing Audit:** Women's safety audits can be adapted (and re-adapted) for the nuances, demographics and typologies of local context and communities and are used internationally (Whitzman et al. 2009: 205–6), for example in Africa, South India, Europe, Australia and the UK. Whitzman found, in her evaluation with 250 individuals and organizations who use women's safety audits, that the tool is most valuable because of: the format flexibility; its application across a "wide variety of groups" and across a range of "different circumstances"; its usefulness in community development; its capacity to address violence against women and against other vulnerable groups; and the larger impact which helps to bring about tangible changes in public places (2009: 205–7).

- **Who Undertakes a Women's Safety Audit?:** The process is for solely for women. Evidence suggests that when safety audits become gender neutral or lose the pointed focus of the experiences of women by failing to flag how women's experiences of oppression limit their access and safety in the built environment, then the audit is less successful (Lambrick et al. 2008: 19).The women undertaking should be representative of the community and the recruitment process may require outreach via media coverage, letters of invitation or emails requesting expressions of interest. Local neighborhood letter box drop may also be useful. Consider publicizing the potential to participate in the women's safety audit in places where women come together, such as libraries, recreational spaces and ethnic shopping strips, or the local schools.

1

Safe and secure

Feel safe here	Very Poor	Poor
Lighting How well illuminated is the space after dark?	Space is dark and gloomy	Space has minimal lighting with many dark spots
Sightlines How well are sightlines considered around pedestrian access areas to ensure visibility and safety?	Numerous blind corners and elements including vegetation blocking sightlines	Minimal clear sightlines, some landscape features causing blocking and blind corners
Openness & entrapment How many choices of pathways & exits are there to move easily through the space in case of an emergency?	No clear path of escape from multiple areas with enclosed walkways and only a single access point into the space	Unclear path of escape with only one option to exit the space
Natural surveillance How well does the site allow for public natural surveillance?	No natural surveillance from surrounding tenancies, no windows or balconies etc.	Minimal natural surveillance from surrounding tenancies or adjacent public spaces
Formal surveillance Is there presence of persons of authority, such as police officers, security etc.?	Formal surveillance is there presence of persons of authority, such as police officers, security etc.?	Police officers constantly present & busy, suggesting site has high crime activity
Technological surveillance How is technological surveillance (CCTV) being utilized to increase safety?	No active security in the space, no accountability for users of the space or way to capture who's in the space	A large number of CCTV cameras, implying the space has potential for high crime activity

FIGURE 7.1 Safety Audit developed by Casey City Council, Australia. This safety audit tool is used to evaluate the public environment through the four categories of "safety and security," "connection and belonging," "access and movement," and the "look and feel" of urban spaces and inform future strategies for the local community.

Average	Good	Excellent
Adequate lighting in some areas, other areas may be over-lit or a little too dark	Adequate lighting in most areas	Lighting is comfortable and sufficient for clear visibility in all areas
One or two blind corners, most landscape features and obstacles meet requirements	Clear sightlines throughout most of the space, all obstacles meet requirements	Clear sightlines throughout the entire space, all landscape features meet requirements
Two pathway options and exits in case of emergency	Clear path of escape with many pathway choices and no dead ends or enclosed areas	Clear wayfinding showing multiple paths of escape with many wide and accessible path and exit options
Some natural surveillance from public spaces or surrounding tenancies with some windows facing towards site	Sufficient natural surveillance with surrounding tenancies looking onto the site	Space is filled with natural surveillance from windows/balconies facing site (if applicable) or nearby amenity that attracts multiple pedestrians/commuters
Security officer/s present	Security officers/staff are present and approachable	Gender diverse, racially diverse and approachable staff present or gender and racially diverse security officers
One to two CCTV cameras visible, no immediate response to incidents that occur in the space	Site has CCTV cameras that are directly linked to an employed security guard, available to respond promptly	CCTV only needed when the site is closed/after hours if at all, due to the high level of natural and formal surveillance during open hours

2

Connection and belonging

Feel welcome here	Very Poor	Poor
Resting What is the availability for people to sit and linger within in a pleasant environment?	No seating, people only passing through promptly	Only uncomfortable seating in an unpleasant environment
Activity What opportunities are there for inclusive social interaction/ activities, such as picnics, casual sports games, events, playgrounds etc.?	Space is only conducive to antisocial behaviour	No clear communal facilities for activities, minimal open space
Adaptability Does the space offer adaptability and variety to provide for different needs and uses?	The space has one use and is not able to adjust to suit other needs and uses	The space has more than one use but is not able to adjust to suit other needs and uses
Amenity (toilets/change rooms) Are there facilities on site that are fully accessible, inclusive and maintained (e.g. soap, toilet paper, sharps container, sanitary bin)	No facilities on site	Minimal facilities available, only male and female toilets

Average	Good	Excellent
One to two available seats within an acceptable environment	A few inclusive spaces to sit and linger within a pleasant environment	Many inclusive spaces to rest within in a well designed, pleasant environment
An opportunity for social activity with places to sit or rest	Opportunities for inclusive social interaction such as picnic tables, shelters and open spaces	A variety of opportunities for inclusive social interaction for an extended period of time, such as BBQ/ kitchen facilities, open space, playgrounds etc.
The space has more than one use and can be adjusted to suit other needs	The space has many uses and spaces that can be somewhat adapted	The space has many uses and spaces that have been designed to be easily adaptable, providing for different needs and uses
well maintained toilets available with a separate inclusive disabled access	Separate gendered toilets and baby change facilities allow for entry with prams and universal access	Facilities positioned close to activity that are inclusive and maintained with multiple fully accessible universal toilets and baby change rooms

3

Access and movement

Can get to and move freely	Very Poor	Poor
Public transport How accessible is the site by public transport?	No public transport options within a 10 minute walk from site	No public transport options within 5 minute walk from the site
Car parking How safe is the car parking in regards to design, location and access to any facilities on the site?	Car park is hidden at the rear of the site/ over 100m from facility entrance and has no paths for pedestrians	Car park is partially hidden, away from the facility entrance with uneven pedestrian paths
Pedestrian access What is the quality of the paths, ramps and crossings, how easy is it for people with all abilities to get around?	No pedestrian paths or ramps	Minimal pedestrian paths in poor condition, no ramps for access into raised areas
Pedestrian priority How prioritized are pedestrians within the space?	Motor vehicles are prioritized, with no consideration of pedestrian access	Pedestrians are somewhat considered in areas of the site
Cycling How have cyclists' amenity and safety been considered within the site?	No cycle lanes, paths or bike storage provided	On-road bike lanes provided with some weather-exposed bike hoops

EXPANDING EXPERTISE

Average	Good	Excellent
There's a public transport stop within five minute walk from the site	The site is within a three minute walk of a bus stop or train station used by people at peak times	The site is in close proximity to a range of bustling public transport options with clear wayfinding & signage
Car park is easy to access from building entrance and has a pedestrian path leading up to it	Car park is nearby and mostly visible from building entrances and has pedestrian paths in most areas	Car park is well presented, visible and accessible from any building or site entrances with wide pedestrian path connections throughout
Sufficient pedestrian paths and ramps in most of the site	Wide pedestrian paths and ramps for prams and wheelchairs to easily access	Good quality, wide pedestrian paths and ramps for prams and wheelchairs to fit side by side
Clear pedestrian connections in the majority of the site	Pedestrians are prioritized with wide, protected footpaths and raised crossings to low traffic	Site has a pedestrianized zone, separating pedestrians from traffic, encouraging walking and social activity in the urban space
On-road protected bike lane with weather protected bike hoops	Off-road bike lanes with secure end of trip bike storage	Off-road bike lanes with secure end of trip bike storage, weather protection and shower facilities

4

Look and feel

Feels good here	Very Poor	Poor
Diversity of people present What variety of people are occupying the space according to age, culture, gender and ability?	No people present in the space dominated by one type of person	The single gender, culture or age group is exclusive and unwelcoming to others
Behaviours What are the common behaviours presented by people on the site?	Presence of unpredictable people participating in anti-social behaviour, drug/ alcohol use or sleeping rough	Evidence of antisocial behaviour, such as alcohol bottles, syringes, rubbish dumping etc.
Sensory Experience What is the user's sensory experience of the space? Smells, sounds and physical comfort	Sensory experience is hostile with bad smells, littered environment and negative sounds, sirens, yelling etc.	User's sensory experience is uncomfortable, unclean environment with loud sounds of traffic and machinery
Sustainability and maintenance How well presented and maintained does the site appear through elements such as (shelter, seating, drinking fountains etc.) impacting the overall sustainability of the site	Site is unmanaged, and unsustainable with no landscape amenities	Site is unmanaged some attempt to contain litter with few bins available
Attention/attractions What visual elements (such as public art, gardens, lighting installations etc.) are present in the site?	No visual elements are present in the site	Visual elements are present in the site that aren't attractive or well maintained
Architecture What is the quality of the architecture or built form present on the site?	Hostile, uninhabitable or partly demolished built form and infrastructure	Low quality building quality with little to no street-facing windows

EXPANDING EXPERTISE

Average	Good	Excellent
Mostly one type of person present in the space, occasionally a mix of people will enter the space	Space has a mix of ages and cultures using the space and passing through	The space has a diverse variety of ages, genders, cultures and abilities using the space
Some evidence of litter and graffiti	People behaving appropriately within the space	A number of people are interacting and communicating positively, possibly participating in organized events or group activities
User's sensory experience is average with a mix of good and bad smells and a mixture of loud and quiet sounds	User's sensory experience is good, pleasant smells and some positive ambient noise from surrounding activity	User's sensory experience is excellent with pleasant smells and lots of positive ambient noise such as people chatting and background music
Site appears managed with gardens and clear paths. Sufficient rubbish and recycling bins provided	Site is well maintained with multiple waste disposal options available and a variety of landscape amenities	Site is well maintained with high quality landscape amenities including tree planting, seating under shelter and in the sun, drinking fountains with dog bowls, etc.
One visual element is present in the site that attracts attention	Two visual elements are present in the site that attract attention and discovery	Two plus quality visual elements are present in the site that give character and attract attention, discovery and interaction
Average quality building, some street facing windows	Good quality building and infrastructure with ground floor activated and opened to the street	Quality and infrastructure with ground floor activated and opened to the street and balconies overlooking street

- **How to Support Women's Participation:** To participate in on-site audit walks, women need practical support, such as childcare, transportation, translators, and sign interpretation and/or support for participants with disabilities. Materials should be provided to women in their preferred language, otherwise translators will need to be engaged to assist with the completion of the process. The audit is, ideally, a dynamic tool. It may be a digital tool (accessed on the smartphone or laptop) or an analogue tool (completed with a pen and paper) or facilitated via a walking interview. It is a methodology that responds to the invisibility of women within city planning and gives voice to a range of diverse positions that have historically been subjugated to male viewpoint. As a participatory process, it aims to engage with a wide and representative cross-section of women to ensure that the localized socio-geographic understanding of the community is captured. Outreach and recruitment are a significant aspect of undertaking a successful audit. Representation of the different demographic backgrounds of the community will ensure that diverse views and needs are gathered, and social inclusion is enhanced (Lindell et al. 2020: 480). Partnership may need to be established through the local communities to gain the confidence of women. As the women's safety audits process must promote the active involvement of diverse women, the community will need to ethically facilitate outreach to women who are financially disadvantaged, from various racial and cultural backgrounds, women with disabilities, and diverse sexualities. Through the engagement with women from different backgrounds and with diverse needs, a wide variety of views will help to understand how different women can have divergent perspectives on the same place (Beebeejaun 2017). In engaging with the lived experiences of women, urban research responds not only to people's experiences, but also to how people live *through* and *respond to* their experiences.

- **Briefing Women on Their Role:** Practically, women are briefed to complete a guided survey form, checklist, rubric, map and/or template (for an example of the criteria see Fig. 7.1), and to share insights and suggestions. Assessing spaces against the audit criteria allows communities and stakeholders to see spaces through the eyes of women users and reveals how spaces may need to be transformed—whether in relation to socio-cultural behavior change or amending the built environment—to better meet women's needs, rights and desires. Whitzman et al. concluded that women's safety audits are "effective for bringing about environment changes, empowering women, and alerting the public and authorities to the shared responsibility for ensuring the safety of women" (Whitzman et al. 2009: 205).

A series of statements will require comment and evaluation, where the women auditors "rate" the spaces to inform designers and planners of the value, needs and fears that women may have when moving through and around their community. As well as examining the built environment, women will be asked to assess the non-physical aspects of the space; for example: the presence of other women and their perceived diversity across, age, race ethnicity, ability, and class; and the activities taking place in the space and whether women are able to dwell and gather comfortably and with a sense of belonging. They may also be required to look at the behavior of people in the area: How many people are about? What is the sex or gender? Are they lingering? Are any people drug-affected?). They may be required to consider if they would feel empowered to dwell in this space, and if not, why not? Where possible, they may assess aspects of the community's diversity, considering, for example, the dimensions of age, ethnicity, and sexuality of people using or passing through the area.

- **Synthesizing the Data:** Responses should be collated, coded, analysed and synthesized for insights that can be transparently shared back to all participants, members of the local community (if ethical considerations allow) and used by policymakers, planners and designers to inform decision making. The mediation of both qualitative insights and quantitative data reflects scholar Sara Ahmed's suggestion that living is a process of data collection, gathering up the everyday with the knowledge that politics (and policy) and the act of living cannot be separated (2017: 214). With regular auditing, this engagement can provide community stakeholders with the ability to measure both the issues as well as the impact of changes implemented through urban design interventions to ensure that the longitudinal needs of women are being met. A women's safety audit will offer a "wide range of benefits to participants, the community at large, decision-makers, planners and the organizations that sponsored the audits" (Whitzman et al. 2009: 205).

> **TIP**
>
> A women's safety audit is a participatory method. Participation and co-design are addressed in **Chapter 11—*Run the world: Participatory design with women and girls***.

- How the Findings and Actions Will Impact the Community: From the local community's perspective, the audit may be applied to tackle priority areas. For example, communities may appraise areas of intended public space investment; they may seek to understand opportunities for improvement; or engage the assessment of spaces for post-occupancy evaluation. The process can identify critical gaps in the ways that "experts" may have been developing local community areas and can renew or challenge commitments from the local community and/or government to ensure that problem spaces identified by women are prioritized and that existing strategies are value for money. Through the feedback from women and girls, the community can work on (or advocate for) improvements using gender-sensitive design.

Building on crime prevention principles, women's safety audits fill a critical role in designing feminist cities, as they engage with feminist principles of participatory urban analysis, involving women with lived experience in the planning and design process. As a "grass roots" and locally-driven consultative approach, a critical strength of the audit process is to engage local women and leverage their insights, but the "government support and follow-up is essential for the success of women's safety audits" (Lambrick et al. 2008: 14).

Elevating Women's Voice?

The aim is to engage with women's lived experience and the process aims to elevate insights from a diverse range of women, to bring about change in the urban environment, to challenge inequity in communities and contribute to positive change (see Fig. 7.2).

Equally, there are risks that the audit process will be used to validate "expert" perspectives rather than engage productively with users of local spaces. As with any kind of group engagement, there

Physical environment is changed through
- better lighting
- signage
- emergency devices
- changes to thoroughfares
- improvement in public infrastructure

Awareness building about
- men's violence against women
- women's perspectives
- women's security
- divergent experiences of public spaces
- discrimination in the urban environment
- collaboration for safer communities
- socioeconomic insecurity
- women's role in planning

Community participation through
- better lighting
- signage
- emergency devices
- changes to thoroughfares
- improvement in public infrastructure

Behavior is changed through
- community action to address unwanted behavior such as public drinking
- creation of new on-site jobs

Participant confidence and agency through
- gaining new skills through undertaking the audit such as collaboration and tech skills
- better understanding of policy and legislation
- decision makers gain skills in understanding and advocating for underrepresented communities
- decision makers have increased access to resources about women and violence

Funding is increase through
- greater understanding of the needs of women and girls in planning and urban design

FIGURE 7.2 The impact of the use of women's safety audits. Table based on findings from Women's Safety Audits: What Works and Where? UN-Habitat: Safer Cities Programme, Melanie Lambrick, & Kathryn Travers, 2008. Research suggests that positive outcomes result from the use of women's safety audits.

will be difficulties and tensions between stakeholders, facilitators and those with lived experiences of the sites. One form of audit and participatory engagement style may be terrific for one group but fall short for another group. Community partnerships are tricky and women's safety audits challenge the embedded hierarchical structures within organizations and will likely ruffle a few feathers.

Diversity is a desirable part of the women's safety audits process, but language can be a barrier to overcome when working with culturally diverse groups, women from broad socio-economic backgrounds, or those who are geographically challenged because of homelessness or precarious housing situations. For example, the dynamics of audit discussions could potentially disadvantage some marginalized women when some others try to dominate. This is where an experienced facilitator will be able to negotiate with the perspectives of groups to capture all positions fairly. All women are occupants of the space and will have specific needs and perspectives. Capturing all viewpoints is difficult and may require directed effort with specialized organizations.

There are risks that undertaking a women's safety audit will create expectations that problematic areas of the built environment will be addressed (Lafont 2015: 38). The process does not address the fact that implementation of the recommendations may be difficult (Whitzman et al. 2009: 207). Despite the challenges, the benefits will amplify the voice of marginalized women, which is vital. As planner and researcher Yasminah Beebeejaun suggests, these temporary occupations and the evaluation of public spaces can contribute to women's right to occupy space and "reveal something about how fear can be productively challenged" (2017: 328). Through the women's safety audits and through the positive encounter that uses "walking as a collaborative and political strategy" (ibid.), women are invited to propose innovative and alternative feminist futures which imagine new possibilities for urban places that draw on women's lived experiences.

PART THREE
Prioritizing Safer Cities

CHAPTER EIGHT

Train Wreck

Public Transport and Women's Safety

Principles
- Incorporate women's rights and a gender lens into transport policy and planning frameworks
- Ensure equal representation of men and women in transport governance
- Address the social and economic costs of ignoring gender issues in public transport spaces
- Evaluate the role of police and authorities to improve the provision of public transport for women and girls
- Use data visualization to undertake intersectional analysis of transport access
- Mandate gender-sensitive training for all front-line staff in public transport
- Instate best-practice methods for women and girls to report concerns and incidents
- Consider if women-only spaces and women-only commercial passenger services that are female-focused and female-employed are appropriate for the cultural context
- Consider blanket ticket concessions to targeted population groups, such as younger or older women who need financial assistance and women with disabilities

- Track sex- and gender-disaggregated transport usage to understand women's mobility in detail
- Understand links between gender, transport and development in relation to sustainability targets
- Adopt use of technologies and real-time data to improve planning and service delivery for women and girls

Practice
- Engage with gender-sensitive design to make public transport spaces hostile to perpetrators
- Ensure equal representation of men and women in transport planning and design
- Increase the expertise, leadership and visibility of women in the sector
- Evaluate change with a gender-sensitive approach across the life of the project from inception to post-occupancy (which may be between 25 and 40 years, in larger rail projects)
- Include the whole of journey and the "last mile home" in the decision-making process, including active transport, commercial passenger vehicles and micro-mobility (for example: bicycles, e-bikes, micro-mobility, and shared systems)
- Engage with women and girls in the design process using an iterative, participatory, feminist co-design methodology
- Install real-time technology into the design of transport infrastructure
- Design streets that are safe for all users, including good environments for walking and cycling

Participation
- Undertake community engagement to gather data from women and girls about their mobility experiences
- Understand and provide for the preferred mobility modes for women and girls in local communities
- Consider implementing community-focused transport interventions to address transport poverty
- Use communication campaigns to announce acceptable behavior on public transport; emphasize that it is not women's responsibility to keep themselves safe when moving through the community; emphasize how women and girls can report issues and the need to communicate public transport-related crime hotspots in local areas

Public Transport And Women's Safety

Safe and accessible public transport provides women and girls with access to education, training, employment, healthcare, social services and leisure activities. Since women and girls are more reliant on public transport (Loukaitou-Sideris 2016: 554), poor public transport can be a hindrance to equity when "access to and use of public transport options is unevenly distributed across society," with safety the key differentiating factor between men and women (Matthewson et al. 2021: 54). While public transport is a basic human right (Currie et al. 2007: 29) it remains one of the most safety-challenged, hostile, and inadequate environments for women in cities.

The assumption that women and men have the same user needs and experiences is the key obstacle to improving public transport for women and girls. Many of the barriers for women when using public transport are the result of applying a gender "neutral" approach to policy, planning and design, which paradoxically results in discrimination. Given that women and men's use of public transport is markedly different, neutrality defaults to a male perspective and refuses to acknowledge women's wants, needs and fears. This tacitly condones (and arguably enables) discrimination and thus feeds systemic gender inequality.

Unsurprisingly, the issues have been raised persistently within feminist scholarship for over forty years and the field of gender and transport does not lack evidence-based research on the issues faced by women. For example, in 1979, transport researcher Genevieve Giuliano noted the differences in opportunities and alternatives between men and women using public transport, and asked questions about the impact of the transportation system on women's choices and agency. A steady evidence-based stream of research has been built since. Urban planning researcher Clara Greed has noted the "mono-dimensional" emphasis of transport that is focused on men's commute (1994: 42). Sociologist Randi Hjorthol has critiqued how a lack of transport options reflects social and economic activities, including the division of labor and paid and unpaid work within each household, and impacts access to resources (2008: 193). In a survey of the victimization of women in transportation settings in North America, urban planners Anastasia Loukaitou-Sideris and colleagues (2009) describe how women are socialized to fear transport spaces. A champion and expert in the field of gender and public transport, Loukaitou-Sideris has been prolific in the field for decades, and in 2016, argued that cultural, physical, economic and psychological barriers reduce women's mobility and inhibit their use of public transport. In 2013, urban researcher Carolyn Whitzman and colleagues outlined public transport as "both an economic development and a human rights issue" where individuals should have "an equitable share of collective resources" (Whitzman et al. 2013: 50). More recently, researcher in transport safety Vania Ceccato (2017) examined the compounding intersectional factors that impact perceptions of safety and fear. In 2019, and with research spanning several decades, Clara Greed reiterated the need to counter the perception that women transport users are a homogenous group, and noted the resistance to change in the system and the ongoing issues faced by women, particularly in relation to managing caring roles. This includes the definition of their use of public transport by multiple short trips (trip-chaining) to accomplish domestic tasks (2019). Greed suggests that there is a need to tackle the contradictions between what planner's *think* is required in public transport spaces and the "realities experienced by the urban population as they seek to access and use" cities (Greed 2019: 27).

A significant obstacle for public transport overhaul has been a continued and blinkered emphasis on safety, but solely in reference to the technical aspects of public transport. The transport-oriented development which has come to dominate cities aims to integrate transport modalities into urban places so that communities, services and public spaces are centered around access and mobility. With a technical focus on the operationalization of transport development, the tendency has been to concentrate on the transactional value of public transport, with the "social" aspect peripheral to transport studies and planning (Levy 2019: 44). By side-lining the social aspect of mobility and disregarding how gender is pivotal to the success and safety of transport environments, women have been excluded and gender inequity deepened. And so, it will be in naming and qualifying women's different needs and wants that public transport policy, planning and design can develop transport frameworks that are responsive to and reflect women's rights and needs and make service providers accountable for women's travel patterns, income levels, housing situations, employment levels, and intersectional perspectives and experiences.

Undervalued and Overlooked: Men's vs Women's Use of Public Transport

Sex and gender influence the patterns of movement through cities. Loukaitou-Sideris has articulated how "physical, economic, cultural, and psychological constraints" are reinforced by inadequate transportation policies that often neglect women's needs (2016: 547). Key differences between the transport experiences of men and women may include inadequate transport services and/or access for women who are transport dependent; inadequate understanding of women's journeys; women's use of public transport and the impact of caring responsibilities; and issues of personal safety and vulnerability when women use public transport, including the risk of sexual violence. These barriers are further influenced by the level of gender inequity within a women's community, and other considerations, where access to transport and mobility is shaped by intersectional oppression related to age, disability, ethnicity, geographic location, income, indigeneity, migratory status, race, religion and sexuality.

- **Transport Poverty:** While transport poverty is an under-explored area of research in relation to sex and gender, it is likely that women are at increased risk of experiencing transport poverty, as they are the dominant users of public transport and tend to be public transport dependent (Blomstrom et al. 2018: 7). Transport poverty affects 10 to 90 percent of people across low- and middle-income countries as well as those living in developed cities, and broadly refers to the "inadequacy, fragmentation, inconsistency, and tokenism" of public transport (Lucas et al. 2016: 353). As members of a household have different needs related to public transport, and since planning data focuses on the male "breadwinner" transport poverty must be determined *individually* and is significantly shaped by gender roles and expectations (Booth et al. 2000: 68). Women's dependency on public transport results in them being "transport captive," meaning they have no choice but to use public transport and "are often the most fearful and the most vulnerable"; usually they are people with intersecting oppressions, such as age, disability and women with caring responsibilities (Wekerle et al. 1995: 62). A dependency on public transport directly relates to the traditional divisions of labor, with men dominant, placing women at even greater risk of transport poverty. Economic and social barriers overlap with physical ones for those who live in outer suburbs or in rural areas, where there is often infrequent or erratic public transport service.

> **Transport poverty**
>
> A woman is transport poor if, to satisfy her daily basic activity needs, at least one of the following conditions applies (adapted from Lucas et al. 2016: 356):
>
> - There is no transport option available that is suited to her physical condition and capabilities
> - The existing transport options do not reach destinations where she can fulfill her daily activity needs and maintain a reasonable quality of life
> - The necessary weekly amount spent on transport leaves the household with a residual income below the official poverty line
> - She needs to spend an excessive amount of time traveling, leading to time poverty or social isolation
> - The prevailing travel conditions are dangerous, unsafe or unhealthy for her.

Women's mobility options—and often the *lack* of options—reflect their socio-cultural and economic positions (Matthewson et al. 2021: 54). Women, for example, may spend a high proportion of their income on transport but be forced to use the poorest quality service. Economic barriers mean that women from lower socio-economic areas may lack the choice to use private transport options and may travel less and walk more and have their travel restricted to mandatory trips only (Lucas et al. 2016: 362). A lack of choice of transportation modes has additional burdens for women and increases "time poverty" (Blomstrom et al. 2018: 7). Transport poverty impacts women internationally and, even in countries considered to be wealthy, the priority given to roads and car ownership means that some of the population will be affected (Lucas et al. 2016: 360).

WOMEN'S STORIES

I rely on public transport. If I am going out or leaving work late in the evening, I am often concerned for my safety at train stations. I don't have any other way to get around though, so I have to use these spots even though I don't feel safe.

- **Use of Service and Inadequate Service:** Public transport is scheduled to align with the formal workday, with priority given to trips between the peripheral areas of the city and the urban center during peak times. Women's transport needs are diminished by the bias toward a gendered system and service focused on the periods of peak commuting times when demand is high for male office work. This focus is disproportionate and does not reflect the needs of women (Booth et al. 2000: 65). The fact that women are the dominant users of public transport is overlooked in most cities. Examining 19 major cities across 13 countries and six continents, Rahul Goel and colleagues found that women are the most likely to use public transport (Fig. 8.1). This includes commuting to work, where the research revealed that that "women's use of public transportation is significantly greater than men's" (Goel et al. 2022). This supports other international research that outlines how women are more reliant on public transport than men (Loukaitou-Sideris 2016: 554; Harumain et al. 2021: 76), are less likely to have access to or own a car (Transport for West Midlands 2022: 4–5; Blomstrom et al. 2018: 7) and are more likely to trip-chain (Blumenberg et al. 2004: 192).

Regardless of the reason for travel, women's use of public transport is likely outside of peak times and centered around the combination of caring roles and/or work (Greed 1994: 42; Sánchez de Madariaga 2013: 35–36; Levy, 2019: 54). Many women's needs are often ignored by service providers and women are forced to negotiate less reliable and less timely services at off-peak times. A continued emphasis on transport for peak hours does not accommodate women's complex journeys and their need to move across multiple destinations (Sánchez de Madariaga 2013: 39). This indicates that the dominance afforded to "peak" travel times

City	Country	Region	Public transport (%) Female	Male
Accra	Ghana	Africa	28.0	23.6
Kisumu	Kenya	Africa	23.5	24.1
Cape Town	South Africa	Africa	32.8	27.3
Delhi	India	Asia	17.3	24
Melbourne	Australia	Australia	8.8	8.8
London	England	Europe	27.4	27.2
Berlin	Germany	Europe	23.7	19.7
Cologne	Germany	Europe	14.4	13.7
Hamburg	Germany	Europe	18.8	17.7
Munich	Germany	Europe	21.9	19.1
Zurich	Switzerland	Europe	17.7	14.5
Buenos Aires	Argentina	Latin America	47.7	41.7
Sao Paulo	Brazil	Latin America	38.2	32.5
Santiago	Chile	Latin America	34.1	31.1
Bogota	Colombia	Latin America	38.3	35.0
Mexico City	Mexico	Latin America	37.8	45.3
Chicago	USA	North America	6.3	6.9
Los Angeles	USA	North America	6.0	6.0
New York City	USA	North America	32.0	30.4

FIGURE 8.1 Gender differences in use of public transport in major cities across the world, adapted from Rahul Goel, Oyinlola Oyebode, Louise Foley, Lambed Tatah, Christopher Millett, and James Woodcock 2022.

requires revision. In her study of urban trips in Spain in 2006–7, gender and planning researcher Inés Sánchez de Madariaga examines women's "mobility of care." By re-aggregating transport trips to include their trips related to caring and domestic work (for example, those related to escorting, shopping, leisure, strolling, visits) she found that the amount of travel undertaken by women is comparable to commuter trips, suggesting that there are assumptions made in transport research which neglect the complexity of women's use of public transport (Sánchez de Madariaga 2013: 39).

- **Caring Responsibilities:** Women users of public transport tend to undertake shorter or more local trips to meet their responsibilities, many of which involve cross-city journeys with multiple stops and interchange points for caring and family duties. They are more likely to be accompanied by someone needing care, including children, the elderly or people with a disability. As such, women's everyday struggles to use public transport are intensified and multiply burdened. As a result, women make shorter but more trips with several stops in one journey. This can be related to the fact that women undertake more household work and continue to bear the load of providing primary caregiving and managing the organization of family life.

For women who are transport dependent with caring responsibilities, they may need regular assistance from strangers to manage prams, wheelchairs and household items, as they are more likely to be carrying goods (Blomstrom et al. 2018: 7). Women organize their route to avoid transport that is not easily accessible or conducive to their additional requirements.

- **Safety versus *Safety*:** Technical priorities dominate transport service provision. Issues of safety are usually centered on recommendations that view mobility as an economic and environmental investment, where gender is relegated to minor importance (Scholten et al. 2019: 10; Matthewson et al. 2021: 55). This neglects the social responsibility of transport service providers to accommodate the specific safety needs of women and girls. Investment in personal safety is likely focused on "slip, trip and fall" hazards, and the ways to separate public users from the dangers of public transport infrastructure.

One of the differentiating factors for women is that they face a disproportionate fear of victimization from male violence, such as

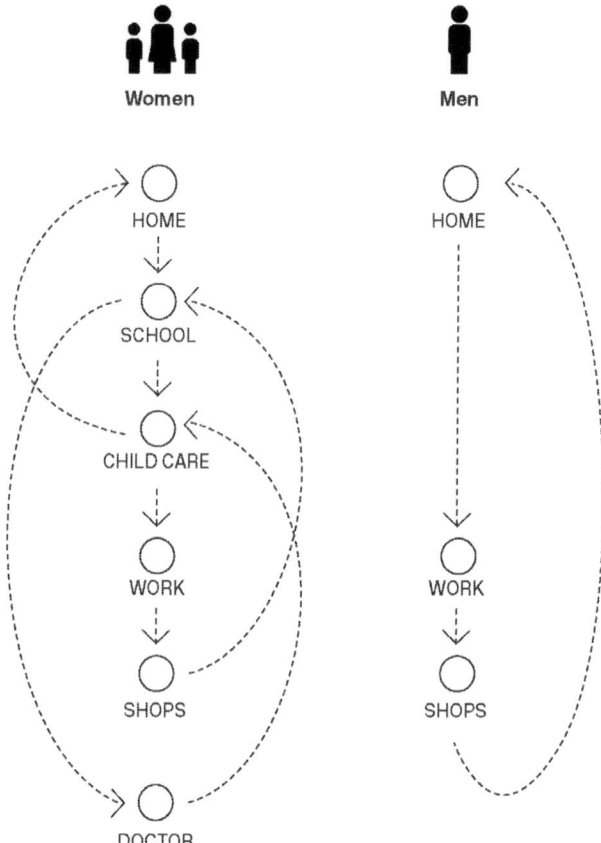

FIGURE 8.2 Women's mobility patterns versus "traditional" commuter mobility. Diagram Isabella Webb, Monash University XYX Lab 2022.

sexual harassment, assault and rape, when using public transport. As women continue to be considered more "open" than men, some men believe that women are available for unsolicited interaction when in the public realm (Goffman 1963). The threat of sexist harassment and assault is a burdensome aspect of using public transport for women and girls, with many facing relentless and even life-threatening encounters when navigating cities. Public transport during peak times can be overcrowded, leading to more harassment (Blomstrom et al. 2018: 7). Reporting on "transit rapes" across cultures including India, South America, North America, Australia and Southeast Asia, Ceccato and Loukaitou-Sideris (2020b: 4) note the concerning fact that across all cities and cultures, public transport is risky for women.

> **DEEPER DIVE**
>
> For a detailed overview of evidence of women's victimization in transit environment across the world, see *Transit Crime and Sexual Violence in Cities – International Evidence and Prevention* (2020a), eds Vania Ceccato and Anastasia Loukaitou-Sideris.

Given that most public transport systems fail to focus on women's experiences of risk when moving around their cities, women's mobility is commonly defined by careful planning, modification and self-restriction. Some women may not use a service due to the perceived risk, and most manage or reduce their access to transport services during times when the services are less frequent, or the behavior of other people may be threatening. As human geographer Rachel Pain notes, for women, it is not whether the space itself is objectively safe or unsafe, but how these spaces are given meaning, what they represent to women, and how they might affect their lives (1991). As women's access is restricted and reduced, as they manage the challenges of sexist harassment (and worse), the disadvantages accumulate and their quality of life, health and wellbeing and access to education and sense of community are diminished.

WOMEN'S STORIES

On public transport I have experienced a lot of sexual harassment, I feel very unsafe when getting off a train in places where there are very few other people around at night. Especially when traveling to get home to the outer suburbs. I think some ideas that might improve feeling safe on public transport are helplines to report sexual harassment and having advertisements on trains to say that sexually harassing behavior is unacceptable.

Along this route, I have been harassed multiple times, had men masturbate at me, follow me off the tram, and shout profanities.

After dark I don't want to leave train station to catch bus. I will catch taxi from rank.

Harassed on the upper deck of the ferry. Wouldn't leave me alone despite my clear non-interest (headphones in, sunglasses on, turned away to look out over the water). Sat directly across from me staring, despite plenty of other seats and wouldn't go away despite multiple requests from me to be left alone.

Intersectionality and Women's Transport

Regular participatory research with women who may be multiply burdened in public transport spaces should be established by all transport service providers, as well as policymakers, planners and designers working in public transport provision. Iterative collaboration with minority groups through local women's organizations should include women with disabilities, women from diverse races and ethnicities, lower socio-economic women, linguistically diverse women, older women and young women, gender-diverse people, and women with divergent cultural beliefs. Below is an overview of some of the challenges facing women with multiple differences that a lack of equity and inclusion construct as a burden.

- **Public Transport and Women with Disabilities:** Women with disabilities are not a homogenous group but share numerous fears and concerns when accessing public transport, due to limitations in their capacity to travel in a normative way. The transport environment has an enormous impact on a disabled woman's access to social interaction, participation, education and work. The whole of journey can be challenging when the built environment presents obstacles from door to door, and not just during the public transport experience. A range of risks often makes navigating a journey impossible.

For some women with disabilities, adequate public transport provision may not be available. While specialist services may be provided for women with disabilities, these services may not be free, therefore, some women may be prevented from access (Lucas et al. 2016: 362). If women with disabilities do have adequate access to public transport, their major concern is the journey time (Park et al. 2022: 188). Alongside reliability, the issues of safety related to much longer wait periods for accessible transport options are significant. This means disabled women may be spending longer periods of time on train platforms, in subways or at bus and tram stops or interchanges, which often lack shelter and lighting.

Women with a disability are more likely to fear crime and be concerned with their personal safety (Delbosc et al. 2011: 3). These challenges, while intensified when women are teenagers and young adults, are often endured across their lifetime, with fear of assault or harassment by men significantly constraining their everyday access to public transport. As such, they are at increased risk of harassment, sexual assault, or a being a victim of crime. Women with mobility needs are vulnerable, especially if they need physical assistance from service providers or the gendered public or are required to discuss their disabilities with a stranger.

- **Racism, Religious Vilification and Women on Public Transport:** There continue to be inequalities in women's access to public transport; these are related to race-based discrimination and continued disinvestment in public transport networks servicing communities of color. As a result of economic and geographic disadvantage, women of color will likely have less (or no) access to a car, will be transport dependent, and face increased commute times.

Women may be targeted racially or because of their religion, with the result that they are reluctant to use public transport and may forgo opportunities, employment and training, due to lack of assurance that their public transport experiences will be respectful and safe. Ongoing vilification resulting from racist stereotypes or slurs confirms that migrant, refugee and First Nations women are at risk of being targeted for both their race and/or religion as well as for their gender. Experiencing racism toward themselves or witnessing racism toward others leaves women feeling unsafe, and women are aware that challenging racist behavior can escalate an incident (Transport for West Midlands 2022: 9).

- **Public Transport Needs for Women from Low Socio-economic Backgrounds:** The polarization of wealth and poverty adversely affects women's access to public transport. As the lower socio-economic areas tend also to be the communities where crime may be high, women's fear of victimization in these areas may be greater and may limit access to public transport. Research indicates that fear for personal safety shapes how different groups travel, especially at night, where women may be excluded from using public transport due to perceived risk (Oviedo Hernandez et al. 2016: 161–162). The capacity to spend disposable income on a car (a choice made by many middle-class people) can provide a "bubble of personal security" for many women (Wekerle et al. 1995: 62). And while some households may own a car, structural inequalities and economic power within the household may mask the fact that women do not have access (or have limited or no access) to a vehicle. Women may therefore be more reliant on walking and public transport. Those who are living in economically vulnerable areas need to be a primary concern for transport planners and policymakers when they are designing safer cities for women and girls.

- **Public Transport Needs for Linguistically Diverse People:** Increasing the use of communication campaigns in dominant and diverse language groups can assist communities to understand the socio-cultural expectations for users of public transport. For example, uncivil behavior can be reduced, and linguistically diverse populations may benefit from on-site behavior campaigns as well as smart phone technology for reporting incidents, creating confidence that offenders will be held accountable. Social media in a range of languages can provide real-time information to assure women that their needs and experiences are central to the service and assistance is at hand.

- **Public Transport needs for Women of Different Ages:** Societal factors leading to feelings of fear in public transport spaces vary across age. Research has shown that negative experiences of public space are overwhelmingly encountered by young women and girls because of sexual harassment (Aruldoss et al. 2019; Plan International 2018; Santoro et al. 2020: 218). The everyday occurrence of harassment reinforces a fear of traversing public spaces and influences mobility and access, so that girls and women with different needs are marginalized.

Older women face significant barriers with public transport and may be prevented from accessing basic social services or recreational activities. While the cost of public transport may limit older women's access to health care and contribute to isolation, this affects older women disproportionately, as they tend to outlive their male partners (if heterosexual and partnered) but are also disproportionately poorer in older age. Older women are more fearful of being victims in public space and are at risk of age-related abuse, which impacts their safety and mobility. There may also be cultural reasons that prevent them from moving through cities on their own. The access around public transport may be inappropriate for their mobility needs and they are subject to trip hazards and falls on moving carriages. Getting on and off public transport may be difficult and stressful when services do not accommodate women's needs.

- **Public Transport, Sexuality and Gender Identity:** Public transport is a key site for harassment of gay, lesbian and bisexual women as well as people who identify as a sexual or gender minority. They experience a high rate of victimization and harassment in public transport spaces and may take risks, be vigilant, or avoid public transport altogether (Weintrob et al. 2021: 785). Many try to hide their sexual or gender identity when on public transport for personal safety reasons (Stack et al. 2021: 40). Entrapment is a common fear for women of minoritized sexuality or gender who are required to manage the unpredictable behavior of other people and may feel the need to be able to exit transport spaces easily. These concerns indicate that public transport design that includes multiple entrance and exit points is preferred.

- **Public Transport and Cultural Practices:** Cultural barriers encompass the norms, practices and expectations of a particular society about how women "should" behave. These might be religious (restrictions on women's access to the public realm) but are also social, where women and girls may only be able to travel with consent from their family or if accompanied by a male relative. Some women from low- and middle-income countries may be unable to leave the house at all (Woodcock et al. 2019: S13). If women's income levels allow, then they may have the option to choose different or preferred travel modes, including using taxis. For others, their vulnerability on public transport may be the motivation to buy a car or to use their car to provide "public transport" in their private car to escort other members of their family because the public transport is inadequate or dangerous (Greed 2019: 33–34). While regulated and safer public transport is vital for women, it will not impact those women who need permission from guardians to travel—safer spaces will not significantly change the cultural barriers to public transport (Harumain et al. 2021: 80–81).

Designing for Transport Spaces Typologies

It is vital to recognize that the decisions of those who design, build, manage and maintain public transport infrastructure have a major impact on women's economic, social and civic participation (Our Watch 2017: 43). Cities internationally fall drastically short of women's needs and expectations. Women's ambitions are reduced and opportunities to engage in public life thwarted by inadequate public transport provision (Transport for West Midlands 2022: 4). Qualitative research undertaken with, for and about women users of public transport spaces indicates a broad range of influential factors that contribute to their fear and vulnerability when using public transport spaces. By understanding these typologies and by following practical strategies, women's risk can be mitigated when moving through cities. Designers can enhance women and girls' experiences on public transport rather than compound the issues of unequal access and usage already faced by women (Matthewson et al. 2021: 55).

- **Underpasses, Tunnels, Bridges and Car Parks:** The spaces and structures which define transport spaces such as underpasses, tunnels, bridges, and associated car parks are consistently identified by

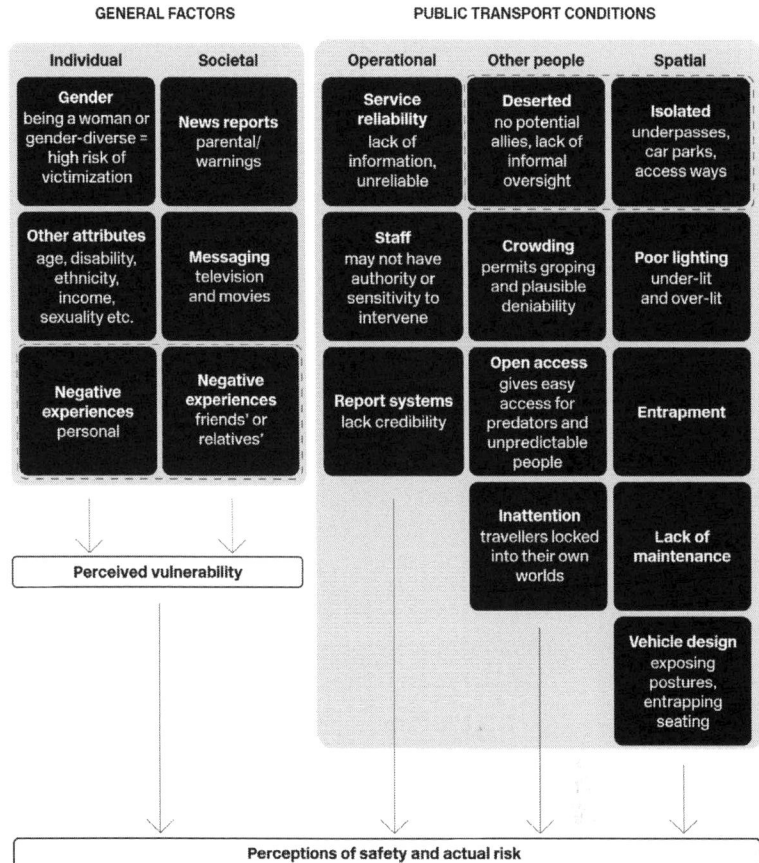

FIGURE 8.3 Factors affecting perceptions of safety on public transport. Adapted and expanded by Gill Matthewson, Monash University XYX Lab from Yavuz and Welch 2010.

women as places of fear and trepidation, particularly at night when they might be poorly lit (Loukaitou-Sideris 2009: 555; Matthewson et al. 2021: 59). While it is necessary to constrain movement of people to reduce danger in the technical and infrastructural system, so too is it to understand that, rather than negotiate feelings of entrapment in underpasses, women may prefer to take more precarious routes and navigate busy intersections where they are more visible, especially at night (Matthewson et al. 2021: 59).

In underground transport spaces, the inability to escape due to spatial limitations or unclear wayfinding shapes women's fear of crime in transport spaces (Kim 2019: 187). Kim suggests that ensuring access to Wi-Fi in public transport spaces—including in carriages and in spaces underground—can decrease women's "feelings of disconnection," as they are able to reach out to family and friends (Kim 2019: 187). "At grade" connections (that is, a junction or intersection where two or more transport/pedestrian axes cross at the same level) are more desirable than the use of underpasses, tunnels and bridges.

WOMEN'S STORIES

This spot is a train underpass with poor visibility in its design. You can't see if someone is walking into the underpass from the other side and you feel trapped. I don't walk through here anymore when I should be able to feel safe to do so.

The car park is dark and smells of urine. It is not safe.

- **Design, Amenity and Maintenance:** Transport infrastructure is vast and often lacks informal oversight—an important element for women's sense of safety. When transport spaces lack maintenance and where there is litter and graffiti, women associate these spaces with increased risk (Wekerle et al. 1995: 71; Yavuz et al. 2010: 303; Cozens et al. 2015: 2). Spaces that are run-down, empty, and desolate are also associated with increased fear (Currie et al. 2007: 303; Yavuz et al. 2010: 2).

Knowledge of the potential for male violence should inform the design of public transport. The design of vehicles and carriages can place women in sitting and standing positions where they are vulnerable—for example, high hand holds which can be exposing (and uncomfortable) and seating arrangements that are so configured that a woman can feel entrapped. Higher stair treads and minimal spaces for prams and strollers may mean that travel during peak times is not possible.

The design of stations, stops and their connection to related forms of transport infrastructure, such as car parks, bike racks and other micro-mobility devices, is often precarious (for example, dark pathways, entrapping bike storage, and underground or remote car parking facilities) and can negatively impact women's perceptions of safety. Wayfinding and signage can alleviate vulnerability by vicinity maps with walk times to destinations and the location of transit police and the use of real-time data displays about departures schedules. Communication campaigns can build awareness of digital systems for connective mobility (like, for example, MaaS—or "mobility as a service") and reporting processes for personal safety issues.

Availability of clean public toilets facilities for women is critical. At present, amenities are poorly located (adjacent to male facilities and in entrapping corridors) with little oversight. Often, they are locked due to maintenance or safety issues. Increasingly, public toilet facilities are "gender-neutral" (meaning the provision is for both men and women). This arrangement is entirely unsuitable for most women and their children, and for many cultures, sex-segregated toilets are required for accessibility and safety (Tyler 2021: 31).

- **Waiting for Transport:** Women's perceived insecurity when waiting for public transport after dark is significantly greater than men's (Brown 1998: 211). Service providers need to be accountable and timely. Services that operate on schedule and are reliable increase women's feelings of safety. If delays do occur, "prompt information about the cause of the delay and service recovery time should be given to users"; this can decrease the women's feelings of uncertainty and lack of control (Kim 2019: 187). As women undertake multiple short trips to complete their daily tasks during off-peak periods, when public transport service is less frequent, women's transport time is dominated by periods of waiting in unpredictable and often unsafe environments where there may be lack of security or presence of other people.

Reducing the sense of isolation while waiting can be achieved by ensuring that bus stops, taxi and ride-share pick up zones are not adjacent to vacant land or set too far back from the street and ensuring that bus stops are clearly visible from the street or have oversight from surrounding active buildings (Wekerle et al. 1995: 64–5).

WOMEN'S STORIES

This area generally feels unsafe, especially waiting by yourself for a bus or to meet friends. For a major transport hub, there are very few cafes, bars etc. open nearby that you could run to if something were to happen. Everything is shut. Have often seen people harassed, stared at or verbally abused.

When I wait for the tram at this tram stop, about 1 in 4 times I will get yelled at from a car, by a man. I'm not sure why it happens so much at this particular tram stop. It makes me feel vulnerable and exposed, and like I am on display for vulgar comments from men.

- **Overcrowding on Public Transport:** The frequent overcrowdedness of public transport services means that people are concentrated into small areas, providing multiple opportunities for perpetrators to grope and rub women with "plausible" deniability and the defense that the spatial context prevents physical distancing (Ceccato 2017: 279; Levin et al. 2019: 4). If women use public transport during the peak times, the problem of overcrowded carriages not only restricts the ability to sit or stand comfortably but may also prevent a quick exit in an unpredictable situation and additional multiple difficulties when traveling with children, if pregnant, or elderly.

DEEPER DIVE: SEX-SEGREGATED PUBLIC TRANSPORT

Women-only transit options have been promoted as a solution to improve the safety of women on public transport. Cities around the world have implemented variations of sex-segregated transport including on trains, buses, taxis and ride-sharing services, with the aim of increasing women's safety by minimizing the potential for assault by men. Women in low- to middle-income countries face problems that may result from gender segregation even if it is not legally prescribed (Harumain et al. 2021: 71). Some may only be able to travel with consent from their family and others may be required to be accompanied by a male relative. Implementation of segregation has, to date, been in countries with low rates of gender equality and where women face high levels of discrimination and sexual harassment, including Belarus, Brazil, Egypt, India, Indonesia, Israel, Japan, Mexico, Philippines and the United Arab Emirates.

Women-only train carriages were first introduced in Tokyo in 2000 to combat the high incidences of groping that occurred on trains, commonly known as *chikan*. Transportation companies offer single-sex carriages in various Japanese cities on selected services at various times; they are indicated on train doors and platforms and usually in force during rush hour and weekdays. Female-only carriages also allow primary school-aged boys and people with a disability and their carers. A 2018 survey of women in Tokyo found that almost 70 percent approve of female-only train carriages because they felt they could travel without fear of sexual harassment or violence (*Japanese Times* 2018: n.p.). The rule is not enforced by law and men are not punished for entering; however, there has been persistent opposition from men, protesting that male exclusion is discriminatory.

In 2016, a private German railway company, Mitteldeutsche Regiobahn (MRB), introduced train compartments exclusively reserved for women, children and the elderly on the line between Leipzig and Chemnitz. The carriages are monitored by railway staff. It was speculated that this was instigated in response to the violent sex attacks that occurred prior to this in nearby Cologne; however, the railway company denied a link. Although the decision for a western European railway to adopt such a measure was highly controversial, and seen as regressive by many commentators, German Twitter users began sharing their experiences of harassment on trains with the hashtag #*imzugpassiert* ("happened on the train") to show their support. Deutsche Bahn, a government-owned rail company, also offers a women-only compartment for its overnight sleeping cars for solo women travelers.

The Dubai Metro, in operation since 2009, is the major rail network of the UAE, and together with the Dubai Tram, operates a three-class system: first class, economy, and dedicated carriages for women and children. Men are fined 100 AED ($US27) for entering the women's carriage. The front seats of buses are also reserved for women and there are taxi services for women with female drivers. Carriages and taxis are colored pink, and signage is displayed to indicate that they are for women only. Sex-segregation on public transport may reflect broader religious and cultural values rather than explicit initiatives to target sexual harassment.

There is limited evidence of the effectiveness of sex-segregation across cultures, and contexts and opinions remain divided. Some support single-sex space as a practical and easy-to-implement way to improve safety for women in transit. However, this approach has been criticized as a "knee-jerk" reaction that is short sighted and paternalistic. Critics argue that sex-segregation returns to outdated modes of victim blaming and reinforces harmful gender stereotypes that ask women to modify their behavior. Problematically, women-only transport is a band-aid solution that does not tackle the more difficult and systemic issues that cause sexual harassment and gender-based violence in the first place (Dunckel-Graglia 2013: 274). There have also been questions about how sex-segregated space serves the transgender and gender-diverse community.

- **Communication Campaigns:** Communication campaigns can be used to convey the expectation for behavior while in public transport spaces. This may include posters, print and online media, digital and social media. Through the use of gender-sensitive messages—and best undertaken in collaboration often with women and girls—targeted communication campaigns can shape behavior on public transport and "play a major role in activating and shifting community attitudes and behaviours to social issues" (TramLab 2020a: 13).

WOMEN'S STORIES

On public transport, I have experienced a lot of sexual harassment, I feel very unsafe when getting off a train in places where there are very few other people around at night. Especially when traveling to get home. I think some ideas to improve feeling safe on public transport are helplines to report sexual harassment and having advertisements on trains to say that sexually harassing behavior is unacceptable.

- **Active Surveillance:** All surveillance should be designed in a way to accommodate the spatial dynamics of public transport environments that are changeable, due to the number of people and time of day (Kim 2019: 186). As a result of the dramatic fluctuations, there are significant stretches of time when spaces lack basic passive surveillance, making the visibility of recognizable and active staff important for women's perception of safety (Kim 2019: 186). The presence of designated public transport authority figures to provide formal surveillance can help to: deter offenders from committing sexual harassment; reduce women's fear of assault; provide swift help for passengers in need; give women somebody obvious to report incidents to; identify and arrest perpetrators (Gekoski et al. 2015: 24).

Research undertaken for the TramLab project (2020c: 15) found that the presence of designated public transport authority figures improves perceptions of safety. Evidence also suggested that authority figures need gender-sensitive training to deliver appropriate responses to women's concerns and to mitigate their potential abuse. For some women, interactions with designated public transport authority figures result in misconduct (like racism) and predatory behavior, where the authority figures misuse the women's personal details (State of Victoria 2016: 17). This may be the result of a lack of diversity in the authority and may result in an increase of sexism, racism and homophobia.

- **Transport after Dark:** The night-time economy has seen many cities emphasize the need for safe and accessible night-time public transport services. Smeds et al. state that this focus lacks an adequate understanding of "how different people move and experience the city at night," where the research and policy has focused on daytime mobility while under-acknowledging equity issues after dark (2020: 1). Not traveling at night or avoiding certain areas of the city has limited women's access and enjoyment of public life (Yavuz et al. 2010: 2491), especially in travel, where women must occupy a restricted space like a carriage. Similarly, many women may be undertaking shift work or be part of the invisible after hours "care economy" dominated by women in areas such as retail, health, cleaning and hospitality, and will require night-time public transport services to meet their specific 24-hour needs.

WOMEN'S STORIES

Constant state of fear at night particularly, no choice to catch public transport to and from work.

Darkness and poor lighting contribute to women's fear of crime (Yavuz 2010: 2494), and so increased lighting is a standard (yet misdirected) response to places that are identified as unsafe (Yang et al. 2022; Kalms 2019). While enhanced lighting in transit environments can increase women's feelings of safety, brighter lighting may not be the answer. Some previous research has shown that women can feel highly exposed under floodlit conditions (Loukaitou-Sideris 2014: 243; Ceccato 2020b: 45; Wekerle et al. 1995: 64) and "poor lighting appears regularly in audits of unsafe spaces more generally" (Matthewson et al. 2021: 59).

> **TIP**
>
> For more information about lighting and CCTV in cities, see **Chapter 10—On the edge of the night: Women and the night-time economy.**

- **CCTV in Public Transport Spaces:** Service providers may view CCTV as a mode to create feelings of safety for women and may believe that it reduces the risk of being a victim of crime (Hale 1996: 79; Brown 1998: 207). Yet, CCTV installed throughout public transport spaces primarily protects assets and covers other legal requirements for technical safety. Many women have different perceptions of CCTV, meaning that it does not address their fear of being the victim of crime or sexual assault (Loukaitou-Sideris et al. 2009: 559; Overington 2017; Brown 1998: 218). To be impactful, CCTV needs to be live-monitored, with women confident that service providers are nearby and able to respond to distress. CCTV, therefore, can only be an effective tool for women in cities when "the distance between users and people in authority" is designed with attention to them being "close in proximity" and having "transparency from the user's point of view" (Kim 2019: 186). This, unfortunately, is rarely the case or even possible, because of the financial burden of what live monitoring would entail.

  Other safety measures may include safety zones with alarm buttons to connect verbally with transit police and give advice to women about "staying safe." However, this mode makes personal safety women and girls' responsibility and—if or when something goes wrong—women are to blame for "not being careful" enough and engaging in "risky behavior."

- **The Last Kilometer Home:** The last kilometer home can be a stressful part of women's public transport journey. It refers to the distance traveled between the end of the public transport service (for example, alighting from the bus or exiting the train station) and the remaining journey home. These transitional and "connective" environments need to be safe and comfortable, with well-designed lighting and traffic-calming measures. Priority should be given to walking and other forms of micro-mobility over the use of motor vehicles. Cycle paths should be networked with separate pedestrian pathways in busy areas. If paths are combined for pedestrian and other modes of active transport combined, these should be signed for slow speeds at critical junctures. Lighting for footpaths and cycling paths is critical, and wayfinding with active street frontages that encourage passive surveillance will positively impact perceptions of safety. When it is not possible to ensure that the last kilometer home is adequate for women's and girls' needs, then alternative modes should be explored, such as community "demand-stops," where buses drop women at their home in high-risk areas, low density suburbs or in after-dark hours (Wekerle et al. 1995: 67).

Access All Areas

Without equitable access and safe public transport, cities and city spaces will continue to materialize a form of gender bias that impacts women's whole-life access to services, education, work, health care and recreation. Given the plethora of research excellence in the field over the last forty years, the lack of acknowledgment and lack of uptake of recommendations indicates that gender inequity is overlooked and undervalued within the transport industry and transport policy (Loukaitou-Sideris et al. 2009: 558; Transport for West Midlands 2022: 5). Transformation will require the development and determination of strong central leadership and governments committed to the prioritization of women-focused strategies to address the safety of women in public transport spaces.

With the fragmentation of networks and the divestment of responsibilities to service providers, ensuring access and safety issues for women on public transport is a complex social problem. Even in Sweden—one of the more advanced countries in terms of gender equality—analysis found that key policies failed to address gender differences in transport beyond somewhat generic statements with gender issues trivialized (Smidfelt Rosqvist 2019). To claim that the socio-political context is "challenging" is an understatement.

Understanding and implementing the different methods for analysis, synthesis and intervention, with a sharp focus on the benefits of designing safer public transport for women, should be clear in the context of increased urbanization and the need for high performing infrastructure, services and social services (Shaw et al. 2013: 8). If safety matters continue to focus on technical and infrastructural issues, women's safety needs will continue to be marginalized from mainstream policy and planning (Levy 2019: 44), with public transport another contributing factor to the spatial inequities of cities.

Safety—from women's perspectives—must be at the forefront of transport policy, planning and design. As women are unlikely to have participated in the design of a city's transport infrastructure or the public spaces that adjoin them (Transport for West Midlands 2022: 5), ensuring women can contribute to policy, planning and design will illuminate problems from their own divergent perspectives. Community consultation can contribute to shifting perspectives, but too often it is co-opted as a token exercise in transport planning and viewed as a necessary hurdle for ticking a box, and without any significant impact on policy, planning or design. Inviting women to work alongside transport planners and designers as experts in their experience—collaborating to define challenges and propose innovative solutions—is imperative for more equitable transport.

> **TIP**
>
> See also **Chapter 7—*Expanding expertise: Women's safety audits*** and **Chapter 11—*Run the world: Co-design in a feminist framework***.

- **Data Bias and Public Transport:** The current modes for collecting mobility data are inadequate in most transport systems internationally. Some transport data may be collected from the heads of households—who are usually male—who have different transport patterns to women and miss the opportunity to capture women's experiences. For women's equitable access to public transport, comparable, high-quality data is essential. Sex- and gender-disaggregated data allow for evaluating and monitoring the effectiveness of gender mainstreaming strategies and prioritizing areas of concern for women and girls. This is essential for understanding the prevalence of violence against women in public transport spaces, for raising awareness and assessing the cost

(TramLab 2020b: 13). Data from mobility diaries or geolocative data can be aggregated with a range of data sets for site-specific information. Data can be gathered from women's interactions with real-time transport information, integrated mobility services and crime reporting statistics.

> **TIP**
>
> For more information about sex- and gender-disaggregation and ways to collect and synthesize qualitative and quantitative data sets, see **Chapter 4—*Missing women: Smart women in the data gap.***

- **Sustainable Mobility and Women:** The relationship between women's public transport ridership and sustainable mobility is shaped by women's experiences of personal safety. Safety is a paramount consideration in the move for women's mobility requirements and has larger implications beyond equitable transport spaces. Women's safety on public transport will progress the sustainability agendas for transport and mobility more adequately as women's travel patterns need less adjustment in order to meet the sustainability goals (Institutionen för globala studier et al. 2016: 709). And yet, the gender-neutral approaches to transport planning reinforce that women's patterns should match those of men. A more accurate position would be the reverse (Sánchez de Madariaga 2013: 79, 83).

One of the benefits of widening the often-utilitarian approach to public transport policy planning and design to include the needs of women and girls is that it will bring broader improvements to cities (Matthewson et al. 2021). Recent research looking at the combined impact of sustainability and mobility seeks to increase the efficient movement of people and reduce car-centric planning and carbon-intensive modes of planning (Harumain et al. 2021: 71; Transport for London 2021: 7–8). In 2021, 28 percent of the US greenhouse gas emissions came from transport (EPA 2021), with road transport accounting for three-quarters of transport emissions and most coming from cars and buses (Ritchie 2020). Urban planner Caren Levy argues that the technical and sustainability challenges of transport mean that we need to equally consider the social positions and multiple identities of transport users (Levy 2019: 45). This means prioritizing the involvement of women in the decision-making processes and examining women's transport use as a mode to meet the sustainability goals. Research suggests that if men engaged in similar transport behavior as women the reduction in CO_2 omission would be significant (Institutionen för globala studier et al. 2016: 710).

Operational Transformation in Transport Policy, Planning and Design

Women's participation in transport is low, especially in the operationalization and technical aspects. It is a sector that is dominated by men and relies on "masculine norms and its activities coded as masculine" (Institutionen för globala studier 2016: 704). As an industry that continues to struggle to attract women professionals, investment needs to be made to generate women's professional representation at all levels of the public transport decision-making process (Levin et al. 2019: 104). Research suggests that increased representation from women in the public transport sector decision-making processes will assist in addressing the lack of equity in public transport systems (Zibell 2013: 83). This long-term change is likely to be slow, but gender balance at the operational end of public transport will influence service provision and engagement with women's experiences.

The application of gender mainstreaming strategies (see **Chapter 5**) will require policymakers, planners and designers to take the different needs of women users of public transport seriously and, if applied correctly, will ensure that the technical needs and gender-neutral mindset will not dominate decision making in the sector. This requires stakeholders to review policies with a gender-sensitive approach and commit to gender mainstreaming for all transport planning (Smidfelt Rosqvist 2019; Levin et al. 2019). Gender mainstreaming remains the policy with the most capacity to bring women into the democratic process of mobility decision making, to initiate gender analysis in the public transport sector, and to evaluate the impacts of gender parity in transport planning.

CHAPTER NINE

Eyes on the Street

Women and Urban Crime Prevention

Principles
- Ensure that all levels of governance understand their role in implementing crime prevention strategies and frameworks
- Assist police to share knowledge about hot spot areas and criminal activity
- Provide oversight and recommendations about the implementation of crime prevention in the built environment that includes the perspectives of women

Practice
- Planners, urban designers, architects and landscape architects to undertake women-centered and intersectional professional development for designing for crime prevention
- Ensure practitioners contribute expertise in crime prevention to new development, redevelopment and retrofit projects

Participation
- Encourage communities to gather insights from minoritized people including the needs and perspectives across age, disability, ethnicity, geographic location, income, indigeneity, migratory status, race, religion and sexuality

- Encourage community precincts and business owners to play an active role in the design of interfaces between public and private spaces
- Gather detailed data about hotspots and areas of concern in communities, including the effectiveness (or not) of current crime prevention measures

Women and Urban Crime Prevention

Cities internationally measure safety and livability and recognize the relationship between the built environment, crime and behavior. Policymakers, planners and designers also acknowledge the social and economic impact of crime, and most agree that "the proper design and effective use of the built environment can lead to a reduction in the fear and incidence of crime, and an improvement in the quality of life" (Crowe 2000: 46). The fear of crime may keep residents from venturing into public spaces and cause them to reduce their physical activities, with negative impacts on physical and mental health (Lorenc et al. 2012: 760; XYX Lab et al. 2021). Many local communities, developers and designers view crime prevention approaches as a preventative measure that benefits all members of the community. As such, they enlist a range of interdisciplinary methods from criminology, psychology, public health and urban geography in a series of frameworks broadly known as "situational crime prevention." The foundation of the approach involves predicting the behavior of offenders to mitigate victimization and crime against both property and people. Situated crime prevention increases the effort, increases the risks, and reduces the rewards, provocations, and excuses for offending (Chiu et al. 2021: 1057). It follows the increasing pressure for designers to use crime prevention principles (Ekblom et al. 2013; Cozens 2016) in communities where violence, offense and fear is often the outcome of inequity and inequality.

Women's fear of crime

Lorenc et al. (2012: 758) suggest that the fear of crime has two aspects: the "perceived likelihood of victimization" and the "emotional response to the possibility of crime."

Certainly, integrating common-sense crime prevention and safety at the beginning of a project can have long-term social and financial benefit for communities and can prevent the need to retrofit public spaces that have been poorly designed at the outset, but evidence of the positive impact—especially in the context of diverse communities—is not clear cut.

Crime Prevention Through Environmental Design (commonly referred to as CPTED)[1] is a part of broader crime prevention strategies and focuses specifically on the manipulation of the built environment and surrounding landscape. The various approaches to designing for crime prevention developed from the community-based and activist approaches during the 1960s and 1970s, when urban designers, architects and planners were encouraged to design passive forms of surveillance. The well-known phrase "eyes on the street," as described by urban commentator Jane Jacobs (1961), aimed to employ opportunities for community observation to reduce the propensity for crime in public space and to minimize feelings of risk in communities. The linking of crime with specific design features was quickly established (Jeffery 1971; Newman 1972) and since that time, designing for crime prevention has been popularized (even mandated) in urban design and underpins the need to protect property, the public realm and citizens themselves (Atlas 2008; Cozens 2016; Johnson et al. 2014).

> **Primary crime prevention**
>
> Primary crime prevention looks to address and change both the social factors (poverty and inequality) and situational factors (built environment and design more broadly). For a discussion on primary prevention as it pertains to urban planning and violence against women, see **Chapter 1–*Women in cities***.

The application of CPTED has slight variations. In the 1990s, the global implementation, commercialization and certification of CPTED as a professional credential saw a rapid growth and expansion, with critique of the new "territories of control" which were designed in response to increased urbanization, population and density. The CPTED principles are prolific and are now deployed in 286 countries throughout Europe, North America, South America, Australia, New Zealand, South Africa and Asia, with a broad counter-crime effect (Morgan et al. 2012). Concepts such as territoriality, natural surveillance, image management and maintenance, access control, activity support, target hardening and geographical juxtaposition have come to dominate and dictate design approaches (Camacho Duarte et al. 2011: 157) in all kinds of spaces in cities and towns. Mixed-use and commercial districts, transportation nodes, schools, hospitals, city centers and recreation spaces have taken up CPTED recommendations with a "plethora of policy guidance and standards" now operationalizing crime prevention tactics in cities internationally (Atlas 2013; Ekblom et al. 2013; Cozens 2016). For crime prevention trainer and researcher Randall Atlas (2013), CPTED is a set of concepts which includes technology security. Recent updates to the framework incorporate social factors related to community connection, cohesion and culture (Cozens 2016: 84).

Situated Crime Prevention (SCP) and Crime Prevention Through Environmental Design (CPTED)

Various measures, strategies and interventions to prevent crime and fear of crime are typically implemented by governing bodies and civil society organizations. Situated (or situational) crime prevention (SCP) is a proactive strategy and refers to efforts undertaken to prevent, deter and reduce specific forms of crime through management of the surrounding environment. The aim is to make the perpetration of crime more challenging, precarious, less worthwhile and defensible (Clarke 1997: 4) and is focused on "changing people's offending behaviour not by influencing the predispositions that they bring to crime situations but by changing those situations themselves" (Armitage et al. 2019: 1).

Urban design is an important part of a crime prevention strategy that influences the built environment and shapes how the community interacts with it. Crime Prevention Through Environmental Design (commonly referred to as CPTED, pronounced "sep-ted") is also described as "Defensive Space" (Newman 1972), "Hostile

> Architecture" and "Designing out Crime" and is used in the context of urban planning, architecture and design for public spaces. It is a series of frameworks that integrate the concepts and practices of design and criminology (Camacho Duarte 2011: 155) to create places where communities feel safer, encouraging ownership and resulting in less crime.

Limitations of CPTED for Women and Girls

While there is evidence to suggest the benefit of CPTED is the reduction of property crime such as theft and vandalism it is difficult to demonstrate the efficacy of designing for crime prevention methods and frameworks in terms of how they serve women and other minoritized groups. Armitage et al. suggest that CPTED now has such currency in policy, planning and design that it can stand in for crime prevention more broadly (2019). Armitage furthers this critique and describes the ways CPTED is applied across cultures as a "devoted" but uncritical method (2008: 280).

Reviewing the status of CPTED, environmental criminologist Paul Cozens and CPTED specialist Terence Love (2015) describe that for policymakers and designers, the complex associations between crime and design mean that there are no simple answers and that the generic approaches to crime prevention through a checklist-style approach like CPTED cannot address the complexity of crime and perceptions of safety. This "top-down" and "one-size-fits-all" approach to community safety in public places (Wekerle et al. 1995: Cozens 2016) has limitations; the key flaw is the prescriptive crime prevention approach (Camacho Duarte 2011: 155). This means that, while there may be some positive impact for some members of communities, there is little acknowledgment of the ways that women experience both public space and the fear of crime differently (Walklate 2018: 285).

> **WOMEN'S STORIES**
>
> *This is a pretty dangerous area. It is fairly secluded, in close proximity to a large live music venue, as well as being on the route toward the train station from the night club strip. There are also rehabilitation centres for offenders, and the remand center for criminals, which adds to the overall unsavoury mix of people. I, and many friends unfortunate enough to work in this area have been abused physically and verbally, stalked at night, had vehicles damaged, and have been robbed.*

Urban planning researchers Gerda Wekerle and Carolyn Whitzman (1995) proposed that safe urban environments need to understand the divergent needs of women. Noting women's exclusion from the process, they called for greater community involvement in the planning process, arguing that those who will likely benefit from urban design should be a part of the solution. Importantly, Wekerle and Whitzman describe the victimization, fear, and their effects on women in urban space, noting the potential for crime prevention to turn its attention to the safety of vulnerable groups. Writing about research with rural women, DeKeseredy et al., for example, calls for a version of crime prevention that recognizes that communities are "contested places" with "differing strands of values, norms, beliefs and tolerance" (2009: 178). They go on to suggest that future revisions to CPTED might address "feminist concerns" and be more effective at increasing "women's security" (ibid.).

This advocates for the incorporation of women's perspectives in crime prevention frameworks. If the only measure is the number of incidents of victimization, then the issue misses where women's experiences of cities and communities are shaped by their perceptions of risk, previous experiences of vulnerability or harm, and the unpredictable behaviors of other people. The lack of engagement with women is evident in the frameworks that resist incorporating gender-sensitive approaches that would surely contribute to increasing safety for women (and more so for women who may be further minoritized because of their age, disability, ethnicity, geographic location, income, indigeneity, migratory status, race, religion and sexuality).

> **DEEPER DIVE**
>
> For an in-depth review of traditional CPTED approaches, see Paul Cozens, *Think Crime! Using Evidence, Theory and Crime Prevention Through Environmental Design (CPTED) for Planning Safer Cities*, 2016.

The CPTED model of crime prevention has directed approaches to design for community safety. The early conception of CPTED includes common sense and practical tactics such as "territoriality," "surveillance," "access control," "target hardening," "activity support," and "image management," and aims to increase the effort of committing an offense through controlling the built environment, or to increase the risk of committing an offense because of third-party oversight (Cornish et al. 2003).

The simplification of the CPTED principles into "terms" misses the complexity and richness provided by an intersectional understanding of the "perceived problems" or "conflict resolution" for nurturing social interactions (Saville et al. 1997) which—as a result—remain absent even in the developed version of CPTED. Armitage et al. suggest that this is a foundational problem with CPTED, where the terminology implies a false simplicity that "serves to confuse" and "deny practitioners tools for thinking, communication, knowledge management and collaboration that are subtle enough to handle the messy complexity of everyday crime prevention" (Armitage et al. 2019: 2).

The later variations to CPTED critique how urban design, architecture and planning generate, attract, precipitate, discourage or facilitate crime, using expanded concepts that look at how best to create social cohesion within neighborhoods. There is minor attention given to concepts of "inclusion" and "identity," indicating that the earlier terminology-driven frameworks missed generating practical ideas for enhancing neighborhoods and therefore delimiting crime. And while the later additions try to update CPTED and the development of expanded concepts aimed to create social cohesion within neighborhoods, there is a shortfall when it comes to women and other minoritized groups. If the aim is to ensure community members actively participate in decision-making processes for managing or modifying their community (Brassard 2003), the enactment of women's inclusion, their equal access to amenities and services is invisible. And this is despite research in aligned fields for many years to establish an evidence base for women's inclusion by understanding their experiences in the built environment.

The lack of accountability for how issues pertaining to gender, race or class may be impacted in CPTED is supported by the research of environmental criminologist Paul Cozens and CPTED specialist Terence Love, who argue that the connections between crime and design are far more complex than many of the policymakers and designers care to admit (2015: 406). When not explicitly reviewing the papers about gender, their comprehensive analysis of over 180 peer reviewed articles from 1961 to 2015 reveals that there has been a disregard for women within CPTED scholarship. Just one of the reviewed articles addresses gender, one includes disability, and none directly address age, ethnicity, race, or sexuality. This reveals how the universal or "neutral" design approaches discount certain groups of people, and more specifically those who are "intersectionally disadvantaged or multiply burdened" (Costanza-Chock 2020: 19).

It is accurate, therefore, to state that the diverse perspectives of women have been excluded from CPTED. This is affirmed in the professional development and pedagogy within the disciplines of planning, urban design and architecture which—more or less—have historically relied on a disciplinary canon dominantly created by European and American male designers that sets the foundation for what is deemed "good" or "bad" and ignores alternative ways of knowing (Khandwala 2019: para 4). This impacts on designing safer cities in two significant ways: First, situated crime prevention actively contributes to inequality through techniques which make women (and likely, to a greater extent, women of color, First Nations women, homeless women, and other women marginalized because of, for example, socio-economic status or religion) feel unwelcome. Second, because of the perceived criminality of certain marginalized groups, situated crime prevention strategies may result in keeping certain groups out of designated areas. This has a flow-on effect where "undesirable" people and activities may be pushed into other communities with the associated risk and vulnerability for women and girls.

And so, while there may be some evidence that CPTED is beneficial for tackling some forms of crime (particularly in terms of protecting the physical assets in urban spaces) the frameworks do not address the ways that women experience and participate in public space markedly differently to men. Like other areas of design research, CPTED problematically invites universal and generic design approaches to urban issues (Ekblom 2011: 9–20; Cozens at al. 2015: 406), where, for example, strategies aimed to make middle-class able-bodied white men feel safe are assumed to also work for all women, children and/or people with disabilities. Added to the issue is the fact that many design professionals optimistically assume that CPTED frameworks account for the safety needs of women and girls. They apply them as a mode to address "inclusive" principles and incorrectly believe that this will support personal safety for minoritized people. CPTED approaches fall seriously short when designing for the safety needs of diverse groups of women and girls who are often living in equally diverse communities where urban planning and design practices lack intersectional awareness (McRobbie 2009: 2).

> **TIP**
>
> For more information on how to center women and girls in urban planning and design process, see **Chapter 11—Run the world: Co-design in a feminist framework**.

Some of the many concerning effects occur through the division and control endorsed by situated crime prevention approaches, resulting in the "othering" of some groups, behaviors, characteristics, and communities (Kawash 1998: 320–37). Many crime prevention strategies risk unjustly punishing marginalized individuals and often require them to simultaneously manage both being "at risk" as well as being viewed as "a risk" (Smith et al. 2005: 11–13; Hughes 2011: 404–5). Thus, already marginalized and vulnerable women and girls are further disadvantaged by the universalized approaches and methods which fail to look at both the specificity of local communities and also the individual user needs and perspectives.

For example, Angeles et al. (2020) drawing on Petra Doan's critique of heteronormative privileges in urban planning (2007; 2011) to call for community-based and participatory approaches to "policing and public safety." In an analysis of Toronto's intersecting social identities, Angeles et al. (2020: 10) examine policing and public safety, noting that gender results in "complex affects and embodiments, which constructively problematize CPTED and feminist discourse around planning safer spaces." In this case study, the meaning of "unsafe" in the context of CPTED is critiqued and, unsurprisingly, the complexity of the meaning is not captured in the CPTED framework (Angeles et al. 2020: 10–11). Angeles et al. argue that there is a conflation of "sex, gender and sexual orientation" that is collapsed into a single category that ignores "differential experiences and layering of these identities" (ibid. 10).

WOMEN'S STORIES

As a Muslim, I've been told not to visit this area because it is hostile toward people of my faith.

The gaps in CPTED need to fully incorporate the diverse perspectives of women users so that professionals resist imagining a default user that is raced, classed and gendered to reproduce a dominant stereotype, otherwise, the issues of situated crime prevention risk being exacerbated by the design profession and "disproportionately allocated to people who occupy highly privileged locations" (Costanza-Chock 2020: 73). Planning and design practice must analyse interventions through the perspectives of oppressed populations and "with multiple markers of alterity to increase its understanding and recognition" (Irazábal et al. 2016: 725). Without redress, the current approaches to personal safety will continue to police minority groups to ensure their invisibility.

A Feminist "Revision" to Crime Prevention

Research exploring the effectiveness of situated crime prevention emerges with mixed results (Reynald et al. 2009) and stressing the need for public participation in progressing safer urban places (Ceccato et al. 2020: 19). Some have posited that the core reason for such inconsistencies across studies is the ambiguity of what situated crime prevention is at a theoretical and conceptual level (Reynald et al. 2009)

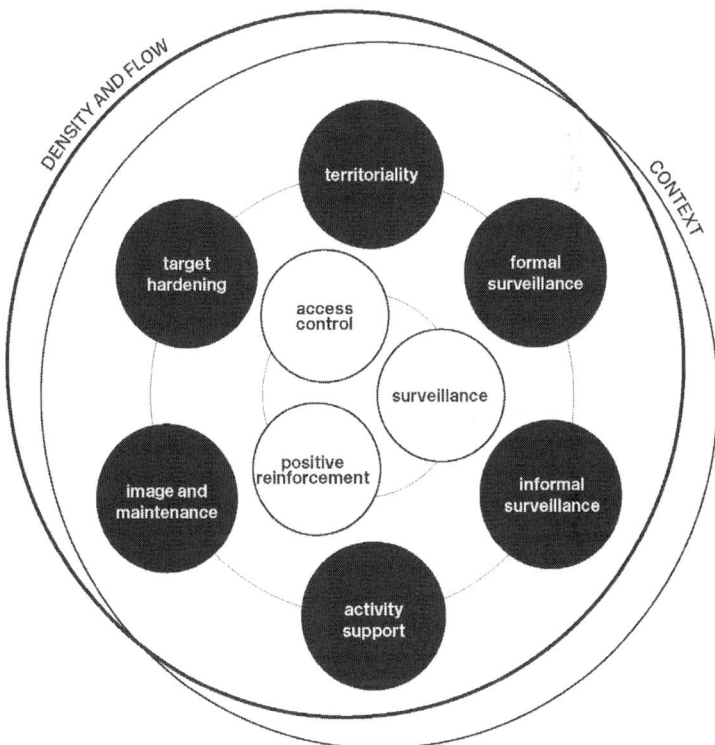

FIGURE 9.1 The principles of crime prevention through environmental design are often viewed as "best-practice" by local government and city stakeholders who implement a series of measures, aimed at assisting designers to meet metrics for safety. This mode fails to seek insights from the diverse communities these practices should ostensibly benefit. The absence of community contribution leads to "neutral" guidelines often uninformed by the influencing factors of race, indigeneity, class, ability, age, sexuality and gender. Diagram Isabella Webb, Monash University XYX Lab 2022.

and furthermore, how these concepts and theories manifest in public space. Studies of CPTED in the context of women's urban experiences of male violence are scarce and when undertaken, are focused on "opportunity rather than propensity" (Chiu et al. 2021: 1056). Planners and designers can show commitment to safe cities for women and girls by deploying strategies that prioritize their feelings of urban fear, risk and insecurity. Rethinking some of the CPTED frameworks can disrupt the continued disregard of women in urban space design. When a women-centered perspective is brought to CPTED, women will be afforded greater access to public spaces and less risk of violence.

Surveillance (Informal and Formal)

Surveillance is a form of guardianship of public spaces that may reduce crime due to offenders' perceptions of being watched—thus increasing the perceived potential for intervention, apprehension and prosecution. Centered around visibility, sightlines and human mobility, surveillance is highly influenced by Jane Jacobs' (1961) position that the safest urban place is where there is continuous observation, and that crime is less likely to occur when natural surveillance is strengthened (Newman 1972).

- **Examples of Informal/Natural/Passive Surveillance:** Informal surveillance includes the configuration of large windows and highly active rooms and street frontages for oversight. Building entries should be visible from the street and demarcated with lighting and signage. Avoid deep recesses on elevations which can be entrapping. Transparency and visibility of shops and business to the street is ideal. Orientation and well-scaled landscaping allow for surveillance of public gatherings. Avoid garages, car parking and/or long blank building elevations at the street frontage.

WOMEN'S STORIES

Walking through here at night the lighting is extremely poor, there is no one around and no signage. The overhanging branches of the trees felt like anyone could easily hide.

- **Examples of Formal/Mechanical/Active Surveillance:** More recently, CCTV monitoring, formal surveillance from police and private security has expanded to include smart city technology. In terms of public space, the evidence suggests that the effectiveness of CCTV "depended very much on the context and the type of crime addressed" and while CCTV can reduce property crime in car parks, it does not appear effective in terms of addressing violence and assault (Bowers et al. 2016: 119).

- **A Feminist "Revision" for Formal and Informal Surveillance:** Surveillance measures may be a mode to target women of color and other marginalized communities by restricting their movement which becomes "authorized" by the built environment through over-policing and criminalization. Researchers Sadowski et al. suggest that this "perceived neutrality of smart city technology uses stories about progress, modernity and innovation to entrench and disguise existing urban injustices" (2020). This may indicate that informal surveillance is more suited to women where presence of other people (particularly other women and women from diverse backgrounds) makes women and girls feel safer.

  Clear sight lines and effective lighting that is not overly bright will maximize observation of public spaces. Ensuring the edges of developments are activated, with business frontages installing double glazing rather than visual screening for noise, will maintain passive surveillance on the street. Public transport bus stops and taxis should be in visible positions and circulation should eliminate entrapping spaces. If pedestrians are moving underground and without adequate passive surveillance, then consider surveillance cameras or active security guards. Car park circulation on the edges of developments can be built in transparent materials with lighting that is well-positioned and bright enough to see into parked cars.

Positive Reinforcement (Activity and Maintenance)

Drawing on the "broken window" theory, the positive reinforcement concept supports "territoriality" and helps define the ownership of spaces (Wilson et al. 1982). When urban environments are not maintained, subject to vandalism, graffiti and/or rubbish, then they may become a hotspot for criminal activities.

- **Examples of Activity Support:** Creating positive behavioral cues for users and increasing activation of public space. Through formal and informal design as well as the use of communication and media, appropriate behavior and safer spaces can be encouraged and endorsed (Cozens et al. 2005: 337). The concept is that active and well-used streets can deter crime.

- **Examples of Image and Maintenance:** The aim should be to promote a positive image and maintenance of the built environment in order to encourage the occupation of public spaces. Regular cleaning and maintenance of public spaces; quick repair of public assets; rapid rectification of vandalism and graffiti; regular removal of rubbish and evidence of drug and alcohol use; maintenance of landscaping and natural environments; use of graffiti-resistant materials are all vital.

- **A Feminist "Revision" for Positive Reinforcement Activity Support and Image Maintenance:** Wayfinding in diverse language groups with strong contrasting colors to support public interaction; pop-up vendors supported to operate at risky times of day/night; making activities mutually visible and complementary; organizing public programs around public transport facilities and recreational spaces. Include maps with key locations and transport hubs on signage. Note distance and walking time between significant buildings, spaces with directions. Locate signage, wayfinding and footpath decals at key nodes, at regular distances and at transport hubs.

Access Control (Hardening and Territoriality)

Access control differentiates public and private spaces to encourage access and use by authorized users and discourage unauthorized people from gaining access. This reduces opportunities for crimes like theft (Sidebottom et al. 2015: 26) by creating an increased perception of risk in offenders. Access can be formal and may use real barriers (for example, lockable gates to control entry to crime hotspots) or informal by using symbolic barriers to create defined boundaries and semi-private community spaces (Lee et al. 2016: 3–4).

- **Examples of Target Hardening:** The use of barriers as a method to "increase the effort associated with committing an offence" (Bowers et al. 2016: 112) can be designed via controlled zoning through signage, fences and pavement color/material/treatment. Other modes include restricting vehicular access and greater definition between public and private spaces.

- **Examples of Territoriality:** A design strategy to create or extend influence over a property or space aims to delineate spaces, whether they are public, semi-public, or private, with the aim to signal ownership, usage and accepted behavior in spaces. Access and entry points to buildings and public places should be designed to ensure visibility for people both entering and exiting. Car parking entry and egress should be well-signed with showing the time it takes to walk to venues with wayfinding instructions.

    Signage, surface texture, entry statements, barriers (landscaping, walls, fences), gardens to create clear boundaries between spaces and provide privacy or to define the use of spaces. Security gates, locked entrances, alarms, building security, as well as use of security guards and patrols.

- **A Feminist "Revision" of Access Control:** Access control must look beyond the physical barriers to access and work with women to understand socio-cultural and intersectional barriers they face—particularly around fear of violence and their perceived vulnerability in public space. Visual markers, signs, wayfinding and communication can be used to guide people to or away from places and should address activity transport, micro-mobility, public transport and private vehicles and car parking. Ill-considered fencing can restrict visibility and surveillance. Access control can interrupt niversal design principles for women with disabilities, older women and women with prams or caring responsibilities.

    The prevention approach to "unwanted" behaviors is fraught when situated crime prevention tactics divert crime elsewhere—either to spaces that are more public or more secluded—with further likelihood of victimization of women and criminalization. Consider dual entry/exits for car parks and bike storage so these spaces are not entrapping. Frontages and fences should avoid recess spaces and fences higher than 1.2m should be semi-transparent. Indicate closing hours or when activity sites shift programs.

The use of hostile architecture (where the material space is designed to prevent people from lingering) makes surviving the precariousness of being homeless, for example, more difficult for people who disproportionately come from marginalized communities

DEEPER DIVE: COMMUNITY SAFETY[2]

The concept of building community safety is addressed by Saville et al. (1997) and extended by Cozens et al. (2015). They raise key issues about the social aspects of communities and a holistic approach to crime prevention.

Social Cohesion: A socially cohesive environment is one that welcomes and supports diversity and positive relationships between community members (Cozens et al. 2015: 397). It is aimed to foster an environment of respect and appreciation of similarities and differences between groups in a community (ibid). Social cohesion can also include positive engagement with authority figures in the community (such as police and security guards) with the aim to develop strategies that involve the broader communities to make positive change in relation to crime.

Community Connectivity: Connections should be made between government and non-government agencies to create activities and programs for the community (Cozens et al. 2015: 397). In theory, this leads to a connected and integrated community with a strong sense of place, which strengthens community self-policing and may discourage criminogenic behavior through collective legitimate activity support (Cozens et al. 2015: 397).

> *Community Culture:* Community culture can be supported or encouraged through festivals, cultural events, or social clubs. A strong sense of community is important, providing a community with a positive outlook/identity, strengthening the "eyes on the street" and can encourage prosocial behavior through residents performing self-policing (Cozens et al. 2015: 397).
>
> *Threshold Capacity:* Neighborhoods and urban spaces are systems with a fixed capacity for land use and activities. It suggests that it is important to recognize and monitor this threshold capacity to maintain ongoing order in a "community ecosystem" through encouraging "human-scale and pedestrian-oriented land uses and activities" (Cozens et al. 2015: 398).

Typology, Context and Fear of Crime

Different urban typologies, the context of the built environment and the programs and people within spaces therefore have the propensity for different kinds of crime which will impact women's feelings of safety. For example, sex districts are likely areas where heterosexist attitudes may dominate after dark, increasing women's risk of crime and sexual assault (Kalms 2017: 111); night-time entertainment precincts where the service of alcohol prevails can shape behavior on the streets and sexist harassment (Fileborn 2016); in transport hubs and infrastructural networks where anonymity is guaranteed, perpetrators may be emboldened (Matthewson et al. 2021: 59). Reducing the capacity for high-risk programs to generate crime by understanding the influence of land use in the adjacent sites, precincts and neighborhoods is part of the CPTED considerations.

To address these issues, recent revisions to designing for crime prevention have begun to draw out the social, political and economic factors for determining risk and safety about behavior and crime. Factors such as social cohesion, community connectivity and threshold capacity are now included as areas for investigation and investment. However, the relationships between all these factors and the design of space are complex. Detailed research is required into the specific conditions and context of a locale to inform careful design responses and to ensure that women's rights, needs and desires are accounted for.

[Not] for Women's Safety: The Problem with CCTV

The growth of surveillance and crime control through closed-circuit television (CCTV) is a significant part of most city strategies and is viewed by many as a crucial tool for safety in cities. It is increasingly the "go-to" intervention for addressing community concerns around unwanted behavior, including vandalism and drug use. Urban designers and planners are often mandated to include CCTV in their designs and are corralled by crime prevention strategies and a range of literature that supports CCTV to assuage fear of crime.

Its installation is supported by government and business owners—especially in the aftermath of serious incidents of crime—who are eager to deter criminal and unwanted behavior. As such, CCTV is used to preserve high-cost infrastructure, such as transport networks or privatized common spaces, from vandalism, theft and damage.

The evidence that CCTV increases safety for the users of shared public space is contested (Overington 2017) and opinions regarding CCTV's role in urban design are increasingly divided. Research into this form of surveillance in relation to making cities safer for women and girls suggests that CCTV may contribute to their anxiety and fear of crime and "the degree to which technological innovation promotes or prevents violence" needs careful analysis; CCTV intervention should not be seen as a "quick fix" (Whitzman 2008: 102). Such a high-cost measure may "actively militate against women's security by reducing the amount of funding available for projects designed to enhance women's security" (Brown et al. 1998: 218)

CCTV works on the principle that if activities and behaviors are monitored (and that people are aware that the space is under surveillance) then crime and anti-social behaviors will be deterred (Ceccato et al. 2020: 16). Live monitoring of CCTV technology certainly provides the capacity to respond to events of crime; but while it is considered best practice, it is mostly impractical, given the number of cameras now installed in urban environments and the cost associated with live monitoring. Unfortunately, some women assume that cameras are live monitored (meaning that someone is watching the footage in real-time) and—should an incident arise—that help will be immediately available. For these women, a false sense of security creates an extra danger, when actually, no one who can intervene is watching in real-time.

As such, CCTV is better understood as a recording device from which material can be retrieved and reviewed after an incident. This confusion reveals that the "importance of women's safety is inadequately acknowledged. CCTV cameras, 'safety zones' and alarm buttons are generalized measures for all users, and only become useful after the sexual harassment or assault has occurred" (Kalms 2017: 114). From women's perspective, CCTV "does far less to prevent violence or the fear of violence" (Whitzman 2008: 102). The greatest use for CCTV for personal safety is as a forensic tool used to recover evidence of an incident to support a case or conviction in the traditional justice system. But even in this form, it falls short and is unable to capture all forms of threats that women and girls face, such as verbal harassment or stalking. What often results—even if unintended—is an *increase* in feelings of vulnerability and hyper-alertness, with the awareness that the camera exists because of preceding unwanted or criminal behavior (Overington 2017) so that the presence of the CCTV signals that there is something to feared.

As a forensic tool, there are other risks and consequences, particularly for women and girls. In some cases, CCTV may provide a short-term solution (for example, it captures some incidents and can potentially be used as evidence). But in public transport, for example, the maintenance of the technology may be problematic, so that the quality of the material is unreliable; in many cases, the cameras are not in working order.

The financial cost of implementation is high. To question its value and whether CCTV is a good investment may provide deeper insights into the cost of women's lack of safety and exclusion from public spaces. The systems in place are variable in quality and their effectiveness for women and girls needs greater research. The importance of transparency in the collection of surveillance data is paramount. Governments and practitioners should be aware of the potential legal risks associated with imperfect technologies.

Any technological responses to crime and the policing of urban spaces must be evidence-based. Certainly, if CCTV is not monitored or working and if help is not immediately available, then nothing can replace the socio-cultural practice of "people keeping an eye on one another" (Whitzman 2008: 102). Welsh and Farrington's review of the scientific evidence for CCTV in crime prevention found that it is effective in reducing property (and especially vehicle) crimes (2009: 736). Other research into surveillance and technology initiatives suggests that this mode impacts marginalized groups in negative ways, when they may already be required to manage some people's fear and suspicion of them when in public. As urban researcher Leslie Kern reminds us, Jane Jacobs' original insight about the important of passive surveillance or "eyes on the street" was not referring to the "eyes of state surveillance"—where CCTV polices identity, sexuality and racial minorities. The city becomes a place which is safe for no one, with the result that it is "impossible to be safe and alone among strangers" (Kern 2020: 93–4).

A Note on Digital Guardians

It is common for women to carry their own forms of surveillance in the form of a smart phone, which provides new modes to "connect and collaborate as well to monitor and moderate participation and practices in cities" (Kalms 2018: 112). While there are positive examples of savvy women snapping a picture of an anonymous perpetrator who went on to be identified and charged, other uses of smart phone tech may be less productive for women in public spaces. Commonly, women may use a smart device as a personal safety tool for managing the risk of violence in public spaces by sharing their destination and mode of transport with family, friends or an intimate partner (sometimes referred to as a "companion" or "guardian") so they can monitor her remotely and communicate during the journey to provide support and ensure that that she arrives safely (Kalms 2018: 113–14). With some devices, either user may be able to trigger an alarm or alert the police, notifying the companion if the user's destination is (or is not) reached.

As a personal safety device, these technologies reinforce "self-surveillance and discipline" and confirm that "violence against women and girls is their own responsibility to manage"; they mimic "ways that women have historically been monitored and may mirror the controlling behaviour of perpetrators, which is part of the disempowerment of women" (Kalms 2017: 115). For example, women express concern about perpetrators filming women without their consent, or the footage of an adverse incident being filmed by a bystander, or, more commonly, that a bystander might be more concerned with filming an incident than with intervening in an emergency.

Cities Interrupted

CPTED can be a useful framework for tackling some of the factors that contribute to safety in the built environment but will only account for the needs of women and girls if supplemented by a range of multi-modal interventions that incorporates their diverse perspectives. Of course, women's safety cannot be accomplished through design alone, but changing the built environment to promote a sense of community, reduce the occurrence of crime in public spaces and address women's vulnerability will support their participation in public life. This requires a proactive promotion of design that is sensitive to gender as well as other intersectional oppressions faced by women, and challenging excuses that justify neutral approaches. Even if unintentionally, CPTED—in its current form—does not account for women in urban spaces and endorses and authorizes the perpetration of male violence, reinforcing gender inequality. To effect change in crime prevention through the built environment, the CPTED framework requires a range of complementary initiatives that are women-centered.

CHAPTER TEN

On the Edge of the Night
Women and the Night-time Economy

Principles
- Lighting specification to address the needs of women and girls after dark
- Engage multi-modal research that aims to increase women's visibility and confidence in accessing public spaces after dark
- Ensure public messaging does not imply that it is women's responsibility to use self-protective behaviors after dark
- Develop safe infrastructure by providing key stakeholders and decision makers in government, local communities, transport providers and business with women-centered after-dark policy guidelines
- Adopt use of technologies and real-time data to improve planning and service delivery of public transport after dark
- Understand the public expectations for the public provision of lighting and ensure policy meets this demand

Practice
- Design strategies and responses that address the specificity of women's safety needs after dark
- Ensure urban lighting design specialists included in all master planning projects and public placemaking
- Understand the cultural and spatial factors that inhibit women's participation in public spaces after dark

- Leverage multidisciplinary expertise, gender-sensitive planning, and women's lived experience to develop innovative frameworks for designing for women's mobility, work and leisure after dark
- Identify cultural and spatial factors of night-time design responses that go beyond traditional approaches such as brighter lighting and CCTV
- Balance the installation of CCTV so that light luminance level can be reduced across urban places and spaces
- Design spaces that are flexible and adaptable with the capacity to work across a range of times of day including the transitional periods at dawn and dusk

Participation
- Appoint a night-time committee of diverse interdisciplinary perspectives– including women advocates—who can provide a lived experience perspective
- Undertake night-time placemaking co-design activities to increase gender-sensitive interventions and perceptions of safety in certain "hotspot" sites
- Reconsider the benefit and effectiveness of CCTV in local communities and redeploy the costs to gender-sensitive initiatives
- Improve participation in the night-time economy by deploying communication design strategies to enhance women's perceptions of safety and confidence in the urban environment at night
- Ensure that staff in business, venues or in public-facing transport roles are trained in gender-sensitive support to assist reporting incidents
- Focusing on improving night-time experiences for women across age, disability, ethnicity, geographic location, income, indigeneity, migratory status, race, religion and sexuality, and especially for women who work in informal sectors
- Emphasize the creative use of public spaces for diverse after-dark arts and cultural events, including multi-generational activities
- Manage myths or exaggeration about night-time safety with gender-sensitive communication campaigns
- Deploy regular street cleaning to manage the results of over-consumption of alcohol in leisure precincts where vomiting and urination occur on the street after hours

Women and the Night-time Economy

Ensuring women have equitable access to the night-time economy is vital to the success of cities after dark, so that the night-time economy meets women's needs and allows them to engage with the possibility of 24-hour cities. Understanding women's complexities and improving their access to cities after dark will further increase women's employment as well as economic and leisure opportunities, in turn bringing substantial economic benefits to cities and communities more broadly. Given that working women will often have to manage sexist harassment on the street and when using public transport and given the importance of women's contributions to the economy of cities, there is a need to go beyond quick-fix solutions such as brighter lighting and more CCTV. Policymakers, planners and practitioners need to consider specific strategies and responses for improving women's perceptions of safety after dark and to increase women's visibility and confidence in accessing and engaging with public amenities after dark.

The concept of the night-time economy has gained increasing interest since the 1990s and originally emerged to address concerns about anti-social practices and decline in cities after dark. It is now a significant growth sector and an area of strategic engagement supported by a flurry of "night mayors," "night councils" and "nighttime governance" (Acuto et al. 2021: 2). For culture, tourism and communities, it plays a crucial role in stimulating "urban revival and regeneration" (Stevenson, 2018: 560), and while the night-time economy is viewed optimistically by business and government, there are ongoing issues related to the safety of women after dark. These issues raise questions about how best to regulate the dynamics of inclusion and exclusion for women, girls and other marginalized groups, making the night-time economy a paradoxical arena. With a complex network of stakeholders, understanding women's rights, needs and fears in the night-time economy involves changes in policy, planning and design, and insights from women who live and work in communities after dark.

Night-time economy

The exact definition of the night-time varies between countries but is generally considered to be "after hours" and/or the industries operating in the hours from dusk until dawn, such as the entertainment and hospitality sectors. While night-time economy

> refers to the economic activity that takes place during this time, it also includes strategies to extend activities traditionally associated with the daytime into the after dark period, such as "shopping, exercise, education or cultural consumption" (Roberts et al. 2009: 4).

Cities after dark are places of "entertainment and excess" (Stevenson 2018: 560) with the rhetoric dominated by "major initiatives ... emerging from the entertainment and hospitality sectors" (Acuto et al. 2021: 2). This attention sits alongside a range of related transformations in mobility, work, education and leisure after dark. Researchers have examined the support systems to the night-time economy such as "office cleaning, street sweeping and the like" all of which must occur "overnight to ensure the city is ready for the next day" and much of which "is rendered invisible in most narratives of the city at night" (Stevenson 2018: 560). Workplaces and cities have become more flexible and responsive as a result. The "care economy" dominated by women in areas such as retail, health, cleaning and hospitality, as well as the transport sectors, has central roles in facilitating the after-dark workforce. This has the potential to increase women's participation in cities after dark with more opportunities in paid work and more disposable income to participate in night-time leisure activities. Despite these shifts, women are less likely than men to benefit, either through work or recreation, from the night-time economy.

WOMEN'S STORIES

This space needs more lighting. There is a bus stop here next to a park with lots of trees and darks spots. Getting off the bus during winter after 6pm always makes me look behind my back. There is no lighting on the street side of this park and is generally very unsafe in this area when there is pitch darkness and you're alone.

I pass through here twice a day to get to work and am routinely verbally abused by men. I feel unsafe and would never go through here at night.

I have to walk here to get home late at night. I feel unsafe walking through a long winding path surrounded completely by bushes with no lighting and I hate it.

Risky Business

Women's experiences will vary from city to city and from street to street. Like other aspects of urban life, women's perceptions of cities—including at night—are the result of geographic location as well as the intersectional factors of age, disability, ethnicity, income, indigeneity, migratory status, race, religion and sexuality (Green et al. 2006: 2). While matters of inclusion and exclusion may differ, there are issues of safety and fear that appear to be universal, with night-time viewed as a time for caution for women internationally. For example, in 2020 the Organisation for Economic Co-operation and Development (OECD) compared the percentage of men and women who say they feel safe walking at night. Men feel markedly safer than women across thirty-eight countries (Fig. 10. 1), with the OECD noting the relationship between personal security and well-being (OECD 2020).

A change occurs in urban spaces as cities move from day to night. Women will calibrate their interactions in cities after dark and will be shaped by their familiarity with places, their habits, needs, challenges and belief systems, which are formed via sociocultural attitudes learned from media, experiences of friends, stories, television and movies that impact women's experiences at night. This heightens anxiety and uncertainty for some people (Hubbard 2007: 120) and can also mean that women who are out at night are viewed as "irresponsible" (Williams 2008: 31). So powerful are these interactions that research suggests that women believe stories shared "directly by family members and friends" (including thorough social media) and that "they automatically interpret it as trustworthy since it's coming from people who care about their well being" (Pulse Lab et al. 2019: 3).

An area that may be deemed "safe" during the day may swiftly become a place of risk and vulnerability at night. Sociologist Deborah Stevenson describes this contradiction, noting how cities

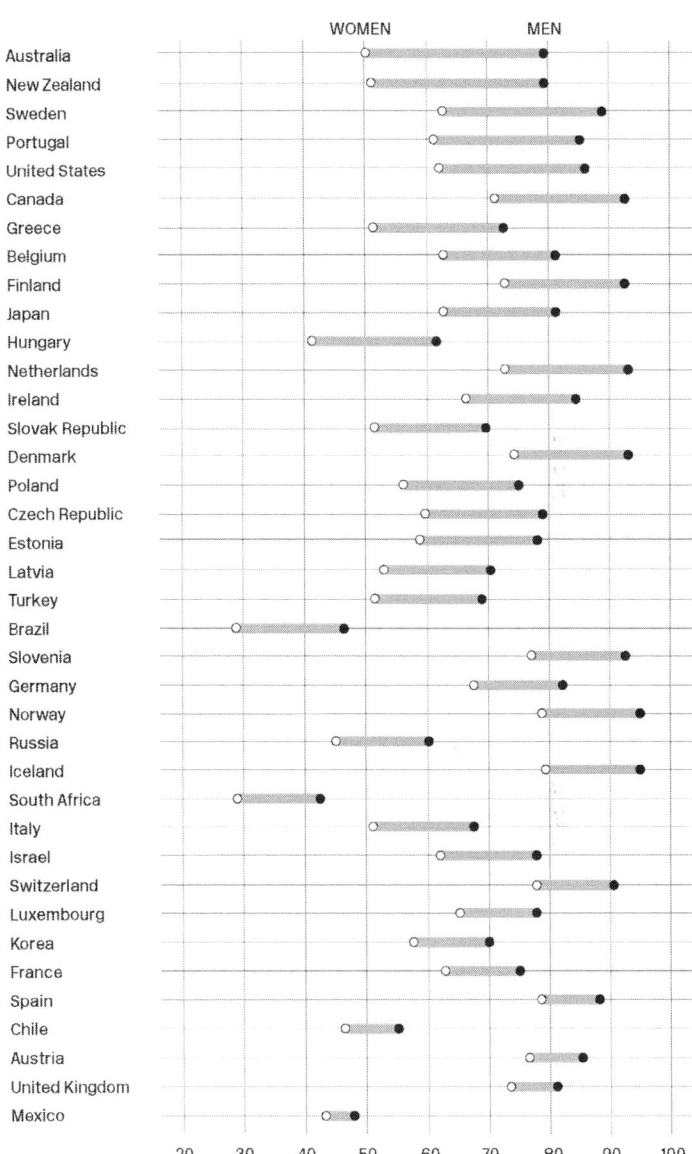

FIGURE 10.1 Proportion of women who say they feel safe walking home at night compared to men. Adapted from OECD Better Life Index (2020).

are "a site of pleasure, opportunity and adventure, as well as of danger and uncertainty" (2018: 560). Urban design scholar Marion Roberts and sociologist Adam Eldridge note the city as a space of "flux," commonly understood as either a place of "danger or pleasure" (2009: 12). Women must balance these paradoxical conditions and consider both the opportunities and the risk as they move through and occupy cities at night. The work required to find this balance undermines their active participation in the night-time economy as they manage their apprehensions about the possible dangers of being in public spaces at night.

Women's primary threat is male violence including rape, which may become the determining factor of how they engage with public space after dark (Stevenson 2018: 557). When women face sexist street harassment, for example, they "explicitly or implicitly" make connections to the possibility of sexual assault and rape (Kelly et al. 1990: 42). As a result, women's perceived vulnerability to sexual violence after dark has been solidified as part of the social policy which "has been underpinned by the aim of controlling/containing women's movement through the city at night to protect them and their reputations" (Stevenson 2018: 560).

> **TIP**
>
> Women's experiences of sexist harassment and their sense of vulnerability in public space because of male violence is a consequence of gender inequality. This is discussed in **Chapter 2—*Don't stand so close to me: Sexist street harassment and women's "safety work"***

For some women, their fear may also sit alongside a sense of defiance and the desire to occupy public spaces in ways that feel more powerful (Koskela 1997: 301). Across culture and countries, many women will have moments engaged in what geographer Hille Koskela describes as the "bold walk" where they develop an articulated practice of resistance and fearlessness as they traverse cities. Using this strategy, women may see themselves as active agents when they decide to go into cities, despite their awareness of the risk (Koskela 1997: 316), but this is not a stable or constant perception. As Koskela describes, there is an elasticity between fear and boldness, with women existing dynamically in an arc between the two (Koskela 1997: 315). Their feelings are shaped by who they pass on the street, and by how they feel at any given moment. The important point to make here is that women are not uniformly vulnerable or passive victims but may find ways to be courageous despite the perceived risks. This can become a tactical practice for women. And of course, they are benefits for women more broadly, because, as women's presence in public space increases, more women feel emboldened to occupy public space (Koskela 1997: 316).

Accountability and Responsibility

Even in the context of resistance and defiance, women's behavior at night continues to be viewed as a form of risk taking and places the responsibility for safety on women. This, in turn, avoids placing accountability on the perpetrators and has been a point of contention via international protests since the 1970s. As a challenge to the self-regulation and constant mitigation of risk required from women, protests such as "Reclaim the Night" speak back to the "protective" measures often adopted and endorsed by authority figures. Women call this doctrine of protective messages into question—not just women's access to city streets, but also the right for women to dress and occupy places as they please without inviting unwanted sexist attention. These outdated ideas of women's "reputation" fail to take into account the rights, needs and desires of women. Women rightly state that making them always undertake risk management contributes further to their exclusion from public spaces at night and limits their use of public transport and access to work, education, and leisure.

Policymakers, practitioners and communities must reposition preconceptions about "risk" so that they do not—even unintentionally—make women accountable for their own safety. Communicating women's right to autonomous use of public space as well as their right to occupy spaces after dark is a critical component to increasing women's safety and presence in cities at night.

> **DEEPER DIVE: RECLAIM/TAKE BACK THE NIGHT MOVEMENT**
>
> The Reclaim/Take Back the Night movement began in 1975 in Philadelphia and quickly developed into a global annual event in cities across the world, with a focus on the threat to women's safety during the hours of darkness (Mackay 2015). The Reclaim/Take Back the Night movement pushes back against women being made responsible for their safety and the fear and alienation from city life that results. The activism to "take back the night" is a way to speak back to the socio-cultural limitations placed on women and challenges the suggested responsibility (often reinforced through media, policing and social stereotypes) that women should be accountable for their own safety. Furthermore, it politicizes how women "fail" if they are unable to mitigate risk or protect themselves—particularly from male violence against women.

Typologies of Darkness

The requirement to understand and design for the changeability of public spaces transitioning from day to night-time is a key factor in urban design after dark. While people's behavior in spaces after dark is a major factor in whether urban space feels safe, the built environment and other physical factors of cities strongly influence their experience of safety (Greed 1994; Wekerle et al. 1995) and—while communities strive for primary prevention of men's violence against women—policymakers, practitioners and communities can support women to feel confident negotiating public space at night (Whitzman et al. 2014).This reinforces previous scholarship on safety in the night-time economy, which has suggested that the "atmosphere" of urban places (as well as the sense of belonging), will shape perceptions of safety for women (Fileborn 2016b, 206;

Committee for Sydney 2019, 16). Importantly, and as Acuto et al. suggest, the night-time economy is not defined by a single sector and cannot be regulated by a top-down approach, but requires diverse input and perspectives via a participatory process with various groups, including women (2021: 107). By leveraging multidisciplinary expertise and collaborating with women who have lived experience of the issues, communities can target site-specific interventions and design for women's mobility, work and leisure needs after dark. Identifying typologies of concern for women at night can assist policymakers, planners and designers to address the cultural factors and perceptions of lack of safety in the built environment.

- **Transport and Mobility After Dark:** Women commute to cities because there may be better job opportunities in city centers and business districts. Their homes may be in places that are more affordable and in outer suburbs, so their travel experiences are critical to safe and successful employment. And yet women's vulnerability and risk of sexist harassment in public transport increase during evening hours, creating significant barriers to their participation in the night-time economy.

Mitigating risk on public transport at night can take many forms. Women are often anxious and may spend considerable time planning journeys and thinking up protective strategies when traveling at night. As women and girls juggle multiple responsibilities and caring duties, they may mix and match different transport modes due to safety considerations and use private options (if the disposable income is available). Yet some taxis and forms of ride-share are dangerous for lone women, for they can be at risk of sexual assault and rape from male drivers (Roberts et al. 2009: 171). Unsurprisingly, many women take particular routes or use modes of transport at night that, even though they may take longer, are perceived to be safer. Other women are unable to mitigate risk and must prioritize financial responsibilities over personal safety and manage fear, despite their sense of vulnerability.

WOMEN'S STORIES

Bus stop felt perfectly safe during the day, but I would not like taking the bus from here at night.

The footpath in this area goes under the highway and has no buildings near it. It's really scary to walk through at night after work as there's no one around and it's pitch black, with the sound of the highway covering everything else.

The lighting is so poor after dusk—people were appearing out of nowhere. There was a suspicious person hanging around the car park, and no one else around. Solar lighting along the walking tracks and bright lighting in the car park would go a long way to making this space feel safer.

Practically, the availability, timeliness and quality of public transport after dark is critical. The spaces around and connecting public transport need sensitive street lighting, and well-defined, well-maintained walkways and the presence of security persons can positively impact women's mobility and travel choices at night.

Women will view formal and informal business in and around public transport spaces as forms of passive surveillance and will, for example, wait in view of shop owners, as they are perceived as potential allies. In this regard, planners and designers can exploit the role of retail and business as assets for safer public transport spaces for women at night.

DEEPER DIVE

For a practical discussion of night-time economies, see *Managing Cities at Night: A Practitioner Guide to the Urban Governance of the Nighttime Economy*, by Michele Acuto et al. 2021.

- **Entertainment Districts: Bars, Pubs and Nightclubs After Dark:** These spaces of leisure and entertainment are places of contradiction for women. For women, visiting bars, pubs and nightclubs in entertainment areas may represent freedom and enjoyment but equally can place them in unpredictable spaces "formed and reformed through the unstable and temporary coming together or meeting of unique material, affective, cultural (and other) factors" (Fileborn 2016b: 11). Research into the impacts of alcohol consumption dominates much of the night-time leisure economy scholarship (Sheard 2011: 620; Fileborn 2016a: 1108) and is associated with violence, which causes concern for women. Research in Sydney in 2018 showed that intoxication may be part of the "fun of a night out"; but alcohol and drug taking is also "strongly associated with sexual violence" (Committee for Sydney 2019: 13). This research suggests that "intoxication can be used to diminish perpetrator's responsibility for their action, while victim-survivors who have consumed alcohol or drugs are often viewed as bearing some responsibility for the violence perpetrated against them"(Committee for Sydney 2019: 13). Equally, there are concerning assumptions that if women consume alcohol in public settings they may be viewed as "asking for it"—that is, they should expect sexual attention and/or harassment (Committee for Sydney 2019: 13).

WOMEN'S STORIES

This is a pretty dangerous area. It is fairly secluded, in close proximity to a large live music venue, as well as being on the route toward the train station from the night club strip. There are also rehabilitation centers which adds to the overall unsavory mix of people. I, and many friends unfortunate enough to work in this area have been abused physically and verbally, stalked at night, had vehicles damaged, and have been robbed.

The interior spaces of night clubs, bars and pubs also have a role to play in what happens in the precincts and on the city streets. While these are not public spaces, these spaces house a culture dominated by intoxication (Seal 2022: 110; Stevenson 2018: 560) where the behaviors from the interior slip onto the street unpoliced, and without oversight by patrons and staff. Women may move through the areas of entertainment precincts and experience masculine aggression and hyper-masculinized performances of male bonding or street fighting (Plan International 2019: 9). Gay and lesbian women may consider the heterosexist hostility or violence based on their sexuality too risky and may avoid traversing specific parts of the city entirely.

While policy, planning and design will not mitigate against all issues in entertainment districts, it is possible to design spaces that can certainly enhance safety (Fileborn 2016b: 206). Indeed, criminologist Bianca Fileborn encourages the evaluation of design impact in relation to entertainment and leisure venues, noting how an "assemblage of elements" can shape spaces and that venue design plays a role in "enabling the actions of perpetrators and in preventing intervention from other patrons"; the same is true for the public realm (2016: 206).

DEEPER DIVE: GOOD NIGHT OUT

With the aim to create safer music, culture, and nightlife spaces, "Good night out" aims to prevent all gender-based harms. Initially part of the Hollaback London campaign (see **Chapter 2**), "Good night out" supported the local anti-sexual harassment policy and then began to work with licensed venues and their staff to deliver "specialist, interactive workshops to bar staff, managers, and security." https://www.goodnightoutcampaign.org/info/#our-work

- **Sex Districts, Street Prostitution, Brothels, Strip Clubs and Illicit Massage Businesses:** While proposing solutions to the issues brought about by prostitution is beyond the scope of this book, it is vital for policymakers, planners and designers to explore how sex services in cities relate to women's inequality. In the night-time economy, sexual services such as brothels, massage parlors, as well as lap-dancing and strip clubs are normalized and exist unquestioned in the urban landscape (Kalms 2017: 140; Larin 2022: 104); most people in sexual services are women and girls (Tyler 2021: 80–1). This uncritical consumption of sex in cities after dark means that women and girls prostituted in legal and illegal sex service are providing paid and unpaid sexual services. Many are victims of trafficking and pedophilia.

In cities internationally, sexual services constitute a "thriving and visible illicit commercial sex trade" (Larin 2022: 67) and yet—despite their normalization—the districts where brothels, strip clubs and/or street prostitution congregate are viewed negatively in the geography of cities and are sites of contestation and political tension.

The tension relates to the divergent positions and perspectives on violence perpetrated against women in sex services. Some policies (for example in parts of Australia and New Zealand) align with third-wave feminists, who believe that women choose to participate in sex services and see the industry of prostitution as a "potentially positive site of women's empowerment, economic and otherwise" (Mackay 2015: 204). The evidence suggests that, while there may be a small minority of women who state that they have choice and agency providing sex services, this is not the case for most women and girls trafficked and exploited in prostitution. Many women may engage in prostitution as "survival sex" because of their personal and extreme need, often related to unstable housing, homelessness or other disadvantage; sex is used to acquire food or drugs, accommodation, and basic needs for themselves and/or their children.

In urban sex districts, women's exploitation in brothels, massage parlors, lap-dancing and strip clubs will "extend to larger territories where the effect operates across sites and suburbs of cities" (Kalms 2017: 228). Previous research has highlighted that the urban relationship to sex service authorizes the "commercial and systemic use of women's bodies" in various industries, where prostitution, including stripping, massage parlors, brothels, street prostitution trafficking and pornography shape cities and normalize exploitative heterosexuality so much that sexist spaces are a routine part of the everyday life of cities (Kalms 2017: 14).

WOMEN'S STORIES

Lots of strip clubs means lots of drunk men, very sleazy along here at night-time, I live nearby so popping out to the shops is only done during the day time, at night-time it's awful.

As prostitution is characterized by intersectional inequality, where geographic location, income, indigeneity, migratory status, race and sexuality may play a significant role in women's exploitation, women who are part of sex services have the right to various kinds of protection, which may include CCTV, security, access to empathetic police support and protection, with the capacity to report crimes including sexual assault and rape (MacKay 2015: 213). The use of CCTV in street prostitution precincts should be discussed with women, as there can be negative impacts on women in the sex service. CCTV is likely to make streets more dangerous and may push women into less safe locations in order to work (Kerns 2019: 162).

WOMEN'S STORIES

Yet another "massage" business opening along Plenty Road—this means there will be five in a 1 km stretch. These businesses are clearly not for regular massage. They make women feel unsafe, and work against a culture of local shopping strips to which all people are drawn and can benefit.

Some may argue that this is a form of everyday labor and that sex services are comparable to any form of "work." They inaccurately argue that—to some extent—everyone is "coerced" and exploited in the workforce and in the context of various power structures and discrimination (Mackay 2015: 214–15). Contrary to the belief that legal brothels and "tolerance zones" protect women and their rights, women are still raped, assaulted and attacked. Despite the use of the terms "industry" (as in sex industry) or "work" (as in sex work), the business of prostitution is not "work like any other," as selling access to one's body is markedly different to selling one's labor (Mackay 2015: 214–215). Thus, the so called "sex wars"—active since the 1980s—with anti- and pro-sex feminism take opposing positions, continue to divide society more broadly on the issue of prostitution.

The exploitation, violence and power structures negotiated by women in prostitution impact all women. In sex districts and precincts, this is particularly relevant, where the interior practices and behaviors of the strip club, massage parlors or brothels are mirrored on the city streets. Inside these venues, the possibility of men's desires not being met is minuscule (Kalms 2017: 143). These sexist attitudes and demands migrate into the surrounding public realm, and some men feel entitled to access women's bodies. Nonprostituted women may be expected to tolerate the sexist intimidation and violence of some men in these urban contexts and beyond (Kalms 2017: 143). Furthermore, women may be punished when they do not meet the gendered and sexualized expectation and stereotypes of strangers on the street (Kalms 2017: 143).

Some of these perspectives and analyses of the urban context are unpopular, but difficult to contest on the ground. The conflict is partly because many policymakers and planners have learned that to speak about this difficult subject is challenging and often attracts harsh penalties from businesses who profit from women's and girls' exploitation. Challenging the push for legalization and decriminalization—and the impact on cities—means that professionals may be stigmatized and labeled anti-sex and prudish.

In contrast to the rhetoric that is pro-sex and pro-prostitution, there are researchers and feminist who suggest a different solution and maintain that the Nordic/Equality model is the most equitable solution at hand. Adopted in Sweden, Canada, Iceland, Ireland, Israel, France and Norway, it is an innovative approach that criminalizes the sex buyer (thereby reducing the demand for prostituted women and sex trafficking more broadly). Women who are prostituted are not criminalized and must be offered support to exit prostitution; communities undertake to provide women with exit support, such as housing, education, training benefits, counseling, family mediation, and police support to prosecute abusers (Mackay 2015: 222). While ending prostitution may seem improbable, that does not mean that communities need to endorse its proliferation or impact on women's equality. Through the emphasis that buying people for sex is unacceptable, the Nordic/Equality model reconfigures the issue of prostitution so that women can exit in a safe and supported way.

• **Homeless Women After Dark:** Homelessness is a universal challenge, and women's homelessness is often intertwined with inequality and male violence, while support services are chronically underfunded (United Nations 2019: 2–3). Homeless women have increasingly complex needs and are a high-risk group who are marginalized because of their biological sex, economic and social inequality, and often as a result of their caring responsibilities. Women may be homeless due to insufficient income or unreliable employment, displacement or migration, family violence, physical or mental health issues, and a range of political and natural crises.

Homelessness impacts women and their children of all ages; housing instability may begin when fleeing harmful and violent environments. Being forced to take refuge in unsafe environments, transitional housing, or to sleep on the street increases women's risk further; "sexual violence, exploitation and survival sex" are common (United Nations 2019: 2). When homelessness is due to sexual violence, women's and girls' basic needs and dignity are paramount and gender-sensitive strategies are required to accommodate their diverse needs. Women-only refuges must be fully funded and include advocacy, legal support, psycho-social support, continued education, and childcare (United Nations 2019: 3). Sex-segregated places to safely take rest and sleep are vital, with support services that can ideally assist in finding more permanent accommodation if requested by women. Harm reduction facilities for drug users and exit programs for women who may be working in sex services are also part of strategies to manage women's homelessness. Basic needs such as access to clean water, sanitation and facilities to charge devices is vital (Roe et al. 2021: 110).

The complexities of homelessness are multiplied when women's vulnerability intersects with age, disability, ethnicity, geographic location, income, indigeneity, migratory status, race, religion and sexuality. These often-multiple oppressions determine "who becomes homeless, how long they are homeless, how they become homeless, how that homelessness is experienced, and whether they remain homeless" (Kawash 1998: 323). Older women are increasingly at risk of homelessness (Donnelly et al. 2022: 5) and older women's entitlement to safe and affordable housing needs to be a priority for policymakers and planners, especially for older migrant and Indigenous women.

Blinding Light: Gender-sensitive Lighting

For women's productive enjoyment of cities after dark, evidence suggests that lighting can discourage crime, enhance natural surveillance, and reduce fear. In this sense, investment in a specialized lighting design with gender-sensitive training is a strategic tool for good placemaking and impacts the value that cities and communities attribute to public places. From the terror of dark, deserted streets through to the crazed spectacle of light and media that blinds urban centers of cities, light (or lack thereof) shapes the night-time economy. Urban lighting is a specialized field and discipline within planning and design and plays a significant role in mitigating feelings of risk and vulnerability for women in cities after dark. While the effect of crime prevention through the installation of lighting, that is, understanding the impact of increased lighting and/ or intensity of lighting, has been studied since the 1960s (Struyf 2020: 347), how lighting relates specifically to women's experiences and their perceptions of safety is less researched. Indeed, most research to date has been undertaken in laboratories that do not represent "diverse real-world urban settings, multiple lighting sources, larger populations and population subgroups" (Svechkina et al. 2020: 2). Certainly, well-designed lighting will enhance the pedestrian experience of urban spaces and lighting technology will emphasize the aesthetic definition of public spaces, but light needs to be correlated with both accessibility and safety rather than assuming that "less public lighting will result in increased crime rates and unsafe public places" (Struyf 2020: 347).

In fact, evidence suggests that higher illuminance does not necessarily enhance feelings of safety (Svechkina et al. 2020: 13) and those over-lit spaces may intensify feelings of risk for women and girls and can exacerbate social inequity and exclusion for marginalized people more broadly (Yang et al. 2022). There is an assumption that brighter urban spaces are safer and urban lighting technology tends toward an "excessive use of light" where extreme brightness can be unsettling (McQuire 2005: 127). For example, and in the case of women and girls, brighter lights can create a "fishbowl effect" where the lighting increases violence against women by making the "victims more visible" (Ceccato 2020: 45).

The nuances of urban lighting therefore require bespoke design specific to site and cannot be a blanket policy or a one-size-fits-all approach (Svechkina et al. 2020: 14). The specification of the type and quantity of light source requires careful analysis of each site condition at various times during dusk, dawn and darkness as well as across seasonal variations. And while lighting is the major factor in perceptions of safety, the alignment with other factors or "surrogate" elements with which lighting interacts is also critical—for example, the landscape and foliage conditions and visibility (Ceccato 2020: 52).

Recent research shows that there are techniques, effects and parameters to consider for improving night-time experience for women and girls. When women have clear visibility throughout their whole after-dark journey and when this is coupled with natural surveillance from other people (especially other women), then there is a significant reduction in women's fear of crime and perception of risk. Critical to visibility is facial recognition, reduced glare, and the color of the light source, all of which are factors in understanding fear of crime (Boyce 2014: 427–58). Over-lit spaces with cold light are usually used for the specification of CCTV and surveillance. It is common, for example, for cities to install LED lighting with the assumption that they are more energy efficient, but this can mark "spaces out as intrinsically problematic, as threatening and risky" (Slaone et al. 2016: 6). The visual spectrum reacts better to warm light and is very sensitive to the blue LED light, so most women feel more comfortable and generally safer under a warmer color temperature (Yang et al. 2022: 96). Site-specific solutions need to be developed within a context of social research, with stakeholders and diverse user groups of the site providing the most inclusive design solutions (Slaone et al. 2016: 4, 21). Street lighting, for example, can benefit women's feelings of safety and influence their feelings about their environment from an aesthetic as well as a safety standpoint. A standardized approach to lighting (especially the tendency toward "brighter" and "whiter" lighting) that overlooks the nuances of public space can make cities feel less safe for women and girls.

DEEPER DIVE

In 2019, research conducted by Arup (international designers of built environments), in conjunction with Monash University's XYX Lab and Plan International, surveyed 84 public sites in Melbourne to identify and quantify how specific elements of lighting contribute to a safe perception of space, particularly for women. Rather than simply measuring the brightness of light, which is the only consideration for compliance with Australia's outdated lighting standards, the researchers considered other elements of lighting such as: color temperature, color rendering, vertical illuminance, horizontal illuminance, uniformity, ambient illuminance, facial illuminance, contrast ratio and vertical plane ratio.

In contrast to popular opinion, the research found that bright lights do not make women feel safe, but instead contribute to women feeling unsafe. This is due, in part, to the drop-off effect between bright light and the dark. Bright lights were also associated with disorienting or blinding glare. The research found that the quality of lighting is more important than quantity, and that a holistic consideration of brightness levels is necessary to allow vision to adapt to changes in light. Multi-layered urban design and a consistent lighting approach were suggested to ensure public spaces are safe and inclusive for women, particularly when walking alone. The research highlights the importance of evidence-based design and the need for the involvement of designers at the policy level.

A consistent, layered lighting approach will make people feel most safe, especially where there are multiple surfaces of different reflectance values that are treated with light. This reduces the floodlit effect and the potential for glare and contrast that may blind and disorientate (Wekerle et al. 1995: 29). Walking into very bright areas can be harsh on people's vision, which can be disorientating.

CHAPTER ELEVEN

Run the World

Co-design in a Feminist Framework

Principles
- Employ participatory co-design to develop, refine and revise women-centered policy
- Conduct longitudinal research into participatory processes undertaken in the public sector to further define impact and benefit

Practice
- Follow evidence-based co-design processes, ensuring that all steps are undertaken
- Challenge traditional practitioner "expertise" where the designer is all-knowing and instead include iterative and participatory co-design with women and girls at all stages of the design process
- Understand that participatory co-design is not only outcomes-driven but also valuable for building meaningful collaboration with stakeholders and women in communities
- Undertake design "with" women (rather than "for" or "about" women)

Participation
- Ensure that a wide range of women are engaged as co-producers to explore and test possible solutions to local placemaking issues

Activating She City

This book has—among other things—discussed how design can be understood as a mode to support the equity of women in cities, with feminist activism providing both the foundation and the scope to shape an alternative future. The role of design in this scenario has been positioned as a role that must move beyond traditional material interventions within the built environment and expanded to examine the intersection of urban space and inequity, where design can address power dynamics. It is a method that galvanizes the "importance of ensuring design meets the needs of users" (Edwards et al. 2017: 159). Critically, this involves moving design from being solely concerned with designing objects (or "things") to considering how design can be powerfully deployed to engage with communities where design responds to and engages with the turn "toward the social" and the "dematerialised practice" (Grocott 2022: 62).

For more equitable cities, designers must engage with women and girls across the design process to examine the concepts and complexity of inequality and work, in order to understand how design practice can contribute to (and positively shape) cultural narratives. By opposing the limitation of top-down approaches, the politics of space can progress women's agency through design processes and practice. This requires design practitioners to employ methods and modes that engage diverse stakeholders, including the people who will benefit from the outcomes of design. Foundational is the understanding that broader participation in the design process that includes the perspectives of women and girls can transform urban experiences.

Participatory design (also broadly referred to as co-design) is a common tool used across multiple stages of the design process with the aim of democratizing urban development. Increasingly (and unfortunately) it is also a buzzword within the public sector, where the method is reinforced by increasing pressure on communities to involve members of the public in decision-making processes (Thinyane et al. 2020: 30). It has come to represent a wide range of techniques and has been subsumed as a "problem solving technique" that is "easily adopted in different context, both to positive and negative effects" (Edwards et al. 2017: 160). This may mean that some of the uses of participatory design are not participatory at all, particularly if aspects of the process are overlooked (such as sketching, modeling, prototyping, etc.) within the research method (Edwards et al. 2017).

Inherent in the methodology is the co-production of knowledge, where the perceived "expert" (usually the policymaker, planner or designer) is required to share the privileges of power via co-learning (Caretta et al. 2016: 260). This moves the design process away from design "for" communities and engages with methods that privilege the process of "designing with" communities (Gheerawo 2016: 304). In this practice, this means that the designer must relinquish their perceived expertise within the hierarchical modes of traditional design practice, with a shared participation intercepting the hegemony of the ambitious and all-knowing "expert."

The process is a means to address the ways that design reproduces "dysfunctional ideologies, coming from a traditionally white heteropatriarchal and capitalist narrative," as participatory co-design can "be a tool" that questions assumptions, assists in reflection, and be a mode for "positive change" (Benbrahim 2021: 109). The evidence for inviting policymakers, planners and designers to work alongside women and girls suggests that participatory co-design is a mode to foster outcomes that are "supportive of the spectrum of gender and intersectional identities" (Kalms et al. 2021: 107).

As a process of "mutual learning," and with the aim to challenge "top-down power structures" (Fuad-Luke 2009: 147; Winschiers-Theophilus et al. 2012: 100) participatory co-design "intertwines" the act of designing a method for "questioning and reconfiguring power relations and notions of expertise" (Huybrechts et al. 2017: 149). When properly implemented in the context of urban placemaking projects, the project outcomes will be more equitable and will center local communities not only as participants in the design process but as evaluators and co-producers of solutions (Gheerawo 2016: 304).

Placemaking

Placemaking refers to a collaborative process undertaken with local communities to ensure that knowledge of the site-specific activities, influences and dynamics is central to public spaces design. Placemaking is both about the material of cities but equally about the social construction. Actively undertaking placemaking

> can uncover shared values, promoting more inclusive urban design through a deepened understanding of "physical, cultural, and social identities that define a place and support its ongoing evolution" (Garau 2016: viii).

Participatory *feminist* placemaking examines relevant urban issues specifically about women and girls and provides a framework to understand their perspectives. Drawing on their experiential knowledge, the process actively positions women and girls at the center of the design process to reconfigure the dynamics that tend to exclude women from urban design and placemaking. This means that design "about" or "for" women and girls moves to a design "with" women and girls, where collaborative tasks between designers and women stakeholders resist assumptions and biases in the design process. The method confronts the assumed disciplinary "expertise" in order to recognize the importance or "using women's experiences as a resource for social analysis" (Harding 1987: 7), which, when centered in placemaking, can progress women's social and political equity.

Participatory co-design

Participatory co-design is a design-led process and a mode for bringing together diverse participants using design principles and practices to solve real-world problems. Co-design is a mode for shared decision-making about the goals and participatory design actively involves all the various stakeholders. When used across the design process, the aim is that "the person who will eventually be served through the design process is given the position of expert of their experience, and plays a large role in knowledge development, idea generation and concept development" (Sanders et al. 2008: 12). The objective of participatory co-design is not solely to achieve an outcome, but to build meaningful collaboration into the design process and between participants. By engaging a range of people in exploring and testing possible solutions, the participatory process is democratic, a form of community engagement. Participatory design can be used for a range of disciplines, including policy development, planning practice, and design more broadly.

There are contrasting perspectives about the benefits of participatory practices and co-design more broadly. Design researchers Elizabeth Sanders and Pieter Stappers suggest that when "practiced at the early front end of the design development process" participatory practices "can have an impact with positive, long-range consequences" (2008: 9). Scholars of social inquiry Anthony Dunne and Fiona Raby suggest that the process leads to discussions about the "kinds of futures people want" (2013: 2). Emma Blomkamp, researcher and strategic designer in policy innovation, suggests that co-design promises "to address long standing social challenges that the public sector is failing to address," but she raises concerns about the limited evidence of its impact in a public policy environment (Blomkamp 2018: 730, 739). Similarly, Caretta et al. (2016: 259 citing Pain et al. 2011) note that, despite the theoretical discussion of participatory feminist methods, knowledge of how exactly to "operationalize greater equality in the process of knowledge production remains rather limited."

Certainly, co-design is suffering from being a business buzzword (often implemented as "co-design light") with industries adopting variations on the theme in all manner of non-research settings which may mine information and ideas from women without reciprocity. This is because the involvement of stakeholders is a "vague concept" and often "highly varied" in practice (Winschiers-Theophilus et al. 2012: 89). It is, therefore, critical to "repoliticise" participatory co-design despite the challenging institutional context (Huybrechts 2017: 149), and to differentiate a feminist participatory co-design model from a commercialized engagement process which is often a diluted form of consultation. The reality is that the

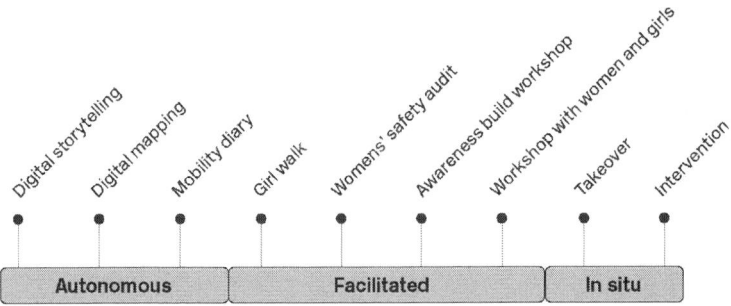

FIGURE 11.1 Modes for feminist participatory co-design.

preparation for engaging with communities involves "legislation-checks, policy-checks, fund-raising, partnership-forming, reporting and assessment" (Huybrechts 2017: 151).

Implemented in a research environment and with appropriate design methods, the process of participatory co-design can be "especially transformational" and "bring together diverse participants and structure activities in a way that allows them to materially engage with ideas in abstract, messy and expressive ways" (Edwards et al. 2017: 158). The value of undertaking the methodology in and through a scholarly setting is that it will not simply be used to build awareness of issues in a "brain storming" session, and ensures that the foundational aims of the practice can create deeper connection within communities who are invited to partake in the creation of alternative futures (Heidaripour et al. 2018: 520).

The process itself can be deeply rewarding for researchers and participants alike, and requires a shared commitment to grappling with the complexities. Stakeholders and facilitators, for example, cannot underestimate the investment in reflexive understanding of the methodology, the ethical responsibilities of engaging with communities, and the limitations present in all methods. When the participatory process is followed, the results can be transformative. Participants can feel empowered, and their insights can lead to innovative collaborations that craft alternative narratives and design solutions (Blomkamp 2018: 739; Bawden et al. 2018: 61; Caretta et al. 2016: 259).

Making Space to Make Space

In the disciplines of policy, planning and design, participatory co-design should be active and dynamic, with the use of bespoke materials designed and crafted as tools to facilitate discursive co-production between participants. Tactile objects prompt reflection, with personal insights and narratives revealing a spectrum of positions which likely result in both friction and confluence (Kalms et al. 2021). Borrowing from the various disciplines of design, participants use two-dimensional materials such as maps, timelines and matrices to plot problems, questions and insights. Three-dimensional modeling creates dynamic narratives and urban solutions that draw out common goals as well as divergent perspectives. This "fosters creative thinking informed by the intersection of academic knowledge, corporate acumen, and lived experience" (Kalms et al. 2021: 109). As a result, the "expert" may gain insight into women's and girls' experiences with a deepened understanding of the challenges they face in urban spaces; solutions to women's spatial inequity are derived from the process. This reflects how "making" is invaluable to the process, as design innovators John Bielenberg, Mike Burn and Greg Galle suggest:

> Something happens when you move from a thought to a thing. You understand the challenge and opportunity more deeply through making which leads to richer solutions. Making triggers a new form of thinking . . . making is essential to understanding.
>
> 2016: 149

This process induces what Myriam Gervais calls "co-production," where participants generate ideas and collaborate around a shared strategy, building and deepening connections to urban problems (2018: 4). This reinforces the importance, not only of the right to occupy cities and communities, but also of the right to "decide how it is developed, managed and used" (Petcou et al. 2015: 250). The perspectives of the participants reveal possible interventions through the building of forms that signify aspects of placemaking and simultaneously transcend the social barriers that are often part of the bias in traditional (non-participatory) urban design processes. The methodology is therefore underpinned by a commitment to "designing with," rather than the expert-centric approach of "designing for."

DEEPER DIVE

For ideas about co-design activities see: *The Design Thinking Toolbox*, by Michael Lewrick, Patrick Link & Larry Leifer, 2020.

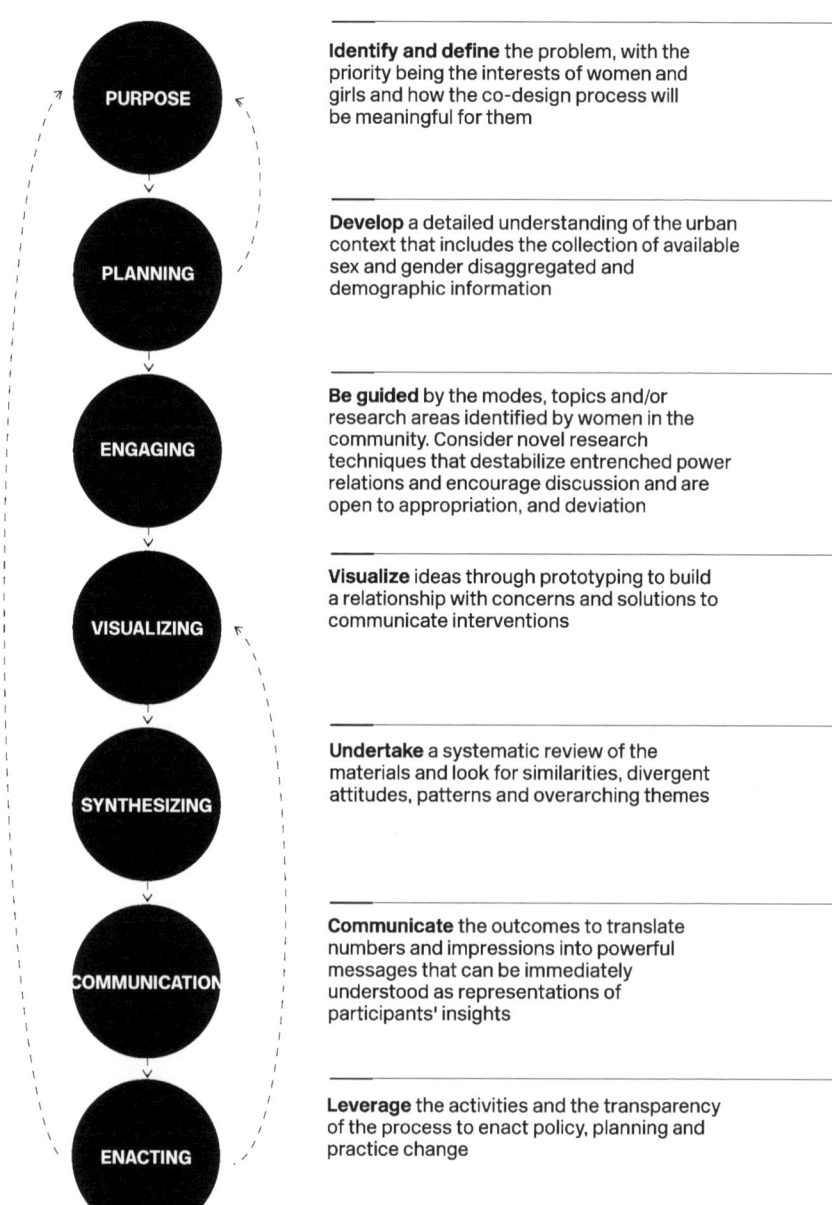

FIGURE 11.2 Feminist participatory co-design process. Diagram Isabella Webb, Monash University XYX Lab 2022.

- Understand how the gender-based systemic biases in the urban context will be addressed
- Questioning assumptions in everyday policy, planning and design is important.
  As is considering how feminist theory will be practically used to reconsider the urban contexts being re-imagined

---

- Plan the outreach to the women experts the reciprocal arrangements and sensitivities
- Design the engagement process with representatives from stakeholder organizations
- Question and communicate the aims of the research and reciprocal commitment between the convener and the women and girls
- Consider obstacles to participation and special needs

- Provide agency to women in all engagements
- Use design tools that are visually engaging and adapted /bespoke to the community group
- Consider the methods for that engagement with communities operate within power dynamics and require facilitators to develop strategies for conducting participatory co-design respectfully

---

- Test through two- and three-dimensional play-based prompts
- Ensure workshops are generative, gender-sensitive processes
- Use hands-on design tools that allow for diverse collaboration
- Encourage discovery; disagreement and novel insight

- The synthesis should aim to translate the outcomes of the participants' perspectives and insights
- Refining the perspectives for recommendations may also be part of this work
- Ensure that the participants receive the synthesis for review – and prior to release – to ensure they feel properly represented

---

- Share information and connect ideas to data visualization to prioritize women's issues
- Outcomes should be shared with all participants in the participatory co-design process to demonstrate their contribution to the process

---

- Advocate for the privatization of women's concerns
- Findings can be used to solicit governments to make changes
- Directly integrate recommendations into policy and planning
- Monitor and measure the impact of interventions
- Develop case studies for best practice
- Share knowledge widely

The women-centered approach to participatory co-design uses applied feminist methodologies to acknowledge women's specific rights and needs in cities. Even the most feminist, gender-aware design process can result in an unintended outcome where new societal inequalities arise. Nonetheless, participatory co-design set within a feminist framework is a solid and efficacious mode from which to conceive, develop and enact public placemaking. This subverts traditional modes where designers may undertake research *for* women, rather than *with* women. Participatory co-design actively develops new modes that can "encourage the sharing of power and a redistribution of research roles" (Gervais et al. 2018: 2). It is a hands-on method that, when used within groups, can "communicate those personal and hard-to-articulate ideas" that can surface within collaborative contexts and "overcome traditional power dynamics and mediate conflict" (Edwards et al. 2017: 165).

Run the World

Feminist participatory co-design processes are defined by bringing women and girls into the design process as the subject matter experts, where their significant (and signified) positionality—that is, their subjective values, views, and occupation of space—becomes the center of the process and rebalances perceived hierarchies between practitioners, researchers and the women themselves. Feminist planners and designers support this. Researchers and activists Sara Ortiz Escalante and Bianca Gutiérrez Valdivia discuss how the intention to empower women must be a "process of affirmation" and one that works to acknowledge "the power that individuals and groups excluded from political action already have" rather than simply handing power over to someone (2015: 117). They state that women must be considered as the "experts about the places where they live" (2015: 116).

Gervais and colleagues suggest that women and girls should be understood as co-producers in the participatory co-design process, as they "play a significant role not only in the collection of information but also in the analysis and the dissemination of the conclusions generated" (2018: 4). Obstacles are often overlooked in generalized participatory design. When working with women and girls who may be marginalized, this often includes neglecting such factors as "language, cultural influences, power dynamics, and personality traits" (Thinyane et al. 2020: 42). A gender-sensitive approach to co-design requires intersectional differentials and recognition that women and girls are not a homogenous group, and therefore, each phase of the participatory process must prompt discussion about the impact of age, disability, ethnicity, geographic location, income, indigeneity, migratory status, race, religion and sexuality.

WOMEN'S STORIES

I wish there were more principles of co-design, led by women, embedded into the council's community consultation.

I wish community consultation would be swapped with community co-design for all new urban planning.

This co-design workshop is really helpful in including everyone's idea about what a safe space means for women, especially a woman of color like myself. Really privileged to be invited to this workshop.

There are caveats with the use and implementation of participatory co-design—specifically, the risk of it being "loosely defined" (Blomkamp 2018: 731). Beyond key words, bubble diagrams and a frenzy of illegible Post-it notes, a women-centered approach to participatory co-design must activate solutions informed by women's studies, sex- and gender-disaggregated data, and the expertise of women who will, hopefully, benefit from a project that is backed up by feminist designers and researchers and in collaboration with attuned stakeholders. The potential for participatory co-design to effect change is directly related to institutional frameworks—many of which are laid out in previous chapters of this book.

In undertaking feminist participatory co-design, the collective empowerment of women and girls means that their stories can be surfaced and amplified, and the transformation of the design process—and the professionals who previously perceived themselves as the experts—can allow for new co-produced concepts, procedures and outcomes. The process, therefore, requires that traditional design methods (even traditional co-design methods) be interrogated and reshaped. Modification of practices will be required, as the feminist method is the foundational guide for the design activities, as is the respect for women participants throughout the process (Rothschild 1995).

The pre-work of co-design is significant and not to be underestimated. Working to understand the participants, their backgrounds, roles and perceived expertise, as well as what kinds of biases may be brought into the co-design space, can inform processes and practices that reduce the risk of disconnection while allowing for a tolerance for friction and irritation. The face-to-face engagement with stakeholders is usually undertaken in a workshop format and "conducted with groups of girls and women to understand a problem that affects them and to propose solutions from which they can benefit, or that will have direct impact on their lives" (Gervais 2018: 2). Through communal making and modeling, workshop participants contribute to our generative design research. Sanders positions the importance of this research approach: "It is about an emerging visual language that people, all people, can use to express and interpret those ideas and feelings that are often so difficult to express in words" (Sanders 2002: 6). This process gives project stakeholders permission to prototype ideas via a range of thoughtfully curated objects that harness a collective and expanding set of ideas (Sanders 2002: 7).

In this environment, "unfixed ideas" can be safely presented, but equally safely challenged. The work often reveals a range of propensities in urban space, but the impact is often about incremental change beyond the interactions, where the "extended impact may be greater – although less traceable and harder to substantiate" as the methods "directly and indirectly play a role in the creation of new institutions as well as the reconfiguration of existing ones" (Huybrechts et al. 2017: 157). Alternative imaginings of the city often emerge in these gender audits in a performative and speculative way. Provisional "take-overs" of city spaces provide a range, from a girls-only bike ride to encouraging a female cyclist culture, to renaming/reclaiming streets and statues with women's names and female champions, to a performative reclamation of a public space. These interventions highlight the current lack of visibility of women in the design and occupation of public space and suggest alternative visions of the city.

A Better Standard than This[1]

This book has shown how feminists continue to intervene across government policy, urban design planning and community activism to encourage the uptake of a women-centered approach to cities and with the aim to accelerate equity in the built environment. For some, it may seem passé to engage a feminist-focused approach, as many will be persuaded that these concerns are somehow resolved in the rhetoric of "equality" (Gamble 2006: 38). And yet, insisting on an appraisal of women's experiences of urban space and the necessity to create cities that prioritize the diverse needs of women and girls is more important than ever.

Assessing the effects of feminist frameworks on women's experiences and equity in cities and communities takes time and is an area that is under-researched. The short-, medium- and long-term impact must be measured through qualitative and quantitative modes with a focus on benefits to women's and girls' quality of life and a fairer distribution of community resources in their cities and communities. It is likely that this measure is dynamic and able to respond to the changing needs of women and girls across their life course. The financial cost of implementing the frameworks as well as the aligned engagement and training need to be appraised in relation to the overwhelming negative impacts on women's health, wellbeing and economic position which is overlooked when cities continue to engage with neutral policy and practice.

To challenge women's exclusion in cities, practitioners need to consider how and why women experience cities differently and how to overcome "cultural and attitudinal bias toward women" (Greed 2006, 276). Through clear and considered understanding of how the built environment contributes to women's oppression—and by engaging with frameworks that are sensitive to women's needs—policymakers, planners and designers will positively impact women's experiences in public life. The integration of participatory feminist co-design can ensure that practitioners understand why women feel at risk in cities, where barriers exist, and what women believe will enable their participation. Centering women to the process will transform design approaches to address inequity in cities.

FIGURE 11.3 Feminist participatory co-design workshop in action. Monash University XYX Lab.

NOTES

Preface

1 Related workshops and engagements include: Gender-Sensitive Training for Inclusive Placemaking (2021 to present), Tram Lab (November 20, 2019), Learning from SHEcity (October 15, 2018), SHEcity (July 25, 2018), Safer Cities (March 9, 2018), Crowd Mapping a New Urban Imaginary (March 21, 2018) and Free to Be: Design Thinking (March 20, 2017). Refer XYX Lab website for partners, funders and collaborators: https://www.monash.edu/mada/research/labs/xyx

Chapter 1

1 This definition is based on three key texts and discussions for defining feminism. These include Denise Thompson (1994), "Defining Feminism," *Australian Feminist Studies*, 9 (20): 171–192; Catharine MacKinnon (1989), *Toward a Feminist Theory of the State*, Harvard University Press, Cambridge, MA; and Jess Megarry (2020), *The Limitations of Social Media Feminism: No Space of our Own*, Palgrave Macmillan, Cham.

2 In Australia, for example, during 2018–19, 97% of sexual assault offenders were men (Australian Institute of Health and Welfare 2020: 1) and likely even higher, given that underreporting is estimated to be around 80%.

3 Thank you to XYX Lab researcher Dr. Tegan Larin for her feedback and insight on this point.

Chapter 2

1 For example, in Egypt, 99% of women have experienced sexual harassment, and in Brazil, 86% of women have been subjected to

sexual harassment (Senthilingam 2017). In the United States, 77% of women encounter verbal sexual harassment, and 51% of women reported unwelcome sexual touching. 66% of women are harassed in the public space (Chira 2018). In 2016, women experienced violence and/or harassment in public places: India 79%, Thailand 86% and the UK 75% (UNU-IIGH 2019: 1).

2 In most places there is only a slight peak in sexist street harassment in the evening or late night (Plan International 2018: 17).

3 Notably, anti-sexist street harassment campaigns are in New York, Sydney, Melbourne, London and Delhi.

Chapter 3

1 In his concurring opinion in the 1964 *Jacobellis v. Ohio* case, Supreme Court Justice Potter Stewart delivered what has become the most well-known line related to the detection of "hard-core" pornography. He stated, "I shall not today attempt further to define the kinds of material I understand to be embraced within that shorthand description; and perhaps I could never succeed in intelligibly doing so. But I know it when I see it."

2 https://www.theguardian.com/fashion/2017/mar/06/saint-laurent-ad-campaign-porno-chic-france, accessed September 10, 2022.

3 Ibid.

4 https://www.galalaw.com/Publication/GazetteArticle?id=1213&utm_source=Mondaq&utm_medium=syndication&utm_campaign=LinkedIn-integration, accessed September 10, 2022.

5 https://wfanet.org/knowledge/item/2019/10/11/Buenos-Aires-Declaration-for-Progressive-Advertising, accessed September 10, 2022.

6 https://www.ana.net/content/show/id/45043

7 https://wfanet.org/knowledge/item/2019/10/11/WFA-and-Latin-American-associations-commit-to-action-on-harmful-ad-stereotypes, accessed September 10, 2022.

Chapter 4

1 UN Women (2021: 14). "Household surveys are the main data source for around one-third of all SDG indicators. In particular, for 80 of the 232 SDG indicators, household surveys are considered a primary/

common source. Approximately 70 percent (55 of 80) of the SDG indicators generated through household surveys have both established standards and questionnaires to measure the indicators. Around 70 percent of the indicators calculated from household survey data have a requirement for at least one level of disaggregation."

Chapter 5

1   This title is borrowed from a few sources: Clara Greed (2005) writes about the "urban question" of who gets "what, where, how and why" in *Making the Divided City Whole: Mainstreaming Gender into Planning in the United Kingdom* and cites Steven Pinch's book, *Cities and Services: The Geography of Collective Consumption* (1985). Aruna Rao and David Kelleher (2005) ask, "Who gets what, who does what, and who decides?" in *Is There Life after Gender Mainstreaming?*
2   Teresa Rees (2005: 570) notes that "The origin of gender mainstreaming as a concept is contested: some commentators identify development projects in the third world as the origin, but the term appears to have come into common usage following the United Nations World Conference on Women at Beijing in 1995."
3   Sweden has a feminist government and is "committed to building a society in which girls and boys, women and men have the same power to shape society and their own lives and live their lives to their full potential". https://www.government.se/information-material/2019/03/a-feminist-government/, accessed May 27, 2022.

Chapter 6

1   Thank you to Dr. Tegan Larin for her input and notes on this tension.
2   I would like to acknowledge PhD Candidate in the XYX Lab, Enira Arvada, whose research into designing for public breastfeeding is yet to be published but will be an important contribution to this area of women's equity.

Chapter 9

1   The term Crime Prevention Through Environmental Design was coined by C. Ray Jeffery in 1971.

2 The social dimension of community safety has been driven by Saville et al. (1997) second generation CPTED and borrows from Cozens et al. (2015) discussion.

Chapter 11

1 Excerpt from the closing statement of former Australian Prime Minister Julia Gillard's "Misogyny Speech" delivered October 9, 2012.

REFERENCES

Chapter One

Australian Institute of Health and Welfare (2020), Sexual assault in Australia. Cat. no. FDV 5. Canberra: AIHW. https://www.aihw.gov.au/getmedia/0375553f-0395-46cc-9574-d54c74fa601a/aihw-fdv-5.pdf.aspx?inline=true#:~:text=The%20rate%20was%20much%20higher,(based%20on%20ABS%202020a), accessed October 10, 2020.

Beebeejaun, Yasminah (2017), "Gender, Urban Space, and the Right to Everyday Life", *Journal of Urban Affairs*, 39(3): 323–334.

Benbrahim, Dina (2021), "Co-designing Meaningful Dialogues on Sexual Harassment", *Temes de Disseny* 37: 106–131.

Crenshaw, Kimberlé (1995), *Critical Race Theory: The Key Writings That Formed the Movement*, New York: New Press.

Criado Perez, Caroline (2019), *Invisible Women: Exposing Data Bias in a World Designed for Men*. UK: Penguin Random House.

Daneshpour, Manijeh (2022), *Gender, Power, and Global Social Justice: The Healing Power of Psychotherapy*. New York: Routledge.

Dawson, Myrna (2021), "'Home Is the Most Dangerous Place For Women,' but Private and Public Violence Are Connected", *The Conversation*, November 25, https://theconversation.com/home-is-the-most-dangerous-place-for-women-but-private-and-public-violence-are-connected-171348, accessed August 19, 2022.

Devlin, Marcia (2021), "Time to Gender Parity Has Blown Out to 135 Years. Here's What Women Can Do to Close the Gap", *The Conversation*, June 2, 2021, https://theconversation.com/time-to-gender-parity-has-blown-out-to-135-years-heres-what-women-can-do-to-close-the-gap-160253, accessed September 5, 2022.

Ditum, Sarah (2015), "The Problem With Men Participating in Feminism? There Is No Risk—But Plenty of Glory", *The New Statesman*, October 25, https://xyonline.net/sites/xyonline.net/files/2020-05/Ditum%2C%20The%20problem%20with%20men%20participating%20in%20feminism%20Oct%2026%202015.pdf, accessed August 23, 2022.

Dobbin, Frank & Alexandra Kalev (2016), "Why Diversity Programs Fail", *Harvard Business Review*, https://hbr.org/2016/07/why-diversity-programs-fail, accessed June 10, 2022.

Dworkin, Andrea (1983), *Right-wing women*, New York: Perigee Books.

Epstein, Dora (1997), "Abject Terror: A Story of Fear, Sex, and Architecture", in N. Ellin, (Ed.), *Architecture of Fear*, 132–142, New York: Princeton Architectural Press.

Fenster, Tovi (2005), "The Right to the Gendered City: Different Formations of Belonging in Everyday Life", *Journal of Gender Studies*, 14(3): 217–231.

Flood, Michael (2018), "Is Gender Equality Good for Men?", August 22, 2020, https://xyonline.net/content/gender-equality-good-men, accessed September 10, 2022.

Flood, Michael (2019), "Gender Equality: Engaging Men in Change", *The Lancet* (British Edition), 393(10189): 2386–2387.

Gamble, Sarah (2006), *The Routledge Companion to Feminism and Postfeminism*, London: Routledge.

Gill, Rosalind (2016), "Post-postfeminism? New Feminist Visibilities in Postfeminist Times", *Feminist Media Studies*, 16(4): 610–630.

Greed, Clara (1994), *Women and Planning: Creating Gendered Realities*, London; New York: Routledge.

Greed, Clara (2005), "Overcoming the Factors Inhibiting the Mainstreaming of Gender into Spatial Planning Policy in the United Kingdom", *Urban Studies*, 42(4): 719–749.

Greed, Clara (2006), "Making the Divided City Whole: Mainstreaming Gender into Planning in The United Kingdom", *Tijdschrift Voor Economische En Sociale Geografie*, 97(3): 267–280.

Grosser, Kate & Meagan Tyler (2022), "Sexual Harassment, Sexual Violence and CSR: Radical Feminist Theory and a Human Rights Perspective", *Journal of Business Ethics*, 177 (2): 217–232.

Heidaripour, Maryam & Laura Forlano (2018), "Formgiving to Feminist Futures as Design Activism", Conference Paper, Design Research Society, June 2018, https://www.researchgate.net/publication/331492222_Formgiving_to_Feminist_Futures_as_Design_Activism, accessed October 14, 2022.

Kalms, Nicole (2017), *Hypersexual City: The Provocation of Soft-Core Urbanism*, London: Taylor and Francis.

Kelly, Liz (1987), "The Continuum of Sexual Violence", in J. Hanmer & Mary Maynard (eds), *Women, Violence and Social Control* (Explorations in Sociology, 23), 46–60, London: Macmillan Press.

Kolysh, Simone (2021), *Everyday Violence: The Public Harassment of Women and LGBTQ People*, New Brunswick: Rutgers University Press.

Levy, Neil (2019), "Taking Responsibility for Responsibility", *Public Health Ethics*, 12(2): 103–113.

Lomazzi, Vera & Isabella Crespi (2019), "Conclusions", in *Gender Mainstreaming and Gender Equality in Europe: Policies, Culture and Public Opinion* (1st edn), 145–152), Bristol University Press.

Mackay, Finn (2015), *Radical Feminism: Feminist Activism in Movement*, London: Palgrave Macmillan.

MacKinnon, Catharine A. (1989), *Toward a Feminist Theory of the State*, Cambridge, MA: Harvard University Press.

MacKinnon, Catharine A. (1991), "From Practice to Theory, or What Is a White Woman Anyway?", *Yale Journal of Law and Feminism* 4, no. 1: 13–22.

Markham, Annette (2012), "Fabrication as Ethical Practice", *Information, Communication & Society*, 15(3): 334–353.

Matthewson, Gill & Nicole Kalms (2021), "Unwanted Sexual Behaviour and Public Transport: The Imperative for Gender-Sensitive Co-design", in Selby Coxon and Robbie Natter (eds), *Advancing a Design Approach to Enriching Public Mobility*, 53–67, Intelligent Systems Reference Library, Cham: Springer International Publishing.

Megarry, Jessica (2020), *The Limitations of Social Media Feminism (Social and Cultural Studies of Robots and AI)*. Cham: Springer International Publishing AG.

Moser, Caroline & Annalise Moser (2005), "Gender Mainstreaming Since Beijing: A Review of Success and Limitations in International Institutions", *Gender and Development*, 13(2): 11–22.

Ortiz Escalante, Sara & Blanca Gutiérrez Valdivia (2015), "Planning from Below: Using Feminist Participatory Methods to Increase Women's Participation in Urban Planning", *Gender and Development*, 23(1): 113–126.

Plan International (2019), "Unsafe on the Streets: Girls' and Young Women's Experience of Group Harassment", https://www.plan.org.au/wp-content/uploads/2020/08/unsafe-on-the-streets-girls-and-young-womens-experiences-of-group-harassment-2019.pdf, accessed May 18, 2022.

Rendell, Jane, Iain Borden, & Barbara Penner (2000), *Gender Space Architecture: An Interdisciplinary Introduction*. Architext Series. London; New York: E & FN Spon.

Ritchie, Hannah & Max Roser (2018), "Urbanization", Published online at OurWorldInData.org. Retrieved from: https://ourworldindata.org/urbanization

Sandberg, Linda & Malin Rönnblom (2016), "Imagining the Ideal City, Planning the Gender-equal City in Umeå, Sweden", *Gender, Place and Culture: A Journal of Feminist Geography*, 23(12): 1750–1762.

Sandercock, Leonie & Ann Forsyth (1992), "A Gender Agenda: New Directions for Planning Theory", *Journal of the American Planning Association*, 58:1, 49–59.

Scala, Francesca & Stephanie Paterson (2018), "Stories from the Front Lines: Making Sense of Gender Mainstreaming in Canada", *Politics & Gender*, 14(2): 208–234.

Sheffield, Carole J. (2020), "Sexual Terrorism in the Twenty-first Century", in Jennifer M. Brown & Sandra L. Walklate (eds), *Book on Sexual Violence*, 190–211, London: Taylor & Francis Group, 2011. Accessed May 16, 2022. ProQuest Ebook Central.

Squires, Judith (2005), "Is Mainstreaming Transformative? Theorizing Mainstreaming in the Context of Diversity and Deliberation", *Social Politics*, 12(3): 366–388.

Stock, Kathleen (2022), "The Importance of Referring to Human Sex in Language", *Law and Contemporary Problems*, 85(1): 25.

Struyf, Pia (2020), "Fear in the Dark: The Potential Impact of Reduced Street Lighting on Crime and Fear of Crime", in Vania Ceccato & Mahesh K. Nalla (eds), "Crime and Fear in Public Places: An Introduction to the Special Issue", *International Journal of Comparative and Applied Criminal Justice*, 44(4): 261–264.

Sweet, Elizabeth L. & Sara Ortiz Escalante (2010), "Planning Responds to Gender Violence: Evidence from Spain, Mexico and the United States", *Urban Studies*, 47(10): 2129–2147.

Thompson, Denise (1994), "Defining Feminism, *Australian Feminist Studies*, 9(20): 171–192.

Tyler, Meagan & Maddy Coy (2021), "Pornographication and Heterosexualisation in Public Space", in J. Berry, T. Moore, N. Kalms, & G. Bawden (eds), *Contentious Cities: Design and the Gendered Production of Space*, 49–59, Oxon: Taylor & Francis Group.

Tyler, Meagan (2021), Can Feminism be Saved from Identity Politics?", Monday 8 March. https://www.abc.net.au/religion/can-feminism-be-saved-from-identity-politics/11646084, accessed May 18, 2022.

UCLA (2011), "How Many People are Lesbian, Gay, Bisexual, and Transgender?", https://williamsinstitute.law.ucla.edu/publications/how-many-people-lgbt/, accessed May 16, 2022.

United Nations (2015), "Transforming Our World: The 2030 Agenda for Sustainable Development", https://sdgs.un.org/publications/transforming-our-world-2030-agenda-sustainable-development-17981, accessed September 10, 2022.

United Nations (2017), "New Urban Agenda from the UN", https://unhabitat.org/sites/default/files/2019/05/nua-english.pdf, accessed September 10, 2022.

United Nations (2022), "Progress on the Sustainable Development Goals: The Gender Snapshot 2022", https://www.unwomen.org/en/digital-library/publications/2022/09/progress-on-the-sustainable-development-goals-the-gender-snapshot-2022, accessed October 10, 2022.

UNODOC (2018), "Global Study of Homicide: Gender-related Killing of Women and Girls", United Nations Office on Drugs and Crime, https://www.unodc.org/documents/data-and-analysis/GSH2018/GSH18_Gender-related_killing_of_women_and_girls.pdf, accessed October 15, 2022.

Valentine, Gill (1989), "The Geography of Women's Fear", *Area* 21(4): 385–390.

Valentine, Gill (2007), "Theorizing and Researching Intersectionality: A Challenge for Feminist Geography", *The Professional Geographer*, 59(1): 10–21.

Vera–Gray, Fiona (2018), *The Right Amount of Panic: How Women Trade Freedom for Safety*, Bristol: Policy Press.

Verloo, Meike (2005), "Displacement and Empowerment: Reflections on the Concept and Practice of the Council of Europe Approach to Gender Mainstreaming and Gender Equality", *Social Politics*, 12(3): 344–365.

Weisman, Leslie Kanes (1981), "Women's Environmental Rights: A Manifesto", *Heresies: A Feminist Publication on Art and Politics*, 3(3).

World Bank (2020), *Book for Gender Inclusive Urban Planning Design*. https://www.worldbank.org/en/topic/urbandevelopment/publication/book-for-gender-inclusive-urban-planning-and-design

WHO (2018), *Global Fact Sheet Violence Against Women Prevalence Estimates*. https://www.who.int/publications/i/item/WHO-SRH-21.6, accessed August 20, 2022.

Yon, Alicia & SriPallavi Nadimpalli (2017), Cities for Whom? Re-examining Identity, to Reclaim the Right to the City for Women, *Australian Planner*, 54(1): 33–40.

Zebracki, Martin (2014), "Sex in the City: Gender Mainstreaming Urban Governance in Europe. The Case of Sweden and Italy", Fennia, 192(1): 54–64.

Chapter Two

Benbrahim, Dina (2021), "Co-designing Meaningful Dialogues on Sexual Harassment", *Temes de Disseny* 37: 106–131.

Carlton, Alexandra (2018), "This does nothing to address Australia's epidemic of coercion, control and violence against women", News.com.au. July 10, https://www.news.com.au/lifestyle/real-life/news-life/this-does-nothing-to-address-australias-epidemic-of-coercion-control-and-violence-against-women/news-story/69b7b6d8274dde7655194d50b119511a, accessed August 24, 2022.

Chira, Susan (2018), "Numbers Hint at Why #MeToo Took Off: The Sheer Number Who Can Say Me Too", *The New York Times*, February 21, https://www.nytimes.com/2018/02/21/upshot/pervasive-sexual-harassment-why-me-too-took-off-poll.html, accessed August 24, 2022.

Chrisafis, Angelique (2018), "France plans on-the-spot fines for sexual harassment in public", *The Guardian*, March 21, https://www.theguardian.com/world/2018/mar/21/france-plans-on-the-spot-fines-for-sexual-harassment-in-public, accessed September 2, 2022.

Coy, Maddy & Meagan Tyler (2021), "Pornographication and Heterosexualization in Public Spaces", in Jess Berry, Timothy Moore, Kalms Nicole, & Gene Bawden (eds), *Contentious Cities: Design and the Gendered Production of Space*, London: Taylor and Francis.

Crenshaw, Kimberlé (1991), "Mapping the Margins: Intersectionality, Identity Politics, and Violence Against Women of Color", *Stanford Law Review*, 43(6): 1241–1299.

di Leonardo, Michaela (1981), "The Political Economy of Street Harassment", *Aegis*, 51–57.

El Nahry, Fatma (2012), "She's not Asking for It: Street Harassment and Women in Public Spaces", *Gender Across Borders: A Global Voice for Gender Justice*, in Christina Lindkvist and Tanja Joelsson (eds) (2019), *Integrating gender into transport planning: from one to many tracks*, Cham: Palgrave Maacmillan.

Epstein, Debbie (1997), "Keeping Them in Their Place: Hetero/Sexist Harassment, Gender and the Enforcement of Heterosexuality", in A. Thomas & C. Kitzinger (eds), *Sexual Harassment: Contemporary Feminist Perspectives*, Buckingham: Open University Press.

Fileborn, Bianca & Fiona Vera-Gray (2017), "'I want to Be Able to Walk the Street Without Fear': Transforming Justice for Street Harassment", *Feminist Legal Studies*, 25, 203–227.

Fileborn, Bianca (2017a), "Justice 2.0: 'Street Harassment Victims' Use of Social Media and Online Activism as Sites of Informal Justice", *British Journal of Criminology*, 57(6): 1482–1501.

Fileborn, Bianca (2017b), "Bystander Intervention from the Victims' Perspective: Experiences, Impacts and Justice Needs of Street Harassment Victims", *Journal of Gender-Based Violence*, 1(2): 187–204.

Fileborn, Bianca (2022), "Mapping Activist Responses and Policy Advocacy for Street Harassment: Current Practice and Future Directions", *European journal on criminal policy and research*, 28(1), 97–116.

Goel, Rahul, Oyinlola Oyebode, & Louise Foley, et al. (2022), "Gender Differences in Active Travel in Major Cities Across the World", *Transportation*, https://doi.org/10.1007/s11116-021-10259-4

Gekoski, Anna., Jacqueline M. Gray, Joanna R. Adler, & Miranda A.H. Horvath (2017), "The Prevalence and Nature of Sexual Harassment and Assault against Women and Girls on Public Transport: An International Review", *Journal of Criminological Research, Policy and Practice*, 3(1): 3–16.

Gekoski, Anna., Jacqueline M. Gray, Miranda A.H. Horvath, Sarah Edwards, Aliye Emirali, & Joanna R. Adler, (2015), *What Works in Reducing Sexual Harassment and Sexual Offences on Public Transport Nationally and Internationally: A Rapid Evidence Assessment*. London: British Transport Police and Department for Transport, http://eprints.mdx.ac.uk/15219

Goffman, Erving (1963), *Behavior in Public Places: Notes on the Social Organization of Gatherings*, New York: Free Press.

Gordon, Margaret T. & Stephanie Riger (1989), *The Female Fear*, New York: Free Press.

Gracia, Enrique, Fernando García, & Marisol Lila (2011), "Police Attitudes Toward Policing Partner Violence Against Women: Do They Correspond to Different Psychosocial Profiles?", *Journal of Interpersonal Violence*, 26(1): 189–207.

Green, Eileen & Carrie Singleton (2006), "Risky Bodies at Leisure: Young Women Negotiating Space and Place", *Sociology* 40 (5): 853–871.

Grosser, Kate & Meagan Tyler (2021), "Sexual Harassment, Sexual Violence and CSR: Radical Feminist Theory and a Human Rights Perspective", *Journal of Business Ethics*, 177(2): 217–32.

Herzog, Sergio (2007), "Public Perceptions of Sexual Harassment: An Empirical Analysis in Israel from Consensus and Feminist Theoretical Perspectives", *Sex Roles*, 57: 579–592.

Hubbard, Phil (2008), "Here, There, Everywhere: The Ubiquitous Geographies of Heteronormativity", *Geography Compass*, 2(3): 640–658.

Jagori & UN Women (2011), *Safe Cities Free of Violence Against Women and Girls Initiative: Report of The Baseline Survey Delhi 2010*, New Delhi, India: Jagori.

Kalms, Nicole (2017), *Hypersexual City: The Provocation of Soft-Core Urbanism*, London: Taylor and Francis.

Kalms, Nicole 2018, "Urban Exposure: Feminist Crowd-mapping and the New Urban Imaginary", in Christoph Lindner & Miriam Meissner, *The Routledge Companion to Urban Imaginaries*, Routledge International Handbooks, London: Taylor and Francis.

Kalms, Nicole (2019), "More Lighting Alone Does not Create Safer Cities. Look at What Research with Young Women Tells", May 28, 2019, *The Conversation*, https://theconversation.com/more-lighting-alone-does-not-create-safer-cities-look-at-what-research-with-young-women-tells-us-113359, accessed September 10, 2022.

Kash, Gwen (2019), "Planners' Visions of Transit Sexual Assault: The Problem of Deproblematizing Beliefs", *6th International Conference on Women's Issues in Transportation*, September 10–13, Los Angeles: Transport Research Board.

Kearl, Holly (2010), *Stop Street Harassment: Making Public Places Safe and Welcoming for Women*, Santa Barbar: Praeger.

Kelly, Liz (1988), *Surviving Sexual Violence*, Cambridge, UK: Polity Press.

Kelly Liz & Jill Radford (1990) "'Nothing really happened': The invalidation of women's experiences of sexual violence", *Critical Social Policy*, 10(30): 39–53.

Kern, Leslie (2020), *Feminist City*, Toronto: Verso.

Kissling, Elizabeth Arveda (1991), "Street Harassment: The Language of Sexual Terrorism", *Discourse & Society*, 2(4): 451–460.

Kissling, Elizabeth Arveda & Cheris Kramarae (1991), "Stranger Compliments: The Interpretation of Street Remarks", *Women's Studies in Communication*, 14(1): 75–93.

Kolysh, Simone (2021), *Everyday Violence: The Public Harassment of Women and LGBTQ People*, New Brunswick: Rutgers University Press.

Larkin, June (1997), "Sexual Terrorism on the Street: The Moulding of Young Women into Subordination", in A. M. Thomas & C. Kitzinger (eds), *Sexual Harassment: Contemporary Feminist Perspectives*, Buckingham: Open University Press.

Lenton, Rhona, Michael Smith, John Fox, & Norman Morra (1999), "Sexual Harassment in Public Places: Experiences of Canadian Women", *Canadian Journal of Anthropology*, 36: 517–40.

Lewis, Ruth, Elizabeth Sharp, Jenni Remnant, & Rhiannon Redpath, (2015), "'Safe Spaces': Experiences of Feminist Women-Only Space", *Sociological Research Online*, 20(4): 1–14.

Macmillan, Ross, Nierobisz, Annette, & Welsh, Sandy (2000), "Experiencing the Streets: Harassment and Perceptions of Safety Among Women", *Journal of Research in Crime and Delinquency*, 37: 306–22.

Madan, Manish & Mahesh K. Nalla (2016), "Sexual Harassment in Public Spaces", *International Criminal Justice Review* 26 (2): 80–97.

Mackay, Finn (2015), *Radical Feminism: Feminist Activism in Movement*, New York: Palgrave Macmillan.

McAllister, Pam (1978), "Wolf Whistles and Warnings", *Heresies* 6.

Merchant, Gabriella (2019), "Many Women Don't Feel Safe Exercising in Public, but Is Bright Lighting The Solution?", November 11, 2019, ABC News Online https://www.abc.net.au/news/2019-11-10/the-emerging-science-behind-lighting-and-womens-safety/11680748?nw=0&r=HtmlFragment, accessed May 19, 2022.

Nast, H. J. (2002), "Queer Patriarchies, Queer Racisms, International", *Antipode*, 34 (5): 874–909.

Pain, Rachel (2001), "Gender, Race, Age and Fear in the City," *Urban Studies (Edinburgh, Scotland)*, 38(5/6), 899–913.

Phipps, Alison (2020), "Reckoning Up: Sexual Harassment and Violence in the Neoliberal University", *Gender and Education* 32, no. 2 (2020): 227–243.

Plan International (2018), "Unsafe in the City: The Everyday Experiences Of Girls and Young Women", https://www.plan.org.au/publications/unsafe-in-the-city-the-everyday-experiences-of-girls-and-young-women/, accessed September 5, 2022.

Plan International (2019), "Unsafe on the Streets: Girls and Young Women's Experience of Group Harassment", https://www.plan.org.au/wp-content/uploads/2020/08/unsafe-on-the-streets-girls-and-young-womens-experiences-of-group-harassment-2019.pdf, accessed 18 May 2022.

Respect Victoria (2022), "Progress on Preventing Family Violence and Violence Against Women in Victoria First Three-Yearly Report to Parliament", https://www.respectvictoria.vic.gov.au/our-publications, accessed April 11, 2023.

Scholten, Lindkvist & Tanja Joelsson (eds) (2019), *Integrating Gender into Transport Planning: From One to Many Tracks*, London: Palgrave MacMillan.

Senthilingam, Meera (2017), "Sexual Harassment: How it Stands Around the Globe", CNN Health, https://edition.cnn.com/2017/11/25/health/sexual-harassment-violence-abuse-global-levels/index.html, accessed September 2, 2002.

Sheffield, Carole J. (2020), "Sexual Terrorism in the Twenty-First Century," in *Gender Violence, 3rd Edition*. NYU Press, 190–211.

Stanko, Elizabeth (1985), *Intimate Intrusions*, London: Routledge Revivals.

Steinbugler, Amy C. (2005), "Visibility as Privilege and Danger: Heterosexual and Same-Sex Interracial Intimacy in the 21st Century", *Sexualities* 8(4): 425–443.

Tanner, Sophie, Nicole Kalms, Hayley Cull, Gill Matthewson, & Anthony Aisenberg (2020), "Disruption and Design: Crowdmapping Young Women's Experience in Cities", *IDS Bulletin*, 51(2): 113–128.

TramLab (2020a), Toolkit 1: *Gender-Sensitive Communication Campaigns – Improving the Safety of Women and Girls on Public Transport*, Melbourne: Victorian State Government, La Trobe University, Monash University XYX Lab, RMIT University.

Deborah, Tuerkhaimer (1997), "Street Harassment as Sexual Subordination: The Phenomenology of Gender-specific Harm", *Wisconsin Women's Law Journal*: 12, 167–206.

UN-HABITAT (2016), "Global Public Space Toolkit from Global Principles to Local Policies and Practice", https://unhabitat.org/sites/default/files/2019/05/global_public_space_toolkit.pdf, accessed August 22, 2022.

UNU-IIGH (2019), "Sexual Harassment: A Global Problem", http://collections.unu.edu/eserv/UNU:7881/n2019-11-22_PB_SH_A_Global_Problem.pdf, accessed August 15, 2022.

Valentine, Gill (1993), "(Hetero)Sexing Space: Lesbian Perceptions and Experiences of Everyday Spaces", in Joanne Sharp & Linda McDowell (eds), *Space, Gender, Knowledge: Feminist Readings*, London: Taylor and Francis.

Valentine, Gill (1996), "(Re)negotiating the 'heterosexual street'", in Nancy Duncan (ed.), *Bodyspace*, New York: Routledge, 146–55.

Vera-Gray, Fiona (2016), "Men's Stranger Intrusions: Rethinking Street Harassment", *Women's Studies International Forum* 58: 9–17.

Vera–Gray, Fiona (2018), *The Right Amount of Panic: How Women Trade Freedom for Safety*, Bristol: Policy Press.

Wånggren, L. (2016), "Our Stories Matter: Storytelling and Social Justice in the Hollaback! Movement", *Gender and Education*, 28(3): 401–415.

West, Robin (2013), "The Difference in Women's Hedonic Lives: A Phenomenological Critique of Feminist Legal Theory," *At the Boundaries of Law: Feminism and Legal Theory*, 115–134.

Wesselmann, Eric. D. & Kelly, Janice. R. (2010), "Cat-calls and Culpability: Investigating the Frequency and Functions of Stranger Harassment", *Sex Roles*, 63(7–8): 451–462.

Yon, Alicia & SriPallavi Nadimpalli (2017), "Cities for Whom? Re-examining Identity, to Reclaim the Right to the City for Women", *Australian Planner* 54 (1): 33–40.

Chapter Three

ASA Advertising Standards Authority (2022), "Tackling Harmful Racial and Ethnic Stereotyping in Advertising : Summary Report", https://www.asa.org.uk/static/dfe6dc19-6499-4b12-9449d07591d68dbb/333a4e95-362a-4ff7-90531a1e4fe9328d/ASA-RES-Summary-Report-Final.pdf, accessed June 4, 2022.

APA American Psychological Association (2007), "The Task Force on the Sexualisation of Girls Report", https://www.apa.org/pi/women/programs/girls/report-summary.pdf, accessed June 4, 2022.

Augé, Marc (1995), *Non-places: Introduction to an Anthropology of Supermodernity*. London: New York: Verso.

Bloor, Robin (2020), "How Many Ads Do We See a Day? The Battle for Our Attention", *Permission*, https://permission.io/blog/how-many-ads-per-day/

Coy, Maddy & Meagan Tyler (2021), "Pornographication and heterosexualisation in public spaces", in Jess Berry, Timothy Moore, Nicole Kalms & Gene Bawden (eds), *Contentious Cities*, London: Taylor and Francis.

Crabbe, Maree & Michael Flood (2021), "School-Based Education to Address Pornography's Influence on Young People: A Proposed Practice Framework", *American Journal of Sexuality Education*, 16(1): 1–37.

Dines, Gail (2010), *Pornland: How Porn Has Hijacked Our Sexuality*, North Melbourne, Victoria: Spinifex Press.

Dines, Gail, Bob Jenson & Ann Russo (1998), *Pornography: The Production and Consumption of Inequality*, New York: Routledge.

Drenten, Jenna, Lauren Gurrieri, & Meagan Tyler (2020), "Sexualized Labour in Digital Culture: Instagram Influencers, Porn Chic and the Monetization of Attention", *Gender, Work, and Organization*, 27(1): 41–66.

Fine, Cordelia (2011), *Delusions of Gender: The Real Science Behind Sex Differences*, New York: Icon Books.

Flood, Michael (2018), "Pornography, Men, and Boys", April 9, https://xyonline.net/content/pornography-men-and-boys, accessed September 10, 2022.

Gill, Rosalind & Akane Kanai (2019), "Affirmative Advertising and the Mediated Feeling Rules of Neoliberalism", in *Neoliberalism and the Media*, 1st edn, 131–146, London: Routledge.

Gill, Rosalind (2008), "Empowerment/Sexism: Figuring Female Sexual Agency in Contemporary Advertising", *Feminism and Psychology*, 18: 35–60.

Greed, Clara (1994), *Women and Planning: Creating Gendered Realities*, London, New York: Routledge.

Grau, Stacey Landreth & Yorgos C. Zotos (2016), "Gender Stereotypes in Advertising: A Review of Current Research", *International Journal of Advertising*, 35(5): 761–770.

Gurrieri, Lauren (2021), "Patriarchal Marketing and the Symbolic Annihilation of Women", *Journal of Marketing Management*, 37(3–4): 364–370.

Gurrieri, Lauren, Mandy McKenzie, & Megan Bugden, (2019), "Community Responses to Gender Portrayals in Advertising: A Research Paper" (Women's Health Issues Paper 15), Women's Health Victoria & RMIT University, https://apo.org.au/node/265496

Harrison, Robert L., Kevin D. Thomas, & Samantha N. N. Cross (2017), "Restricted Visions of Multiracial Identity in Advertising", *Journal of Advertising*, 46:4, 503–520.

Jackson, Sue & Tiina Vares (2015), "'Too Many Bad Role Models for Us Girls': Girls, Female Pop Celebrities and 'Sexualization'", *Sexualities*, 18(4): 480–498.

Jeffreys, Sheila (2015), *Beauty and Misogyny: Harmful Cultural Practices in the West*, London: Routledge.

Kalms, Nicole (2017), *Hypersexual City: The Provocation of Soft-Core Urbanism*, London: Taylor and Francis.

Kohrs, Kirsten & Rosalind Gill (2021), "Confident Appearing: Revisiting Gender Advertisements in Contemporary Culture," in Angouri, Jo & Judith Baxter (eds), *The Routledge Handbook of Language, Gender, and Sexuality*, 528–542.

Lamb, Sharon & Julie Koven (2019), "The Sexualization of Girls: An Update, Culture Reframed", https://www.culturereframed.org/wp-content/uploads/2019/01/CultureReframed-SexualizationOfGirls Report-2019.pdf, accessed September 10, 2022.

Lampen, Claire (2017), "Council of Paris Approves Citywide Ban of Sexist Outdoor Advertisements", *MIC*, March 30, https://www.mic.com/articles/172449/council-of-paris-approves-citywide-ban-of-sexist-outdoor-advertisements, accessed September 10, 2022.

McNair, Brian (2002), *Striptease Culture: Sex, Media and the Democratisation of Desire*, London: Routledge.

McQuire, Scott (2008), *The Media City: Media, Architecture and Urban Space*, Melbourne: Sage.

Papadopoulos, Linda (2010), "Sexualisation of Young People Review", London: UK Home Office, http://www.homeoffice.gov.uk/documents/Sexualisation-young-people.

PILPG, Public International Law & Policy Group (2015), "Legal Frameworks Regarding Sexism in Advertising: Comparison of National Systems", https://pilpnjcm.nl/wp-content/uploads/2015/12/150609-PILP-sexism-comparative-practice-memo.pdf, accessed September 10, 2022.

Rath, Julien (2017), "Paris Voted to Ban 'Sexist and Discriminatory' Outdoor Ads", *Business Insider*, March 29, https://www.businessinsider.com/paris-voted-to-ban-sexist-and-discriminatory-outdoor-ads-2017-3, accessed September 10, 2022.

Rich, Adrienne (1980), "Compulsory Heterosexuality and Lesbian Existence", *Signs: Journal of Women in Culture and Society*, 5(4): 631–660.

Ringrose, Jessica & Kaitlyn Regehr (2020), "Feminist Counterpublics and Public Feminisms: Advancing a Critique of Racialized Sexualization in London's Public Advertising", *Signs: Journal of Women in Culture and Society*, 46(1): 229–257.

Rosewarne, Lauren (2007a), *Sex in Public Women: Outdoor Advertising and Public Policy*, Newcastle: Cambridge Scholars Publishing.

Rosewarne, Lauren (2007b), "Pin-ups in Public Space", *Women's Studies International Forum* 30(4): 313–25.

Rossi, Leena–Maija (2007), "Outdoor Pornification: Advertising Heterosexuality in the Street", in Susanna Paasonen, Kaarina Nikunen & Laura Saarenmaa (eds), *Pornification Sex and Sexuality in Media Culture*, 127–139, Oxford: Berg.

Rudloff, Maj (2020), "Legitimizing Sexist Advertising: A Critical Focus on the Danish Consumer Ombudsman's Guidelines and Adjudications of Complaints of Gender Discrimination", *NORA: Nordic Journal of Women's Studies*, 28(4), 329–342.

Sørensen, Anette Dina (2005), "Pornophication and Gender Stereotyping in Mass Culture in Denmark", paper presentation at *Nordic Forum*, June 8, Tallinn: Estonia. https://www.norden.ee/images/heaolu/info/inimkaubandus/anette_dina_sorensen.pdf, accessed October 10, 2022.

Sorrow, April Reece (2012), "Magazine Trends Study Finds Increase in Advertisements Using Sex", University of Georgia, https://news.uga.edu/magazine-trends-study-finds-increase-in-advertisements-using-sex/, accessed September 10, 2022.

TramLab (2020a), Toolkit 1: *Gender-Sensitive Communication Campaigns – Improving the Safety of Women and Girls on Public Transport*, Melbourne: Victorian State Government, La Trobe University, Monash University XYX Lab, RMIT University.

Tyler, Meagan & Kaye, Quek (2016), "Conceptualizing Pornographication", *Pornographication, Media and Society*, 2(2): 1–14.

UN Women (2022), "The Levers of Change – Gender Equality Attitudes Study 2022", https://www.unstereotypealliance.org/en/resources/research-and-tools/the-levers-of-change-gender-equality-attitudes-study-2022, accessed September 10, 2022.

UNICEF (2021), "Promoting Diversity and Inclusion in Advertising: A UNICEF Playbook", https://www.unicef.org/media/108811/file/UNICEF-PLAYBOOK-Promoting-diversity-and-inclusion-in-advertising.pdf, accessed October 10, 2022.

Ward, L. Monique (2016), "Media and Sexualization: State of Empirical Research, 1995–2015", *The Journal of Sex Research*, 53(4–5): 560–577.

Women's Health Victoria (2019), "Addressing & Preventing Sexist Advertising: A Snapshot of Promising Practice", https://womenshealthvic.com.au/resources/WHV_Publications/Issues-Paper_2019.10.29_Addressing-and-preventing-sexist-advertising-a-snapshot-of-promising-practice_(Fulltext-PDF).pdf, accessed August 25, 2022.

Chapter Four

Bourdieu, Pierre (1977), *Outline of a Theory of Practice*, Cambridge, New York: Cambridge University Press.

Clements, Estelle (2020), "A Conceptual Framework for Digital Civics Pedagogy Informed by the Philosophy of Information", *Journal of Documentation*, 76(2): 571–585.

Criado Perez, Caroline (2019), *Invisible Women: Exposing Data Bias in a World Designed for Men*, UK: Penguin Random House.

D'Ignazio, Catherine & Lauren F. Klein, (2020), *Data Feminism*, Cambridge: MIT Press.

D'Ignazio, Catherine & Lauren F. Klein (2022), "Introduction: Why Data Science Needs Feminism", published March 2017, https://datafeminism.mitpress.mit.edu/pub/frfa9szd/release/6, accessed April 26, 2022.

Data2x (2017), "Gender Data: Sources, Gaps, and Measurement opportunities", https://www.data4sdgs.org/sites/default/files/2017-09/Gender%20Data%20-%20Data4SDGs%20Toolbox%20Module.pdf, accessed May 25, 2022.

Data2x (2022), "Where are the Gaps?", https://data2x.org/where-are-the-gaps/, accessed October 10, 2022.

Data2x and Open data Watch (2022), *Solutions to Close Gender Data Gaps*, United Nations Foundation, https://data2x.org/wp-content/uploads/2022/04/Solutions-to-Close-Gender-Data-Gaps-FINAL.pdf, accessed September 10, 2022.

Fileborn, Bianca (2014), "Online Activism and Street Harassment: Digital Justice or Shouting into the Ether?", *Griffith Journal of Law and Human Dignity*, 2(1): 32–51.

Gartner (n.d), "Glossary", *Big Data*, https://www.gartner.com/en/information-technology/glossary/big-data, accessed October 14, 2022.

Global Partnership for Sustainable Development (2017), "Without data equality. There is no gender equality", https://www.data4sdgs.org/blog/without-data-equality-there-no-gender-equality, accessed October 10, 2022.

Grove, Nicole Sunday (2015), "The Cartographic Ambiguities of HarassMap: Crowdmapping Security and Sexual Violence in Egypt", *Security Dialogue*, 46(4).

Guyan, Kevin (2022) *Queer data: Using gender sex and sexuality data for action*, London: Bloomsbury.

Hawken, Scott, Hoon Han, & Chris Pettit (2019), *Open Cities Open Data*, Singapore: Springer.

Hawken, Scott, Simone Z. Leao, Ori Gudes, Parisa Izadpanahi, Kalpana Viswanath, & Christopher Pettit (2019), "Safer Cities for Women:

Global and Local Innovations with Open Data and Civic Technology", in Scott Hawken, Christopher Pettit, & Hoon Han (eds), *Open Cities Open Data: Collaborative Cities in the Information Era*, Singapore: Springer Singapore Pte. Limited, 85–105.

Hummel, Patrik, Matthias Braun, Max Tretter, & Peter Dabrock (2021), Data sovereignty: A review, *Big Data & Society*, 8(1).

Kalms, Nicole (2018), "Digital Technology and the Safety of Women and Girls in Urban Spaces: Personal Safety Apps or Crowd-sourced Activism Tools?", in Helene Frichot, Catharina Gabrielsson, & Helen Runting, *Architecture and Feminisms: Ecologies, Economies, Technologies*, 1st edn., Oxon, United Kingdom: Routledge, 112–121.

Kitchin, Rob (2014), *The Data Revolution: Big Data, Open Data, Data Infrastructures and Their Consequences*, London: Sage Publications.

Leurs, Koen (2017), "Feminist Data Studies: Using Digital Methods for Ethical, Reflexive and Situated Socio-cultural Research", *Feminist Review* 115(1): 130–154.

Mendes, Kaitlynn, Ringrose, Jessica, & Keller, Jessalynn (2019), *Digital Feminist Activism: Girls and Women Fight Back against Rape Culture*, New York: Oxford University Press.

Mumford, Densua (2021), "Data Colonialism: Compelling and Useful, but Whither Epistemes?", *Information, Communication & Society*, 25(10): 1511–1516.

Perera, Sachini (2022), "White Paper on Feminist Internet Research", Association for Progressive Communications Women's Rights Programme: Recommendations for Action, https://www.apc.org/sites/default/files/firn-whitepaper-2022.pdf

Rabie, Sara (2013), *Crowd-Feminism_Crowdmapping as a Tool for Activism*, (Masters Thesis, Goldsmiths University).

Rothschild, Joan (1995), "Designing Technology to Meet Human Needs: Feminist Visions in Practice", *Icon*, 1: 99–105.

Stephens, Monica (2013), "Gender and the Geoweb: Divisions in the Production of User-Generated Cartographic Information", *GeoJournal* 78: 981–996.

UN Broadband Commission for Sustainable Development (2017), Working Group on the Digital Gender Divide: Recommendations for Action: Bridging the Gender Gap in Internet and Broadband Access and Use, https://broadbandcommission.org/publication/recommendations-for-action-bridging-the-gender-gap-in-internet-and-broadband-access-and-use/, accessed May 26, 2022.

United Nations (2015), Transforming Our World: The 2030 Agenda for Sustainable Development, https://sdgs.un.org/publications/transforming-our-world-2030-agenda-sustainable-development-17981

UN Women, (2018), Gender Equality and Big Data, https://www.unwomen.org/sites/default/files/Headquarters/Attachments/Sections/Library/Publications/2018/Gender-equality-and-big-data-en.pdf, accessed September 10, 2022.

UN Women, Women Count (2021), "Counted & Visible Toolkit to Better Utilize Existing Data from Household Surveys to Generate Disaggregated Gender Statistics", https://data.unwomen.org/sites/default/files/documents/Publications/Toolkit/Counted_Visible_Toolkit_EN.pdf, accessed May 22, 2022.

Viswanath, Kalpana & Ashish Basu (2015), "SafetiPin: An Innovative Mobile App to Collect Data on Women's Safety in Indian Cities", *Gender & Development*, 23(1): 45–60.

Chapter Five

Brouwers, Ria (2013), *Revisiting Gender Mainstreaming in International Development: Goodbye to an Illusionary Strategy*, Working Paper 556, The Hague, Netherlands: Institute of Social Studies.

Caglar, Gülay (2013), "Gender Mainstreaming", *Politics & Gender*, 9(3), 336–344.

Cavaghan, Rosalind (2017), *Making Gender Equality Happen*, 1st edn, vol. 1, New York: Routledge.

City of Vienna (2021), *Gender Mainstreaming – Made Easy*, A Manual, file:///Users/nkalms/Downloads/AC16355202%20(1).pdf, accessed September 10, 2022.

Collins, Patricia Hill (1990), *Black Feminist Thought: Knowledge, Consciousness, and the Politics of Empowerment*, Florence: Taylor & Francis Group.

Council of Europe (1998), Committee of Members: Recommendations No. R (98)6, https://rm.coe.int/16804fc569, accessed September 3, 2022.

Crenshaw, Kimberlé (1989), "Demarginalizing the Intersection of Race and Sex: A Black Feminist Critique of Antidiscrimination Doctrine, Feminist Theory and Antiracist Politics." *University of Chicago Legal Forum*, (1)8: 139–167.

Daly, Mary (2005), "Gender Mainstreaming in Theory and Practice", *Social Politics: International Studies in Gender, State, and Society*, 12(3): 433–450.

Davids, Tine, Francien van Driel, & Franny Parren (2014), "Feminist Change Revisited: Gender Mainstreaming as a Slow Revolution", *Journal of International Development*, 26: 396–408.

Eveline, Joan & Carol Bacchi (2005), "What Are We Mainstreaming When We Mainstream Gender?", *International Feminist Journal of Politics*, 7(4): 496–512.

Greed, Clara (2000), "Women in the Construction Professions: Achieving Critical Mass", *Gender, Work, and Organization*, 7(3): 181–196.

Greed, Clara (2005), "Overcoming the Factors Inhibiting the Mainstreaming of Gender into Spatial Planning Policy in the United Kingdom", *Urban Studies*, 42(4): 719–749.

Greed, Clara (2006), "Making the Divided City Whole: Mainstreaming Gender into Planning in the United Kingdom", *Tijdschrift Voor Economische En Sociale Geografie*, 97(3): 267–280.

Hankivsky, Olena (2005), "Gender vs. Diversity Mainstreaming: A Preliminary Examination of the Role and Transformative Potential of Feminist Theory", *Canadian Journal of Political Science / Revue Canadienne de Science Politique*, 38(4): 977–1001, http://www.jstor.org/stable/25165888

Horelli, Liisa, Christine Booth, & Rose Gilroy (2000), "The EuroFEM Toolkit for Mobilizing Women into Local and Regional Development", Helsinki University of Technology, Centre for Regional Studies. https://issuu.com/eva_alvarez/docs/12_eurofem_toolbox, accessed October 3, 2022.

Hosein, Gabriella, Tricia Basdeo-Gobin, & Lydia Rosa Gény (2020), "Gender Mainstreaming in National Sustainable Development Planning in the Caribbean Gabrielle", ECLAC Subregional Headquarters for the Caribbean, https://repositorio.cepal.org/bitstream/handle/11362/45086/1/S1901209_en.pdf, accessed September 7, 2022.

Huning, Sandra, Barbara Zibell, Doris Damyanovic, & Ulrike Sturm (eds) (2019), *Gendered approaches to spatial development in Europe: Perspectives, similarities, differences*, Taylor & Francis Group.

Kern, Leslie (2020), *Feminist City: Claiming Space in a Man-Made World*, La Vergne: Verso.

Lacy, Anita, Rebecca Miller, Dory Reeves, & Yardena Tankel (2013), "From Gender Mainstreaming to Intersectionality: Advances in Achieving Inclusive and Safe Cities", in Carolyn Whitzman, Legacy Crystal, Caroline Andrew, Fran Klodawsky, Margaret Shaw, & Kalpana Viswanath (eds), *Building Inclusive Cities: Women's Safety and the Right to the City*, [page range], Earthscan: London.

Lomazzi, Vera, & Isabella Crespi (2019), "Conclusions", in *Gender Mainstreaming and Gender Equality in Europe: Policies, Culture and Public Opinion*, 1st edn, Bristol: Polity Press, 145–152.

Low, Setha and Kurt Iveson (2022), "Propositions for More Just Urban Spaces", in Kate Bishop, and Nancy Marshall (eds), *The Routledge*

Handbook of People and Place in the 21st Century City, New York: Routledge.

McRobbie, Angela (2009), *The Aftermath of Feminism: Gender, Culture and Social Change* (Culture, Representation and Identity series), Los Angeles, London: Sage.

Milward, Kirsty, Maitrayee Mukhopadhyay, & Franz F. Wong (2015), "Gender Mainstreaming Critiques: Signposts or Dead Ends?" *IDS Bulletin*, 46(4): 75–81.

Palit, Natalya (2018), "Gender Mainstreaming in Urban Planning: What Can the UK Learn from Vienna with Regards to Adopting a Gender Mainstreaming Approach to Shape Built Outcomes?" https://www.rtpi.org.uk/media/4471/george-pepler-report_200301_final.pdf, accessed April 16, 2023.

Pinch, Steven (1985), *Cities and Services: The Geography of Collective Consumption*, Routledge & Keagan Paul: London, England.

Pollack, Mark A. & Emilie M. Hafner-Burton, (2010), "Mainstreaming International Governance: The Environment, Gender, and IO Performance in the European Union", *Review of International Organizations*, 5(3): 285–313.

Rao, Aruna & David Kelleher (2005), "Is There Life After Gender Mainstreaming?" *Gender and Development*, 13(2): 57–69.

Rees, Teresa (2005), "Reflections on the Uneven Development of Gender Mainstreaming in Europe", *International Feminist Journal of Politics*, 7(4): 555–574.

Rieker, Martina & Linda Peake (2013), *Rethinking Feminist Interventions into the Urban*, London: Taylor and Francis.

Sánchez de Madariaga, Inés (2016), "Looking Forward, Moving Beyond Trade-offs", in Marion Roberts & Inés Sánchez de Madariaga (eds), *Fair Shared Cities: The Impact of Gender Planning in Europe*, UK: Routledge, 325–333.

Scala, Francesca & Stephanie Paterson (2018), "Stories from the Front Lines: Making Sense of Gender Mainstreaming in Canada", *Politics & Gender*, 14(2): 208–234.

Shaw, Margaret, Caroline Andrew, Carolyn Whitzman, Fran Klodawsky, Kalpana Visanath, & Legacy Crystal (2013), "Introduction: Challenges, Opportunities and Tools", in Carolyn Whitzman, Legacy Crystal, Caroline Andrew, Fran Klodawsky, Margaret Shaw, & Kalpana Viswanath (eds), *Building Inclusive Cities: Women's Safety and the Right to the City*, Earthscan: London.

Sidorova, Milota, Zdenka Lammelova, Alevitina Bainakova, Veronika Fajmonova, Miha Mazzini, & Kristyna Stara (2016), "How to Design a Fair Shared City: 8 Short Stories on Equitable Urban Planning in Everyday Life", Heinrich Boll Stifting Prana & WSP Prague, https://cz.boell.org/sites/default/files/komix.hbs_a5_en.pdf, accessed September 7, 2022.

Tummers, Lidewij., Sylvette Denefle & HeidWankiewicz H. (2019), "Gender Mainstreaming and Spatial Development: Contradictions and Challenges", in Sandra Huning, Barbara Zibell, Doris Damyanovic, & Ulrike Sturm (eds) in *Gender Approaches to Spatial Development in Europe*, London: Routledge, 78–98.

Tyler, Meagan (2021), "Can Feminism Be Saved from Identity Politics? March 8, *ABC Religion and Ethics*, https://www.abc.net.au/religion/can-feminism-be-saved-from-identity-politics/11646084, accessed June17, 2022.

Urban Development Vienna (2013), "Manual for Gender Mainstreaming in Urban Planning and Urban Development", https://www.wien.gv.at/stadtentwicklung/studien/pdf/b008358.pdf, accessed September 10, 2022.

United Nations Economic and Social Council (1997), "Report of the Economic and Social Council for 1997: New York and Geneva", https://digitallibrary.un.org/record/245497?ln=en

UN Women (2021), "Progress on the SDGs Progress – A Gender Snapshot", https://www.unwomen.org/sites/default/files/Headquarters/Attachments/Sections/Library/Publications/2021/Progress-on-the-Sustainable-Development-Goals-The-gender-snapshot-2021-en.pdf

Whitzman, Carolyn, Crystal Legacy, Caroline Andrew, Fran Klodawsky, Maragaret Shaw, & Kalpana Viswanath (eds) (2013), *Building Inclusive Cities: Women's Safety and the Right to the City*, London: Earthscan.

World Bank (2020), *Handbook for Gender Inclusive Urban Planning Design*. https://www.worldbank.org/en/topic/urbandevelopment/publication/handbook-for-gender-inclusive-urban-planning-and-design

Women's Advisory Committee of the Senate Department for Urban Development (2011), "Gender Mainstreaming in Urban Development", Kulturbuch-Verlag GmbH, Berlin. https://civitas.eu/sites/default/files/berlin_gender_mainstreaming_0.pdf, accessed October 3, 2022.

Yon, Alicia & SriPallavi Nadimpalli (2017), "Cities for Whom? Re-examining Identity, to Reclaim the Right to the City for Women", *Australian Planner*, 54(1): 33–40.

Zalewski, Marysia (2010), "'I don't even know what gender is': A Discussion of the Connections Between Gender, Gender Mainstreaming and Feminist Theory, *Review of International Studies*, 36(1): 3–27.

Zebracki, Martin (2014), Sex in the City: Gender Mainstreaming Urban Governance in Europe. The Case of Sweden and Italy, Fennia, 192(1): 54–64.

Chapter Six

Andersdotter, Elin Fabre, Emelie Anneroth, & Caroline Wrangsten (2019), *Urban Girls Catalogue: How Cities Planned for and by Girls Work for Everyone*, Botkyrka Municipality, Iteam, Mistra Urban Futures, Un-Habitat, https://globalutmaning.se/wp-content/uploads/2022/03/Urban-Girls-Catalogue_rapport_Global-Utmaning.pdf, accessed August 30, 2022.

Daneshpour, Manijeh (2023), *Gender, Power, and Global Social Justice: The Healing Power of Psychotherapy*. New York: Routledge.

Devlin, Marcia (2021), "Time to Gender Parity has Blown Out to 135 Years. Here's What Women Can Do to Close the Gap", *The Conversation*, June 2, 2021, https://theconversation.com/time-to-gender-parity-has-blown-out-to-135-years-heres-what-women-can-do-to-close-the-gap-160253, accessed September 5, 2022.

Donovan, Jenny, Julie Rudner. & Lisa Amir (2019), "Here's How to Make Our Cities Breastfeeding-friendly", *The Conversation*, June 20, 2019, https://theconversation.com/heres-how-to-make-our-cities-breastfeeding-friendly-110176, accessed September 7, 2022.

Dunne, Anthony & Fiona Raby (2013), *Speculative Everything: Design, Fiction, and Social Dreaming*, Cambridge, Massachusetts, London: MIT Press.

Fileborn, Bianca (2016), "Doing Gender, Doing Safety: Young Adults' Production of Safety on a Night out," *Gender, Place and Culture*, 23(8): 1107–1120.

Greed, Clara (1994), *Women and Planning: Creating Gendered Realities*. London; New York: Routledge.

Greed, Clara (1999), *Social Town Planning*, London: Routledge.

Greed, Clara (2005), "Overcoming the Factors Inhibiting the Mainstreaming of Gender into Spatial Planning Policy in the United Kingdom", *Urban Studies* (Edinburgh, Scotland), 42(4): 719–749.

Kalms, Nicole (2017), *Hypersexual City: The Provocation of Soft-Core Urbanism*, London: Taylor and Francis.

Kalms Nicole (2019), "More Lighting Alone Does Not Create Safer Cities. Look at What Research with Young Women Tells Us", *The Conversation*, May 28, https://theconversation.com/more-lighting-alone-does-not-create-safer-cities-look-at-what-research-with-young-women-tells-us-113359, accessed September 7, 2022.

Kennedy, Russell, Meghan Kelly, Jefa Greenaway, & Brian Martin (2018), "International Indigenous Design Charter: Protocols for Sharing Indigenous Knowledge in Professional Design Practice", https://www.theicod.org/storage/app/media/resources/International_IDC_book_small_web.pdf, accessed September 10, 2022.

Make Space for Girls (2022), https://makespaceforgirls.co.uk/, accessed September 7, 2022.

OECD (2022), "Feeling Safe Walking Alone at Night", *OECD Better Life Index*, https://www.oecdbetterlifeindex.org/topics/safety/, accessed September 7, 2022.

Overington, Caitlin (2017), *The Atmosphere of CCTV: Visibility, Narrative, Encounter*, PhD diss: University of Melbourne, https://rest.neptune-prod.its.unimelb.edu.au/server/api/core/bitstreams/d4c448d7-75ea-5630-af0e-e8677216e24a/content

Plan International (2018), *Unsafe in the City: The Everyday Experiences of Girls and Young Women*, Surrey: United Kingdom.

RTPI (2007), "Good Practice Notes 7: Gender and Spatial Planning", *The Royal Town Planning Institute*, https://policy-practice.oxfam.org/resources/gender-and-spatial-planning-rtpi-good-practice-note-7-112350/, accessed October 14, 2022.

TramLab (2020b), Toolkit 2: "Toolkit for Gender Sensitive Placemaking – Improving the Safety of Women and Girls on Public Transport", Melbourne: Victorian State Government, La Trobe University, Monash University XYX Lab, RMIT University.

Sidorova, Milota, Zdenka Lammelova, Alevitina Bainakova, Veronika Fajmonova, Miha Mazzini, & Kristyna Stara (2016), "How to Design a Fair Shared City: 8 Short Stories on Equitable Urban Planning in Everyday life", Heinrich Boll Stifting Prana and WSP Prague, https://cz.boell.org/sites/default/files/komix.hbs_a5_en.pdf, accessed September 7, 2022.

Whitzman, Carolyn, Legacy Crystal, Caroline Andrew, Fran Klodawsky, Margaret Shaw, & Kalpana Viswanath (eds) (2013), *Building Inclusive Cities: Women's Safety and the Right to the City*, London: Earthscan.

XYX Lab and CrowdSpot (2021), *YourGround Victoria Report*, Melbourne: Monash University XYX Lab, https://www.yourground.org/, accessed October 14, 2022.

Yang, Hoa, Jess Berry, & and Nicole Kalms (2022), "Perceptions of Safety in Cities after Dark", ed. Shanti Sumartojo, *Lighting Design in Shared Public Spaces*, New York: Taylor and Francis.

Chapter Seven

Ahmed, Sara (2017), *Living a Feminist Life*, United States: Duke University Press.

Beebeejaun, Yasminah (2009), "Making Safer Places: Gender and the Right to the City", *Security Journal*, 22(3): 219–229.

Beebeejaun, Yasminah (2017), "Gender, Urban Space, and the Right to Everyday Life", *Journal of Urban Affairs*, 39(3): 323–334.

Berry, Jess (2021), "Catwalking the City: The pleasures and politics of fashioning the metropolis", in Jess Berry, Timothy Moore, Kalms Nicole, & Gene Bawden (eds), *Contentious Cities: Design and the Gendered Production of Space*, London: Taylor and Francis.

Evans, James, & Phil Jones (2011), "The Walking Interview: Methodology, Mobility and Place", *Applied Geography* 31: 849–858.

Gervais, Myriam, Weber, Sandra, & Caron, Caroline (2018), *Guide to Participatory Feminist Research* – Abridged version, https://www.mcgill.ca/igsf/files/igsf/gervais_et_al_guide_to_feminist_participatory_research_2020.pdf, accessed 9 August 2022.

Greed, Clara (1994), *Women and Planning: Creating Gendered Realities*, London; New York: Routledge.

Harding, Sandra G., (1987), *Feminism and Methodology: Social Science Issues*, Bloomington: Indiana University Press.

Kelly, Liz & Jill Radford (1990), "Nothing Really Happened': The Invalidation of Women's Experiences of Sexual Violence", *Critical Social Policy*, 10(30): 39–53.

Lafont, Cristina (2015), "Deliberation, Participation, and Democratic Legitimacy: Should Deliberative Mini-publics Shape Public Policy?", *The Journal of Political Philosophy*, 23(1): 40–63.

Lambrick, Melanie & Kathryn Travers (2008), "Women's Safety Audits: What Works and Where?" *UN-Habitat: Safer Cities Programme*, https://unhabitat.org/womens-safety-audit-what-works-and-where, accessed October 14, 2022.

Lindell, Marina & Peter Ehrström (2020), "Deliberative Walks: Citizen Participation in Local-level Planning Processes", *European Political Science*, 19(3): 478–501.

Whitzman, Carolyn, Shaw, Margaret, Andrew, Caroline, & Kathryn Travers (2009), "The Effectiveness of Women's Safety Audits", *Security Journal*, 22(3): 205–218.

Chapter Eight

Aruldoss, Vinnarasan & Sevasti-Melissa Nolas (2019), "Tracing Indian girls' Embodied Orientations Towards Public Life," *Gender, Place and Culture: A Journal of Feminist Geography*, 26(11): 1588–1608.

Blomstrom, Eleanor, Aimee Gauthlier, & Christina Jang (2018), "Access and Gender", *Institute for Transportation and Development Policy* (ITDP), https://www.itdp.org/publication/access-for-all-gender/, accessed July 4, 2022

Blumenberg, Evelyn & Michael Manville (2004), "Beyond the Spatial Mismatch: Welfare Recipients and Transportation Policy", *Journal of Planning Literature*, 19(2): 182–205.

Both, David., Lucia Hanmer & Elizabeth Lovell (2000), "Poverty and Transport: A Report Prepared for the World Bank in Collaboration with DFI", *Overseas Development Institute*, London, UK.

Brown, Sheila (1998), "What's the Problem, Girls? CCTV and the Gendering of Public Safety", in Clive Norris & Jade Moran (eds), *Surveillance, Closed Circuit Television and Social Control*, Florence: Routledge.

Ceccato, Vania (2017), "Women's Transit Safety: Making Connections and Defining Future Directions in Research and Practice", *Crime Prevention and Community Safety* 19(3–4): 276–287.

Ceccato, Vania & Anastasia Loukaitou-Sideris (2020a), *Transit Crime and Sexual Violence in Cities*, Milton: Taylor and Francis.

Ceccato, Vania (2020b), "The Architecture of Crime and the Fear of Crime: Research Evidence on light, CCTV and CPTED Features", in Vania Ceccato & Mahesh K. Nalla (eds), *Crime and Fear in Public Places: Towards Safe, Inclusive and Sustainable Cities*, 38–71, London, New York: Routledge.

Cozens, Paul & Terence Love (2015), "A Review and Current Status of Crime Prevention through Environmental Design (CPTED)", *Journal of Planning Literature*, 30(4): 393–412.

Cresswell, Tim & Tanu Priya Uteng (2008), "Gendered Mobilities: Towards a Holistic Understanding", in Tim Cresswell & Tanu Priya Uteng (eds), *Gendered mobilities*, 1–12, London: Ashgate.

Currie, Graham, John Stanley, & Janet Stanley (2007), *No Way to Go – Transport and Social Disadvantage in Australian Communities*, Clayton, VIC: Monash University.

Delbosc, Alexa & Graham Currie (2011), "Modelling the Causes and Consequences of Perceptions of Personal Safety on Public Transport Ridership", *Australasian Transport Research Forum*, Proceedings 28–30 September, https://australasiantransportresearchforum.org.au/wp-content/uploads/2022/03/2011_Delbosc_Currie.pdf, accessed September 15, 2022.

Dunckel-Graglia, Amy (2013), "'Pink Transportation' in Mexico City: Reclaiming Urban Space Through Collective Action Against Gender-based Violence", *Gender and Development*, 21(2): 265–276.

EPA (2021) Sources of Greenhouse Gas Emissions: Transportation Sector Emissions, https://www.epa.gov/ghgemissions/sources-greenhouse-gas-emissions, accessed September 15, 2022.

Gekoski, Anna, Jackie Gray, Miranda Horvath, Sarah Edwards, Allye Emirali, & Joanna Ruth Adler (2015), *What Works in Reducing Sexual Harassment and Sexual Offences on Public Transport Nationally and*

Internationally: A Rapid Evidence Assessment, London: British Transport Police and Department for Transport.

Goel, Rahul, Oyinlola Oyebode, Louise Foley, Lambed Tatah, Christopher Millett, & James Woodcock (2022), "Gender Differences in Active Travel in Major Cities Across the World", *Transportation* 50(2): 733–749 (Dordrecht).

Goffman, Erving (1963), *Behavior in Public Places: Notes on the Social Organization of Gatherings*, New York: Free Press.

Greed, Clara (1994), *Women and Planning: Creating Gendered Realities*, London & New York: Routledge.

Greed, Clara (2019), "Are we still not there yet? Moving further along the gender highway", in Christina Lindkvist Scholten & Tanja Joelsson (eds), *Integrating Gender into Transport planning: From One to Many Tracks*, London: Palgrave MacMillan.

Giuliano, Genevieve (1979), "Public Transportation and the Travel Needs of Women", *Traffic Quarterly* 33(4): 607–616.

Hale, Chris (1996), "Fear of Crime: A Review of the Literature", *International Review of Victimology*, 4(2): 79–150.

Harumain, Yong Adilah Shamsul, Deana McDonagh, Andree Woodcock, Nikmatul Adha Nordin, & Komal Faiz (2021), in Jess Berry, Timothy Moore, Nicole Kalms, & Gene Bawden (eds), *Contentious Cities* [page range], Milton: Taylor and Francis.

Hjorthol, Randi (2008), "Daily Mobility of Men And Women – A Barometer of Gender Equality", in Tim, Cresswell & Tanu Priya Uteng (eds), *Gendered Mobilities* [page range], Ashgate: Aldershot.

Institutionen för globala studier (2016), "Achieving Climate Objectives in Transport Policy by Including Women and Challenging Gender Norms: The Swedish Case", *International Journal of Sustainable Transportation*, 10(8): 703–711.

Kalms, Nicole (2019), "More Lighting Alone Does not Create Safer Cities. Look at What Research with Young Women Tells us", *The Conversation*, May 28, https://theconversation.com/more-lighting-alone-does-not-create-safer-cities-look-at-what-research-with-young-women-tells-us-113359, accessed July 5, 2022.

Kim, Hyunjin (2019), "Service Design for Public Transportation to Address the Issue of Females' Fear of Crime", *Transportation* (Dordrecht), 48(1): 167–192.

Levin, Lena & Charlotta Faith-Ell (2019), "How to Apply Gender Equality Goals in Transport and Infrastructure", in Christina Lindkvist Scholten & Tanja Joelsson (eds), *Integrating Gender into Transport Planning: From One to Many Tracks*, London: Palgrave MacMillan.

Levy, Caren (2019), "Travel Choice Reframed: 'Deep Distribution' and Gender in Urban Transport", in Christina Lindkvist Scholten & Tanja

Joelsson (eds), *Integrating Gender into Transport Planning: From One to Many Tracks*, London: Palgrave MacMillan.

Loukaitou-Sideris, Anastasia & Camille Fink (2009), "Addressing Women's Fear of Victimization in Transportation Settings: A Survey of US Transit Agencies", *Urban Affairs Review* 44(4): 554–587.

Loukaitou-Sideris, Anastasia (2014), "Fear and Safety in Transit Environment from the Women's Perspective", *Security Journal* 27(2): 242–256.

Loukaitou-Sideris, Anastasia (2016), "A Gendered View of Mobility and Transport: Next Steps and Future Directions", *Town Planning Review* 87(5): 548–552.

Lucas, Karen, Giulio Mattioli, Ersilia Verlinghieri, & Alvaro Guzman (2016), "Transport Poverty and its Adverse Social Consequences," *Proceedings of the Institution of Civil Engineers, Transport*, 169(6): 353–365, https://doi.org/10.1680/jtran.15.00073

Matthewson, Gill & Nicole Kalms (2021), "Unwanted Sexual Behaviour and Public Transport: The Imperative for Gender-Sensitive Co-design", in Selby Coxon and Robbie Natter (eds), *Advancing a Design Approach to Enriching Public Mobility*, 53–67, Intelligent Systems Reference Library, Cham: Springer International Publishing.

"Our Watch (2017), Counting on Change: A Guide to Prevention and Monitoring", https://media-cdn.ourwatch.org.au/wp-content/uploads/sites/2/2019/06/27043538/OurWatch_Counting-on-Change_AA.pdf, accessed September 15, 2022.

Overington, Caitlin (2017), *The Atmosphere of CCTV: Visibility, Narrative, Encounter*, PhD diss., The University of Melbourne.

Oviedo Hernandez, Daniel & Helena Titheridge (2016), "Mobilities of the Periphery: Informality, Access and Social Exclusion in the Urban Fringe in Colombia", *Journal of Transport Geography*, 55, 152–164.

Pain, Rachel (1991), "Space, Sexual Violence and Social Control: Integrating Geographical and Feminist Analyses of Women's Fear of Crime", *Progress in Human Geography*, 15(4): 415–431.

Park, Jun & Subeh Chowdhury (2022), "Towards an Enabled Journey: Barriers Encountered by Public Transport Riders with Disabilities for the Whole Journey Chain", *Transport Reviews*, 42(2): 181–203.

Plan International (2018), "Unsafe in the City: The Everyday Experiences of Girls and Young Women", https://www.plan.org.au/publications/unsafe-in-the-city-the-everyday-experiences-of-girls-and-young-women/, accessed September 5, 2022.

Reid, Michael & Beh Lih Yi (2018), "Nearly 70% of Women in Tokyo Back Single-sex Train Cars, Survey Finds", *Japanese Times*, https://www.japantimes.co.jp/news/2018/11/15/national/nearly-70-women-tokyo-back-single-sex-train-cars-survey-finds/#.XvAFYPJS9t8, accessed September 15, 2022.

Ritchie, Hannah (2020), "Cars, Planes, Trains: Where Do CO_2 Emissions from Transport Come From?", *Our World in Data*, https://ourworldindata.org/co2-emissions-from-transport, accessed September 15, 2022.

Sánchez de Madariaga, Inés (2013), "Mobility of Care: Introducing New Concepts in Urban Transport", in Inés Sánchez de Madariaga & Marion Roberts(eds), *Fair shared cities: the impact of gender planning in Europe*, Abingdon, Oxon: Taylor & Francis.

Santoro, Paula Freire, Marina Kohler Harkot, Anastasia Loukaitou-Sideris, Vania Ceccato, Catherine Sundling, Javier Romero-Torres, & Asha Weinstein Agrawal (2020), "Intersectionality of Transit Safety", in Vania Ceccato & Anastasia Loukaitou-Sideris (eds), *Transit Crime and Sexual Violence in Cities: International Evidence and Prevention*, 217–236, New York: Routledge.

Scholten, Lindkvist & Tanja Joelsson (eds) (2019), *Integrating Gender into Transport Planning: From One to Many Tracks*, London: Palgrave MacMillan.

Shaw, Margaret, Carolyn Whitzman, Fran Klodawsky, Kalpana Viswanath, Caroline Andrew, & Crystal Legacy (2013), *Building Inclusive Cities: Women's Safety and the Right to the City*, Earthscan: London.

Smeds, Emilia, Enora Robin, & Jenny McArthur (2020), "Night-time Mobilities and (In)Justice in London: Constructing Mobile Subjects and The Politics of Difference in Policymaking", *Journal of Transport Geography*, 82: 102569.

Smidfelt Rosqvist, Lena (2019), "Gendered Perspectives on Swedish Transport Policy-Making: An Issue for Gendered Sustainability Too", in Lindkvist Scholten & Tanja Joelsson (eds), *Integrating Gender into Transport Planning: From One to Many Tracks*, 69–87, London: Palgrave MacMillan.

Stack, Lindsey & Richard Adams (2021), "Queer Mobility", *Logistics and Transport Focus*, 23(9): 38.

State of Victoria (2016), "Transit Protective Services Officers: An Exploration of Corruption and Misconduct Risks", *Melbourne: Independent Broadbased Anti-corruption Commission*, https://www.ibac.vic.gov.au/docs/default-source/research-documents/transit-protective-services-officers---an-exploration-of-corruption-and-misconduct-risks.pdf?sfvrsn=4, accessed September 15, 2022.

TramLab (2020a), Toolkit 1: *Gender-Sensitive Communication Campaigns – Improving the Safety of Women and Girls on Public Transport*, Melbourne: Victorian State Government, La Trobe University, Monash University XYX Lab, RMIT University.

TramLab (2020c), Toolkit 3: *Gender Sensitive Data – Improving Safety of Women and Girls on Public Transport*, Melbourne: Victorian State

Government, La Trobe University, Monash University XYX Lab, RMIT University.

TramLab (2020d), Toolkit 4: *Gender-Sensitive Training – Improving the Safety of Women and Girls on Public Transport*, Melbourne: Victorian State Government, La Trobe University, Monash University XYX Lab, RMIT University.

Transport for London (2021), *Vibrant Places: Sustainable Development Framework*, available at: https://content.tfl.gov.uk/dim01vibrantplaces.pdf, accessed August 1, 2022.

Transport for West Midlands (2022), "Transport Champions for Tackling Violence Against Women and Girls: Recommendations to Make Our Transport Networks Safer for Women and Girls", https://beta.wmca.org.uk/media/ymxjimhw/violence-against-women-and-girls-recommendations-by-the-transport-champions-final-version-1.pdf, accessed July 5, 2002.

Tyler, Meagan (2021), "Shared Bathrooms: Moving from Rhetoric to Redesign", *Architecture Australia*, Architecture Media, 109(5): 31.

Weintrob, Amos, Luke, Hansell, Martin Zebracki, Yvonne Barnard, & Karen Lucas, (2021), "Queer Mobilities: Critical LGBTQ Perspectives of Public Transport Spaces", *Mobilities* 16(5): 775–791.

Wekerle, Gerda R. & Carolyn Whitzman (1995), *Safe Cities: Guidelines for Planning, Design and Management*, New York: Van Nostrand Reinhold.

Whitzman, Carolyn (2013), "Women's Safety and Everyday Mobility", in Margaret Shaw, Carolyn Whitzman, Fran Klodawsky, Kalpana Viswanath, Caroline Andrew, & Crystal Legacy (eds), *Building Inclusive Cities: Women's Safety and the Right to the City*, 35–52, London: Earthscan.

Woodcock, Andree, Deana McDonagh, Sana Iqbal, Komal Faiz, Binti Shamsul Harumain, & Yong Adilah (2019), "Gender Transport Poverty in Low-middle Income Countries, and Its Effects on Women's Health and Wellbeing", *Journal of Transport & Health*, 14: 100716.

Yang, Hoa, Jess Berry, & Nicole Kalms (2022), "Perceptions of Safety in Cities After Dark, in Shanti Sumartojo", *Lighting Design in Shared Public Spaces*, Milton: Taylor and Francis.

Yavuz, Nilay & Welch Eric W. (2010), "Addressing Fear of Crime in Public Space: Gender Differences in Reaction to Safety Measures in Train Transit", *Urban Studies* 47(12): 2491–2515.

Zibell, Barbara (2013), "The Model of the European City in the Light of Gender Planning and Sustainable Development, in Inés Sánchez de Madariaga & Marion Roberts(eds), *Fair shared cities: the impact of gender planning in Europe*, Abingdon, Oxon: Taylor & Francis.

Chapter Nine

Angeles, Leonora C & Jennifer Robertson (2020), "Empathy and Inclusive Public Safety in the City: Examining LGBTQ2 Voices and Experiences of Intersectional Discrimination", *Women's Studies International Forum*, 78: 102313, 1–12.

Atlas, Randall I. (2008), *21st Century Security and CPTED: Designing for Critical Infrastructure Protection and Crime Prevention*, Boca Raton, FL: Auerbach Publications.

Atlas, Randall (2013), *21st Century Security and CPTED: Designing for Critical Infrastructure*, 2nd edn, Boca Raton: CRC Press.

Armitage, Rachel (2008), "Crime Prevention through Environmental Design", in Richard Wortley & Lorraine Green Mazerolle *Environmental criminology and crime analysis* (Crime science series), Cullompton, UK; Portland, OR: Willan.

Armitage, Rachel & Paul Ekblom (2019), *Rebuilding Crime Prevention Through Environmental Design*, Crime Science Series, Florence: Routledge.

Bowers, Kate & Rob Guerette (2016), "Effectiveness of Situational Crime Prevention", in Gerben Bruinsma & David Weisburd (eds), *Encyclopedia of Criminology and Criminal Justice*, 1318–1329, New York: Springer Reference.

Brassard, Anna (2003), "Integrating the planning process and second-generation CPTED", *The CPTED Journal* 2(1): 46–53.

Brown, Sheila. (1998), "What's the Problem, Girls? CCTV and the Gendering of Public Safety", in C. Norris, J. Moran & G. Armstrong (eds), *Surveillance, Closed Circuit Television and Social Control*, 219–232, Aldershot, UK: Ashgate.

Camacho Duarte, Olga, Rohan Lulham, & Lucy Kaldor (2011), "Co-designing out crime", *CoDesign*, 7(3–4): 155–168.

Ceccato, Vania & Mahesh. K. Nalla (2020), *Crime and Fear in Public Places; Towards Safe, Inclusive and Sustainable Cities*, London: Routledge.

Chiu, Yi-Ning, Benoit Leclerc, Danielle Reynald, M., & Richard Wortley (2021), "Situational Crime Prevention in Sexual Offenses Against Women: Offenders Tell Us What Works and What Doesn't", *International Journal of Offender Therapy and Comparative Criminology*, 65(9): 1055–1076.

Clarke, Ronald (1997), *Situational Crime Prevention Successful Case Studies*, Albany: NY: Harrow and Heston.

Cook, Alana, Danielle M. Reynald, Benoit Leclerc & Richard Wortley (2019), "Learning about Situational Crime Prevention from Offenders: Using a script Framework to Compare the Commission of Completed and Disrupted Sexual Offenses", *Criminal Justice Review*, Atlanta, Ga, 44(4): 431–451.

Cornish, Derek B. & Roland V. Clarke. (2003), "Opportunities, Precipitators and Criminal Decisions: A Reply to Wortley's Critique of Situational Crime Prevention", in Martha J. Smith & Derek B. Cornish (eds), *Theory for practice in situational crime prevention. Crime Prevention Studies* (vol. 16), 1331–1368, Monsey: Criminal Justice Press.

Costanza-Chock, Sasha (2020), *Design Justice: Community-led Practices to Build the Worlds We Need*, Cambridge: Massachusetts: MIT Press.

Cozens, Paul & Terence Love (2015), "A Review and Current Status of Crime Prevention Through Environmental Design (CPTED)", *Journal of Planning Literature* 30(4): 393–412.

Cozens, Paul (2016), *Think Crime! Using Evidence, Theory and Crime Prevention Through Environmental Design (CPTED) for Planning Safer Cities*, 2nd Ed., Western Australia: Praxis Education.

Cozens, Paul M., Gwyn Saville, & David Hillier (2005), "Crime Prevention Through Environmental Design (CPTED): A Review and Modern Bibliography", *Property Management* 23: 328–356.

Crowe, Timothy D. (2000), *Crime Prevention Through Environmental Design: Applications of Architectural Design and Space Management Concepts*, Oxford: Butterworth-Heinemann.

DeKeseredy, Walter S, Donnermeyer, Joseph F., & Schwartz, Martin D. (2009), "Toward a gendered Second Generation CPTED for preventing woman abuse in rural communities," *Security journal*, 22(3): 178–189.

Doan, Petra L. (2007), "Queers in the American City: Transgendered Perceptions of Urban Space", *Gender, Place and Culture: A Journal of Feminist Geography* 14(1): 57–74.

Doan, Petra L., (2011), *Queerying Planning Challenging Heteronormative Assumptions and Reframing Planning Practice*, Burlington, Vt.: Ashgate.

Ekblom, Paul (2011), "Deconstructing CPTED . . . and Reconstructing it for Practice, Knowledge Management and Research", *European Journal on Criminal Policy and Research*, 17(1): 7–28.

Ekblom, Paul, Rachel Armitage, Leanne Monchuk and Ben Castell (2013), "Crime Prevention Through Environmental Design in the United Arab Emirates: A Suitable Case for Reorientation?", *Built Environment* 39(1): 92–113.

Fileborn, Bianca (2016), *Reclaiming the Night-Time Economy*, London: Palgrave Macmillan UK.

Guerette, Rob (2009), "The Pull, Push and Expansion of Situational Crime Prevention Evaluation: An Appraisal of Thirty-Seven Years of Research", in J. Knutsson & N. Tilley (eds), *Evaluating Crime*

Reduction Initiatives: Crime Prevention Studies, 24: 29–58, Monsey: Criminal Justice.

Hughes, Nathan (2011), "Young People 'as Risk' or Young People 'at Risk': Comparing Discourses of Anti-social Behaviour in England and Victoria", *Critical Social Policy*, 31(3): 388–409.

Irazábal, Clara & Claudia Huerta (2016), "Intersectionality and Planning at the Margins: LGBTQ Youth of Color in New York", *Gender, Place and Culture: A Journal of Feminist Geography*, 23(5): 714–732.

Jacobs, Jane (1961), *The Death and Life of Great American Cities*, New York: Random House.

Jeffery, C. Ray (1971), *Crime Prevention Through Environmental Design*, Beverly Hills, CA: Sage Publications.

Johnson, Derek, Victoria Gibson, & Emma Stevens (2014), "Developing & Maintaining Sustainable Communities: Managing the Output Focus of Crime Prevention Through Environmental Design (CPTED)", in *Caribbean Urban Forum*, May 14–17, Barbados.

Kalms, Nicole (2017), *Hypersexual City: The Provocation of Soft-Core Urbanism*, London: Taylor and Francis.

Kalms, Nicole (2018), "Digital technology and the safety of women and girls in urban space", in H. Frichot, C. Gabrielsson, & H. Runting, H. (eds), *Architecture and Feminisms: Ecologies, Economies, Technologies*, 112–121, Milton: Routledge.

Kawash, Samira (1998), "The Homeless Body", *Public Culture* 10(2): 319–339.

Kern, Leslie (2020), *Feminist City: Claiming Space in a Man-Made World*, Canada: Verso.

Khandwala, Anoushka (2019), "What Does It Mean to Decolonize Design? Dismantling Design History 101", https://eyeondesign.aiga.org/what-does-it-mean-to-decolonize-design/, accessed September 22, 2022.

Lee, Jae, Sungjin Park, & Sanghoon Jung (2016), "Effect of Crime Prevention Through Environmental Design (CPTED) Measures on Active Living and Fear of Crime", *Sustainability* 8(9): 872.

Lorenc, Theo, Stephen Clayton, David Neary, Margaret Whitehead, Mark Petticrew, Hilary Thomson, Steven Cummins, Amanda Sowden, & Adrian Renton (2012), "Crime, Fear of Crime, Environment, and Mental Health and Wellbeing: Mapping Review of Theories and Causal Pathways", *Health & Place* 18(4): 757–765.

Lorenc, Theo., Mark Petticrew, Margaret Whitehead, David Neary, Stephen Clayton, Kath Wright, Hilary Thomson, Steven Cummins, Amanda Sowden, & Adrian Renton (2013), "Environmental Interventions to Reduce Fear of Crime: Systematic Review of Effectiveness", *Systematic Reviews*, 2(1): 30.

Matthewson, Gill & Nicole Kalms (2021), "Unwanted Sexual Behaviour and Public Transport: The Imperative for Gender-Sensitive Co-design", in Selby Coxon and Robbie Napper (eds), *Advancing a Design Approach to Enriching Public Mobility*, 53–67, Cham: Springer International Publishing.

McRobbie, Angela (2009), *The Aftermath of Feminism: Gender, Culture and Social Change*, Los Angeles, London: Sage.

Morgan, Anthony, Hayley Boxall, Kym Lindeman, & Jessica Anderson (2012), "Effective Crime Prevention Interventions for Implementation by Local Government", *Research and Public Policy* 120: 91.

Newman, Oscar (1972), *Defensible Space: Crime Prevention Through Urban Design*, New York, NY, USA: Macmillan.

Overington, Caitlin (2017), *The Atmosphere of CCTV: Visibility, Narrative, Encounter*, PhD diss., The University of Melbourne.

Perkins, Douglas D., Abraham Wandersman, Richard C. Rich, & Ralph B. Taylor (1993), "The Physical Environment of Street Crime: Defensible Space, Territoriality and Incivilities", *Journal of Environmental Psychology*, 13(1): 29–49.

Reynald, Danielle M. & Henk Effers (2009), "The Future of Newman's Defensible Space Theory: Linking Defensible Space and the Routine Activities of Place", *European Journal of Criminology*, 6(1): 25–46.

Sadowski, Jathan, Anna Carlson, & Natalie Osborne (2020), "Darwin's 'smart city' project is about surveillance and control", Parkville, Vic, Australia: *The Conversation*, February 4, 2020, https://theconversation.com/darwins-smart-city-project-is-about-surveillance-and-control-127118, accessed October 15, 2022.

Saville, Gregory & Gerry Cleveland (1997), "2nd Generation CPTED: An Antidote to the Social Y2K Virus of Urban Design", paper presented at the 2nd Annual International CPTED Conference, Orlando, FL, 3–5 December, https://www.safegrowth.org/uploads/4/8/5/5/48559983/saville_cleveland-2nd_generation_cpted_4.pdf, accessed October 14, 2022.

Sidebottom, Aiden, Lisa Tompson, Amy Thornton, Karen Bullock, Nick Tilley, Kate Bowers, & Shane D. Johnson (2015), "Gating Alleys to Reduce Crime: A Meta-Analysis and Realist Synthesis, *Justice Quarterly*, 35(1): 55–86.

Smith, Neil & Setha Low (2005), "Introduction: The Imperative of Public Space", in Setha Low & Neil Smith (eds), *The Politics of Public Space*, 1–16, New York: Routledge.

Walklate, Sandra (2018), "Reflections on Community Safety: The Ongoing Precarity of Women's Lives", *Crime Prevention and Community Safety*, 20(4): 284–295.

Wekerle, Gerda & Carolyn Whitzman (1995), *Safe Cities: Guidelines for Planning, Design and Management*, New York: Van Nostrand Reinhold.

Welsh, Brandon C. & David P. Farrington (2009), "Public Area CCTV and Crime Prevention: An Updated Systematic Review and Meta-Analysis", *Justice Quarterly*, 26(4): 716–745.

Whitzman, Carolyn (2008), *The Handbook of Community Safety, Gender and Violence Prevention*, London: Routledge.

Wilson, James & George Kelling (1982), "Broken Windows: The Police and Neighborhood Safety", *Atlantic Monthly*, 29–38, https://www.theatlantic.com/magazine/archive/1982/03/broken-windows/304465/

XYX Lab & CrowdSpot (2021), "YourGround Victoria Report" Melbourne: Monash University XYX Lab. yourground.org

Chapter Ten

Acuto, Michele, Andreina Seijas, Jenny McArthur, & Enora Robin (2021), *Managing Cities at Night: A Practitioner Guide to the Urban Governance of the Night-Time Economy*, UK: Bristol University Press.

Boyce, Peter R. (2014), *Human Factors in Lighting*, Baton Rouge: CRC Press.

Ceccato, Vania (2020), "The Architecture of Crime and the Fear of Crime: Research Evidence on Light, CCTV and CPTED Features", in Vania Ceccato & Mahesh K. Nalla (eds), *Crime and Fear in Public Places: Towards Safe, Inclusive and Sustainable Cities*, 38–71, London, New York: Routledge.

Committee for Sydney (2019), *Safety After Dark: Creating a City for Women Living and Working in Sydney*, Sydney: Committee of Sydney.

Donnelly, Samantha & Sophie Dyring (2022), *A Design Guide for Older Women's Housing*, Melbourne: Monash University XYX Lab.

Edensor, Tim (2012), "The Gloomy City: Rethinking the Relationship Between Light and Dark," *Urban Studies* 52(3): 422–438.

Fileborn, Bianca (2016a), "Doing Gender, Doing Safety: Young Adults' Production of Safety on a Night Out," *Gender, Place and Culture*, 23(8): 1107–1120.

Fileborn, Bianca (2016b), *Reclaiming the Nighttime Economy*, London: Palgrave Macmillan UK.

Greed, Clara (1994), *Women and planning: Creating gendered realities*. London; New York: Routledge.

Green, Eileen & Carrie Singleton (2006), "Risky Bodies at Leisure: Young Women Negotiating Space and Place", *Sociology*, 40(5): 853–871.

Hubbard, Phil (2007), "The Geographies of Going Out: Emotion and Embodiment in the Evening Economy," in Joyce Davidson, Liz Bondi, and Mick Smith (eds), *Emotional Geographies*, 117–134, Hampshire: Ashgate.

Kalms, Nicole (2017), *Hypersexual City: The Provocation of Soft-Core Urbanism*, London: Taylor and Francis.

Kawash, Samira (1998), "The Homeless Body", *Public Culture* 10(2): 319–339.

Kelly, Liz & Jill Radford (1990), "'Nothing really happened': the invalidation of women's experiences of sexual violence", *Critical Social Policy*, 10(30): 39–53.

Kerns, Leslie (2020), *Feminist City: Claiming Space in a Man-Made World*, Canada: Verso.

Koskela, H. (1997), "'Bold walk and breakings': women's spatial confidence versus fear of violence", *Gender, Place and Culture*, 4(3), 301–319.

Larin, Tegan Maree (2022), *Behind the Masquerade: Illicit Massage Businesses in Melbourne*, PhD diss., Monash University.

Mackay, Finn (2015), *Radical Feminism*, UK: Palgrave Macmillan.

McQuire, Scott (2005), "Immaterial Architectures: Urban space and Electric Light," *Space and Culture*, 8(2): 126–140.

New South Wales Treasury (2020), 24-hour Economy Strategy, Sydney: Global New South Wales and New South Wales Government.

Nicholls, Emily (2017), "Dulling it Down a Bit: Managing Visibility, Sexualities and Risk in The Nighttime Economy in Newcastle, UK", *Gender, Place and Culture*, 24(2), 260–273.

OECD (2020) From OECD Better Life Index, https://www.oecdbetterlifeindex.org/topics/safety/, accessed August 6, 2022.

Plan International (2019), "Unsafe on the Streets: Girls and Young Women's Experience of Group Harassment", https://www.plan.org.au/wp-content/uploads/2020/08/unsafe-on-the-streets-girls-and-young-womens-experiences-of-group-harassment-2019.pdf, accessed May 18, 2022.

Pulse Lab Jakarta & UN Women (2019), *After Dark: Encouraging Safe Transit for women Travelling at Night*, Pulse Stories, https://asiapacific.unwomen.org/sites/default/files/Field%20Office%20ESEAsia/Docs/Publications/2019/11/id-After-Dark_FINAL-compressed.pdf, accessed September 22, 2022.

Roberts, Marion & Adam Eldridge (2009), *Planning the nighttime city*, London: Routledge.

Roberts, Marion & Clara Greed (2014), *Introducing Urban Design*, Abingdon, Oxon: Taylor and Francis.

Roe, Jenny & Layla McCay (2021), *Restorative Cities*, London: Bloomsbury Publishing USA.

Shaw, Robert (2015), "Controlling Darkness: Self, Dark and Domestic Night," *Cultural Geographies*, 22(4): 585–600.
Seal, Lizzie (2022), *Gender, crime and justice*, Cham, Switzerland: Palgrave MacMillan.
Sheard, Laura (2011), "Anything Could Have Happened: Women, the Nighttime Economy, Alcohol and Drink Spiking," *Sociology*, 45(4): 619–633.
Slaone, Mona, Don Slater, & Joanne Entwistle (2016), "Tackling Social Inequalities in Public Lighting", A Report by the Configuring Light/ Staging the Social Research Programme, London School of Economics, http://eprints.lse.ac.uk/66626/1/__lse.ac.uk_storage_LIBRARY_ Secondary_libfile_shared_repository_Content_Sloane%2C%20M_ Tackling%20Social%20inequalities_LSE-Tackling-Social-Inequalities-in-Public-Lighting-May-2016.pdf, accessed September 23, 2022.
Stevenson, Deborah (2018), "Feminism and its Places: Women, Leisure and the Nighttime Economy," in Louise Mansfield, Jayne Caudwell, Belinda Wheaton & Beccy Watson (eds), *The Palgrave Handbook of Feminism and Sport, Leisure and Physical Education*, 557–570, London: Palgrave Macmillan.
Struyf, Pia (2020), "Fear in the Dark: The Potential Impact of Reduced Street Lighting on Crime and Fear of Crime", in Vania Ceccato, & Mahesh K. Nalla, (eds), "Crime and Fear in Public Places", *International Journal of Comparative and Applied Criminal Justice*, 44(4): 261–264.
Svechkina, Alina, Tamar Trop, & Boris A. Portnov (2020), "How Much Lighting is Required to Feel Safe When Walking Through the Streets at Night?" *Sustainability*, 12(8): 3133.
Tyler, Meagan (2021), "All Roads Lead to Abolition? Debates About Prostitution and Sex Work Through the Lens of Unacceptable Work", *Labour & industry*, 31(1): 66–86.
United Nations (2019), "Affordable Housing and Social Protection Systems for all to Address Homelessness", Economic and Social Council, https://digitallibrary.un.org/record/3869551?ln=en, accessed 23 September 2022.
van Rijswijk, Leon & Antal Haans (2018), "Illuminating for Safety: Investigating the Role of Lighting Appraisals on The Perception of Safety in the Urban Environment", *Environment and Behavior*, 50(8): 889–912.
Wekerle, Gerda R. & Carolyn Whitzman (1995), *Safe Cities: Guidelines for Planning, Design and Management*, New York: Van Nostrand Reinhold.
Whitzman, Carolyn, Caroline Andrew, & Kalpana Viswanath (2014), "Partnerships for Women's Safety in the City: 'Four Legs for a Good Table'", *Environment and Urbanization*, 26(2): 443–456.

Williams, Robert (2008), "Night Spaces", *Space and Culture*, 11(4): 514–532.
Yang, Hoa, Jess Berry, & Nicole Kalms (2022), "Perceptions of Safety in Cities After Dark", in Shanti Sumartojo, (ed.), *Lighting Design in Shared Public Spaces*, 83–104, Milton: Taylor and Francis.

Chapter Eleven

Bawden, Gene & Alison Edwards (2018), "Pride of Place: Co-design, community engagement and the Victorian Pride Centre", *Fusion Journal,* 13: 43–63.
Benbrahim, Dina (2021), "Co-designing Meaningful Dialogues on Sexual Harassment, *Temes de Disseny*, 37: 106–131.
Bielenberg, John, Mike Burn, & Greg Galle (2016), *Think Wrong. How to Conquer the Status Quo and Do Work That Matters*, San Francisco: Instigator Press.
Blomkamp, Emma (2018), "The Promise of Co-Design for Public Policy", *Australian Journal of Public Administration*, 77(4): 729–743.
Caretta, Martina A. & Yvonne Riaño (2016), "Feminist participatory methodologies in geography: Creating spaces of inclusion", *Qualitative Research*, 16(3): 258–266.
Dunne, Anthony & Fiona Raby (2013), *Speculative Everything: Design, Fiction, and Social Dreaming*, London: MIT Press.
Edwards, Allison & Hannah Korsmeyer (2017), "Communication with Self, with Others, and with Futures: Making Artefacts in Design Thinking Workshops", *LEA – Lingue e Letterature D'Oriente e D'Occidente*, 6(6): 157–798.
Fuad-Luke, Alastair (2009), *Design Activism: Beautiful Strangeness for a Sustainable World,* London: Earthscan.
Gamble, Sarah (2006), *The Routledge Companion to Feminism and Postfeminism*, London; New York: Taylor & Francis.
Garau, Pietro (2016), *Global Public Space Toolkit: From Global Principles to Local Policies and Practice Revision*, https://unhabitat.org/sites/default/files/2019/05/global_public_space_toolkit.pdf, accessed September 23, 2022.
Gervais, Myriam, Sandra Weber, & Caroline Caron (2018), "Guide to Participatory Feminist Research Institute for Gender", *Sexuality and Feminist Studies* (IGSF), McGill University.
Gheerawo, Rama (2016), "Socially Inclusive Design: A People-Centred Perspective", in Penny Sparke & Fiona Fisher (eds), *The Routledge Companion to Design Studies*, 326–338, London: Routledge.

Greed, Clara (2006), "Making the Divided City Whole: Mainstreaming Gender into Planning in The United Kingdom", *Tijdschrift Voor Economische En Sociale Geografie*, 97(3): 267–280.

Grocott, Lisa (2022), *Design for Transformative Learning: A Practical Approach to Memory-making and Perspective-shifting*. Design for Social Responsibility Series, Oxon: Routledge.

Harding, Sandra (1987), *Feminism and Methodology: Social Science Issues*, Bloomington: Indiana University Press.

Heidaripour, Maryam & Laura Forlano (2018), "Formgiving to Feminist Futures as Design Activism", in C. Storni, K. Leahy, M. McMahon, P. Lloyd, & E. Bohemia (eds), *Design as a catalyst for change – DRS International Conference 2018*, 25–28 June, Limerick, Ireland.

Huybrechts, Liesbeth, Henric Benesch, & Jon Geib (2017), "Institutioning: Participatory Design, Co–Design and the Public Realm", *CoDesign,* 13(3): 148–159.

Kalms, Nicole & Gene Bawden (2021) "Lived Experience: Participatory practices for gender-sensitive spaces and places", in Jess Berry, Timothy Moore, Nicole Kalms & Gene Bawden (2020), *Contentious Cities: Design and the Gendered Production of Space*. Abingdon, Oxon: Routledge.

Lewrick, Michael, Patrick Link, & Larry Leifer (2020), *The Design Thinking Toolbox*, Newark: John Wiley & Sons, Inc.

Ortiz Escalante, Sara & Blanca Gutiérrez Valdivia (2015), "Planning from Below: Using Feminist Participatory Methods to Increase Women's Participation in Urban Planning", *Gender and development*, 23(1): 113–126.

Petcou, Constantin & Doina Petrescu, (2015), "R-URBAN or How to Co-produce a Resilient City, *Ephemera*, 15(1): 249–262.

Rothschild, Joan (1995), "Designing Technology to Meet Human Needs: Feminist Visions in Practice", *Icon*, 1: 99–105.

Sanders, Elizabeth (2002), "From User-Centered to Participatory Design Approaches", in Jorge Frascara (ed.), *Design and the Social Sciences*, 18–25, London, New York: Taylor & Francis.

Sanders, Elizabeth & Pieter Stappers (2008), "Co-Creation and the New Landscape of Design", *CoDesign International Journal of Co-Creation in Design and the Arts*, 4(1): 5–18.

Thinyane, Mamello., Karthik Bhat, Lauri Goldkind, & Vikram Cannanure (2020), "The Messy Complexities of Democratic Engagement and Empowerment in Participatory Design – An Illustrative Case with a Community-Based Organisation", *CoDesign*, 16(1): 29–44.

Winschiers-Theophilus, Heike., Bidwell, Nicola J., & Blake, Edwin (2012), "Community Consensus: Design Beyond Participation," *Design issues*, 28(3): 89–100.

INDEX

Page numbers in italics refer to figures.

accountability and responsibility 215–16
Acuto, Michele et al. 210, 211, 217
Advertisers' Association (ABA) 80
Advertisers' Chamber (Paraguay) 80
advertising 63–4, 81–2
 co-regulation 80–1
 hypersexualization 66–72, *68*, *70*, *79*
 infrastructures 72–3, *73*
 legislating 75–8
 normalization of violence against women 74–5
 self-regulation of advertising 75, 76, 77, 78
 sexist 35, 64–6
Advertising Standards Authority (United Kingdom) 71
age
 crime prevention 194, *197*, 201
 data collection 83, 85–6, 91, 103
 gender-sensitive design 122, 128, 133, 134, 151, 157, 209, 225
 public transport 131, 161–2, 165, 168, 169, 170–1, 176, 177–8
 sexist advertising 66, 71

sexist street harassment 9, 42, 47, 49, 50, 60
Ahmed, Sara 151
Alliance for Family Entertainment (AFE) 80
Angeles, Leonora, and Jennifer Robertson 196
Armitage, Rachel, and Paul Ekblom 190, 191, 193
Association of National Advertisers (ANA) 78, 80
Atlas, Randall 190
Autorité de Régulation Professionnelle de la Publicité (Authority for Self-Regulation of Advertising; ARPP) 76, 77

Basu, Ashish, and Kalpana Viswanath 95
Beebeejaun, Yasminah 136, 154
Benbrahim, Dina 16, 38, 231
Berry, Jess 138
Bielenberg, John et al. 235
Blomkamp, Emma 233, 239
Blomstrom, Eleanor et al. 162
Bowers, Kate, and Rob Guerette 199, 201
breastfeeding 128, 130
Buenos Aires Declaration for Progressive Advertising 78, 80

INDEX

camera surveillance. *See* closed-circuit television (CCTV)
car parks 48, 172–3, 175, 199, 202
Caretta, Martina, and Yvonne Riaño 231, 233
Cavaghan, Rosalind 105, 106, 108
Ceccato, Vania 160, 167, 226
Chiu, Yi-Ning et al. 198
Chrisafis, Angelique 56
Clements, Estelle 84, 99
Cleveland, Gerry, and Gregory Saville 202, 247 n.2
closed-circuit television (CCTV) xi, 121, 209, 210, 226
  lack of contribution to women's safety 133, 181, 199, 204–6, 222
co-design 59, 125, 229–43, *242–3*
  participatory 232–3, *233, 236–7*
co-regulation 75
collective action *54–5*
Collins, Patricia Hill 114, *115,* 116
Committee for Sydney 216–17, 219
communication campaigns 53, 57–8, *58,* 62, 64, 94, *95,* 209, 220, 245 n.3 (chap. 2)
  public transport 158, 170, 175, 179
community advocacy and complaints 75, 81, 96, 99, 118, 119, 124, 127, 152, 192, 209. *See also* safety audits
community education and media literacy 64, 75, 81
community safety 191, 193, 202–3, 247 n.2
Connelly, Tracey xi
Costanza-Chock, Sasha 194, 196
Council of Europe 105

counter-reporting of sexist street harassment. *See* reporting sexist street harassment
Coy, Maddy 17, 66–7, 67–8, 74–5
Cozens, Paul, and Terence Love 191, 194, 202–3, 247 n.2
Crabbe, Maree, and Michael Flood 69
Crenshaw, Kimberlé 15, 16, 114, 116
Criado Perez, Caroline 13, 86
crime prevention 47, 121, 132. *See also* closed-circuit television (CCTV); Crime Prevention Through Environmental Design (CPTED)
Crime Prevention Through Environmental Design (CPTED) 136, 189–96, 198, 203, 207, 246 n.1 (chap. 9), 247 n.2
  definition and principles *197*
  limitations for women and girls 191–6
  See also closed-circuit television (CCTV)
Crowe, Timothy 188

D'Ignazio, Catherine, and Lauren F. Klein 84–5, 93
Daly, Mary 105, 109
Daneshpour, Manijeh 124
data
  artificial intelligence (AI) 90–1
  collection 83–7, 96–8
  feminist 89–93
  gap 84–6
  sex/gender disaggregated 83, 85–6, *88,* 99, 103, 124
Davids, Tine et al. 106, 109, 110, 113
DeKeseredy, Walter et al. 192
digital guardians 206–7
Dines, Gail 67

disability
- crime prevention 194, 195, 201
- gender-sensitive design 128, 150
- public transport 157, 161–2, 165, 168–9, 177
- sexist advertising 66
- sexist street harassment 34, 43

Dixon, Eurydice xi
Doan, Petra 196
domestic violence. *See* family violence
Donovan, Jenny et al. 130
Dunne, Anthony, and Fiona Raby 127, 233

Edwards, Allison, and Hannah Korsmeyer 230–31, 234, 238
Ekblom, Paul, and Rachel Armitage 190, 191, 193
Eldridge, Adam, and Marion Roberts 211, 214
El Nahry, Fatma 36
Epstein, Debbie 34
Epstein, Dora 8
equality *versus* equity 17–18
ethnicity 34, 71, 77, 194
eyes on the street. *See* crime prevention

family violence 9–11, 58, 224
Farrington, David, and Brandon Welsh 206
feminism, definition 2
Fenster, Tovi 11
Fileborn, Bianca 59, 94, 219, 220
Fine, Cordelia 75
First Nations women 169–70, 194. *See also* Indigenous women
Flood, Michael, and Maree Crabbe 69
Forlano, Laura 13, 14–15
Forsyth, Ann 3

Garau, Pietro 232
gender, definition 13–15
gender audits 103, 105, 123, 140, 240
gender-based violence vs. male violence against women 12–13
gender diverse people 12, 43, 44, 66, 90, 128–9, 168, 178
gender mainstreaming 103–17, 107, 246 n.2 (chap. 5)
gender-neutral design 12–14, 119–20, 121, 128–9, 135, 141, 175, 184, 185, 194
gender-sensitive budgeting 103, 124
gender-sensitive design
- best practices for 120–7
- definition 119–20
- role of practice and communities 127–34, 127

Gervais, Myriam 138, 235, 238, 240
Gill, Rosalind 13
- and Kirsten Kohrs 72
Gillard, Julia 247 n.1
Giuliano, Genevieve 159
Goel, Rahul et al. 46, 163, 164
Goffman, Erving 36
Greed, Clara 3, 119, 241, 246 n.1
- gender mainstreaming 107–8, 109
- public transport 159, 160, 172
- safety audits 105–6, 137
Green, Eileen 34
Grocott, Lisa 230
Grosser, Kate 17, 37–8
Grove, Nicole Sunday 95
Guerette, Rob, and Kate Bowers 199, 201
Gurrieri, Lauren 67, 76–7, 81

Hafner-Burton, Emilie, and Mark Pollack 106

HarassMap (online map) 95
Harding, Sandra 138, 232
Harrison, Robert L. et al. 71
Heidaripour, Maryam 13, 14–15
heteronormativity 16, 19, 34, 44, 64–5, 72, 196. *See also* heterosexism
heterosexism 22, 43, 44, 64–5, 76, 82, 203, 220. *See also* heteronormativity
Hjorthol, Randi 159
Hollaback! *See* Right to Be
homelessness and women's safety 45, 154, 194, 202, 221, 224–5
hooks, bell 116
Hubbard, Phil 36, 44
Huerta, Claudia, and Clara Irazábal 196
Hummel, Patrick et al. 98
Huning, Sandra et al. 105, 108, 109, 113, 116
Huybrechts, Liesbeth et al. 231, 233–4, 240
hypersexual cities. *See* advertising; pornographication

inclusive design 109, 119, 135, 195, 226, 231–2. *See also* co-design; gender-sensitive design
Indigenous women 15–16, 122–3, 140, 225. *See also* First Nations women
International Indigenous Design Charter 122–3
intersectionality, definition 15–17
Irazábal, Clara, and Claudia Huerta 196
Iveson, Kurt 116–17

Jacobs, Jane 189, 198, 206
Jeffreys, Sheila 65, 69, 74

Kalms, Nicole, and Gill Matthewson, "Unwanted Sexual Behaviour and Public Transport" 11, 16, 159, 180
Kelly, Liz, and Jill Radford 38–9, 49, 136, 214
Kern, Leslie 113, 206
Kim, Hyunjin 174, 175, 181
Kitchin, Rob 97
Klein, Lauren, and Catherine D'Ignazio 84–5, 93
Kohrs, Kirsten, and Rosalind Gill 72
Kolysh, Simone 43, 44
Korsmeyer, Hannah, and Allison Edwards 230–31, 234, 238
Koskela, Hille 214–15

Lacy, Anita et al. 114
Lambrick, Melanie, and Kathryn Travers 137, 152, *153*
Lampen, Claire 77
Larin, Tegan 221
Lau, Renae xi
laws. *See* legislation
legislation 53, 56–7, 75–8, 82, 120, 121, 234
Lenton, Rhona, et al. 37
lesbian, gay, and bisexual women 43–4, 72, 90, 99, 171. *See also* heteronormativity; heterosexism
Leurs, Koen 91
Levy, Caren 184–5
lighting
 disability and 169
 gender-sensitive 130, 133, 134, 225–8
 inadequacy 48, 60, 62, 132, 211, 212
 night-time economy 208–9, 210, 211–12
 public transport and 181–2, 218

safety audits and rating lighting 123, 140, 180
surveillance 198, 199. *See also* closed-circuit television
linguistically diverse women 104, 154, 168, 238–9
materials for 96–7, 98, 132, 150, 170, 200
Lorenc, Theo et al. 188
Loukaitou-Sideris, Anastasia 159–60, 161, 167
Love, Terence, and Paul Cozens 191, 194, 202–3, 247 n.2
Low, Setha 116–17
Lucas, Karen et al. 161, 162

Mackay, Finn 221, 222–3
MacKinnon, Catharine 2, 16
Madan, Manish, and Mahesh K. Nalla 45
Markham, Annette 28
masculinities 7, 13–15, 36, 66, 185, 220
Massawre, Alia xi
Matthewson, Gill, and Nicole Kalms, "Unwanted Sexual Behaviour and Public Transport" 11, 16, 159, 180
McAllister, Pam 36
McQuire, Scott 226
McRobbie, Angela 104–5
Meagher, Jill xi
media literacy. *See* community education and media literacy
Mendes, Kaitlynn et al. 93
#MeToo movement 51, 94
Milward, Kirsty et al. 106, 117
mobility as a service (MaaS) 131, 175
mobility of women 45, *46*
 data about 87, 91, 124, 158, 183–4
 gender-sensitive design 106, 121, 127, 131, 158, 185, 209
 micro-mobility 131, 158, 175, 181, 201
 public transport 160, 161–3, *164*, 165–8, *166*, 169–71, 175, 180, 184–5, 217–18
 and sexist street harassment 45

Nadimpalli, SriPallavi, and Alicia Yon 43, 113, 117
Nalla, Mahesh, and Manish Madan 45
neoliberalism 61, 64, 104–5
night-time economy
 definition 210–11
 lighting 208–9, 210, 211–12, 225–8
 perception of risk 212–15, *213*, 216
 transport and mobility 216–25

Organisation for Economic Co-operation and Development (OECD) 212, *213*
Ortiz Escalante, Sara 12–13, 238
Osez le Feminisme! (Dare to Be Feminist!) 77

Pain, Rachel 167, 233
parks 45, 123, 130, 140
Paterson, Stephanie, and Francesca Scala 105, 108, 110, 117
Peake, Linda, and Martina Rieker 109
Petcou, Constantin, and Doina Petrescu 235
Petrescu, Doina, and Constantin Petcou 235
Phipps, Alison 51
placemaking 99, 112, 122–3, 208, 235

definition 231–2
gender-inclusive 104, 209, 225, 229, 238
Plan International 60
police responses to reporting of harassment 49, 50
Pollack, Mark, and Emilie Hafner-Burton 106
porn chic 67, 77
pornographication 64–75, *68, 70,* 79, 81, 82, 245 n.1 (chap. 3)
definition 67, 69
pornography. *See* pornographication
prostitution 64, 74, 220–4
public space, definition 3
public toilets 72, 128–9, 140, 175
public transport
auditing 123, 140
design 131–2, 172–83, *173,* 183–5, 199, 200, 201
gender mainstreaming and 106, 114
intersectionality 168–72
night-time economy 208, 210, 215, 217–18
poverty 161–2, 170
sex-segregated 177–8
women's safety 43, 48, 57, 82, 159–60, 165–8, *173*
women's use of service 161–5, *164, 166*

Raby, Fiona, and Anthony Dunne *127,* 233
racism 15, 22, 33, 43, 114
and pornography 65
and public transport 169–70, 180
and sexist street harassment 35
Radford, Jill, and Liz Kelly 38–9, 49, 136, 214
Reclaim/Take Back the Night movement 215, 216

recreational facilities and spaces 45, 130, 141, 171, 182, 190, 200
religion 34, 77, 98, 169–70, 171–72, 178, 194
Rees, Teresa 246 n.2 (chap. 5)
Rémy-Leleu, Raphaëlle 77
Rendell, Jane et al. 2
reporting sexist street harassment 49–52, *50,* 54–5, 56–7, 61
Respect Victoria 57
Riaño, Yvonne, and Martina Caretta 231, 233
Rieker, Martina, and Linda Peake 109
Right to Be (originally Hollaback!) 52, 220
risk, women's perceptions 7–8, *20.* See also safety, women's perceptions
Roberts, Marion, and Adam Eldridge 211, 214
Robertson, Jennifer, and Leonora Angeles 196
Rosewarne, Lauren 65, 81
Rothschild, Joan 84

Sadowski, Jathan et al. 199
Safe in Her City safety audit (Casey City Council) 140–1, *142–9*
safe space concept 43, 59–60, 62, 129, 239
Safetipin (app) 95
safety, women's perceptions *20,* 133, 137, 179, *179,* 209, 210. *See also* safety audits
safety audits 135–41, *142–9,* 150–2, *153,* 154
safety work 39–41, *40,* 131
Sánchez de Madariaga, Inés 114, 116, 165
Sandercock, Leonie 3

Sanders, Elizabeth 240
   and Pieter Stappers 232, 233
Saville, Gregory, and Gerry
   Cleveland 202, 247 n.2
Scala, Francesca, and Stephanie
   Paterson 105, 108, 110, 117
#SeeHer movement 78, 80
sex, definition 13–15
sexist street harassment
   definition 35–6
   intersectional experiences 41–4
   managing the risk of 38–41, *40*
   reporting, under-reporting and counter-reporting 49–51, *50*
   typologies and hotspots 44–9, *46*
   women's "safety work" 33–8, *37*
   See also sexual assault; sexual harassment
sexual assault 11, 35, 37, 38, 56, 169, 181, 203, 214, 217, 222, 244 n.2. *See also* sexual harassment; sexist street harassment
sexual harassment 45, 244 n.1 (chap. 2), 245 n.2 (chap. 2)
   advertising and 65, 74–5
   campaigns against 51, *54–5*, 57–9, *58*, 245 n.3
   definition 35, *37*
   design to address 114, 220
   policies 53, 59–60
   public transport 165–6, 167–8, 170–71, 177–9
   reporting 49–52, *50*, 94–5
   See also sexist street harassment; sexual assault
Sheffield, Carole 7–8, 42
situated (or situational) crime prevention (SCP) 188, 190–1, 194, 195, 196, 197, 201–2
Slaone, Mona et al. 226

Smeds, Emilia et al. 180
socio-economic status 41, 45, 154, 168, 170, 194
Sørensen, Anette 67
Stanko, Elizabeth 38
Stappers, Pieter, and Elizabeth Sanders 232, 233
Stevenson, Deborah 210, 211, 212, 214
Stewart, Potter 245 n.1 (chap. 3)
Stock, Kathleen 14
Struyf, Pia 8, 225
surveillance, 179–80. *See* closed-circuit television (CCTV); eyes on the street
surveys 9, 87, 95, 124, 159–60, 177, 227, 245 n.1 (chap. 4)
   as practice, 84, 89, 150
Svechkina, Alina et al. 225–6
Sweden 106, 182, 223–4, 246 n.3

tactical walking. *See* walking, tactical
Task Force on the Sexualisation of Girls Report 65
The Female Quotient (TFQ) 80
Thinyane, Mamello et al. 239
toilets. *See* public toilets
trafficking of women and girls 74, 221, 223
training
   bystanders 33, 59
   frontline staff 33, 56–7, 157, 179–80
Travers, Kathryn, and Melanie Lambrick 137, 152, *153*
Tummers 109
Tyler, Meagan 16–17, 66–7, 69

under-reporting of sexist street harassment. *See* reporting sexist street harassment

United Nations (UN)
  2030 Agenda for Sustainable Development 5, 5–6
  New Urban Agenda 6
  Sustainable Development Goals (SDGs) 21, 90, 114, 245 n.1 (chap. 4)
  Women and Unstereotype Alliance 78
  World Conference on Women, Beijing, 1995 246 n.2 (chap. 5)
universal design 120, 135, 194. *See also* gender-neutral design
Unstereotype Alliance Brazil 80
Urban Girls Catalogue 134
urban planning, gender mainstreaming and 64, 106–8, *107*, 110–11. *See also* co-design; crime prevention; gender-neutral design

Valdivia, Blanca Gutiérrez 12–13, 238
Valentine, Gill 2–3, 35, 38, 43
Vera-Gray, Fiona 39, 41, 42, 53
victim blaming 49–50, *50*, 61, 178, 181
violence against women. *See* gender-based violence vs. male violence against women; risk, women's perceptions; safety, women's perceptions; sexist street harassment; sexual assault; sexual harassment; vulnerability, women's perceptions
violence, continuum *10*, 11–12
Viswanath, Kalpana, and Ashish Basu 95

Vukotic, Maša xi
vulnerability, women's perceptions 7–8, *20*, 73. *See also* safety

walking *46*
  recreational activity 45
  tactical 135, 137, 138
  transport and wayfinding 131, 132, 170, 181
  See also lighting; wayfinding
Wånggren, L. 51–2
Ward, L. Monique 69
wayfinding 132, 174, 175, 182, 200, 201
Weisman, Leslie Kanes 2, 7
Wekerle, Gerda 161, 170, 182, 192
Welsh, Brandon, and David Farrington 206
Whitzman, Carolyn et al. 107, 141, 151, 160, 192, 204, 205, 206
Winschiers-Theophilus, Heike et al. 233
women of color 41–2, 169–70, 194, 199, 239. *See also* intersectionality
women with disabilities. *See* disability
Women's Health Victoria 76
women's safety audits. *See* safety audits
World Federation of Advertisers (WFA) 78, 80
World Health Organization (WHO) 9

Yon, Alicia, and SriPallavi Nadimpalli 43, 113, 117
Yves Saint Laurent (company) 77

Zalewski, Marysia 109
Zebracki, Martin 106, 117